SAILING
A SERIOUS OCEAN

You know it by the northern look of the shore
By the salt worried faces,
By an absence of trees,
By an abundance of lighthouses,
It's a serious Ocean.

—Ann Stevenson, "North Sea off Carnousti"

SAILING
A SERIOUS OCEAN

**SAILBOATS, STORMS, STORIES, AND LESSONS
LEARNED FROM 30 YEARS AT SEA**

John Kretschmer

International Marine / McGraw-Hill Education

Camden, Maine | New York | Chicago | San Francisco | Lisbon | London | Madrid |
Mexico City | Milan | New Delhi | San Juan | Seoul | Singapore | Sydney | Toronto

12 13 14 15 LCR 24 23 22 21 20
ISBN 978-0-07-170440-3
MHID 0-07-170440-X
Color ebook ISBN 0-07-171812-5

Library of Congress Cataloging-in-Publication Data
Kretschmer, John.
  Sailing a serious ocean : sailboats, storms, stories, and lessons learned from 30 years at sea / John Kretschmer.
    pages cm
  Includes index.
  ISBN 9780071704403
  1. Kretschmer, John—Travel. 2. Sailing. 3. Boats and boating. 4. Heavy weather seamanship. 5. Sailors—United States—Biography. I. Title.
  GV810.92.K74A3 2014
  797.124—dc23

                                                                            2013040619

McGraw-Hill Education books are available at special quantity discounts to use as premiums and sales promotions or for use in corporate training programs. To contact a representative, please e-mail us at bulksales@mheducation.com.

Questions regarding the content of this book should be addressed to www.internationalmarine.com

Questions regarding the ordering of this book should be addressed to
McGraw-Hill Education
Customer Service Department
P.O. Box 547
Blacklick, OH 43004
Retail customers: 1-800-262-4729
Bookstores: 1-800-722-4726

Contents

To everyone who has stood a watch aboard Quetzal.
Some of you are mentioned in the pages that follow, most are not. But we are shipmates one and all. I thank you for your hard work, for putting up with my cooking, and mostly for your friendship and support. You have allowed me to keep sailing and without you this book would not exist.

Foreword
by Dallas Murphy

IF *SAILING A SERIOUS OCEAN* is your first meeting with John Kretschmer and his work, it's probably John's own fault. He's a modest, self-deprecating man. He doesn't advertise himself or his business or tout his eminently toutable nautical accomplishments. So I'll take up some of that slack.

Kretschmer is an original. Who else has for decades and without serious incident captained a one-man charter operation specializing in long-distance, open-ocean sailing? Who else would have thought to sail from New York to San Francisco with a windward slog around Cape Horn aboard a Contessa 32, perhaps the smallest boat ever to do so? As a charter operator and delivery skipper, Kretschmer has made some twenty Atlantic crossings, many long Pacific passages, and multiple transits of the Med. He annually puts more nautical miles on his beloved Kaufman 47 *Quetzal* than statute miles on his car; he quit counting those nautical miles at 300,000. He's a brilliant seaman who's handled most every condition that serious oceans mete out to sailboats, but that alone is not what makes him an original. It's that in combination with this: *the man can write.* Which brings us to *Sailing a Serious Ocean.*

Kretschmer is a skillful storyteller, and with those 300,000 miles of experience to draw on, he doesn't need to make anything up. Some of his stories are downright frightening, like that terrible trip through Hurricane Mitch, and some are hilarious, like the time shortly after 9/11 when his brand-new life raft suddenly inflated at the check-in desk at Heathrow, prompting nervous security guards to level machine guns at his head ("Don't shoot him!" cried the desk clerk). In addition to being well told, the sea stories share another characteristic. They're charmingly modest and self-deprecating—as I said, like John; the joke's usually on John.

However, this book is not only a memoir of a lifetime at sea in sailboats, nor was it meant to be. No, John takes the ocean too seriously to leave it at that. He explores in depth the aspects of hull and rig design that make for good sea boats and bad ones; and he makes a sound case for his list of favorite boats, most all of which he's sailed across oceans. He explains his well-honed storm strategies (in the event, we're talking about beasts in excess of 70 knots, not just heavy weather). He also makes a compelling case for his somewhat unorthodox man-overboard procedure. But the difference between this and other books concerned with practical knowledge is that Kretschmer lodges the lessons solidly in first-person narratives. His is a very pleasing voice of experience. And, in fact, ocean education is a fundamental concept behind John Kretschmer Sailing—you sign on as crew to sail the boat, not to sit and sip cocktails at the taffrail while John does so (well, sometimes you might—say, during "Captain's Hour"). In *Sailing a Serious Ocean*, he writes this about his clients/crew: "They are searching for the sea and, in the brutal honesty that flows through its currents, hoping to catch a reflection of themselves."

So if this is your first meeting with John, the treat still in store, I know you'll want to read more after you finish *Sailing a Serious Ocean*. And be warned, you'll very likely want to sail with him, perhaps across an ocean, all of which are serious. And if you've read Kretschmer or sailed with him, well, then you already know why you want to read this book.

Dallas Murphy is the author of Rounding the Horn *and other ocean-related books. He met John Kretschmer on a panel at the Miami Book Fair in 2009 and subsequently had the pleasure of circumnavigating Newfoundland with him. He learned much from John on that and other voyages.*

Foreword

by Tania Aebi

OVER THE YEARS, along with Joshua Slocum and Moitessier, John Kretschmer has secured an iconic place in my pantheon of inspirational sailors. Even though we didn't meet until about ten years ago, as speakers invited to the same seminar weekend, our story goes way back.

I was seventeen years old, during my first Atlantic crossing from the Canaries to the Caribbean, when we were first introduced on paper. The satellite navigation (satnav) broke, and just as the conversational instruction of John's mail order celestial navigation course guided my father through all the sight reduction, plotting, and running fixes, his words taught me the simpler mechanics of just the noon sight.

When this trip ended and my own circumnavigation was about to begin, the outstanding qualifications of the Contessa 26 that I was planning to sail were substantiated by another John story that my father had read and liked to talk about with great flair, the one about his rounding of Cape Horn on a Contessa 32. It only followed that if a Contessa 32 could withstand such a harrowing journey in the notoriously difficult Southern Ocean, then the 26 could certainly handle the trade wind belt I faced.

On my first passage from New York to Bermuda, beset as I was with rookie mistakes and navigational difficulties, it was his celestial navigation manual that I used for solace, for reassurance, for learning. The loose pages were clamped together in a red cardboard binder that still sits on a shelf above my desk almost thirty years later, and I can reread the words of his introduction that were nearly memorized while trying in vain to locate my position out in the middle of all that water. "Even today, although I've sailed thousands of miles in both the Atlantic and Pacific Oceans, I remember my first landfall distinctly," he writes.

He describes a passage from the East Coast to Bermuda. Shortly before landfall, a terrible storm drops in, and hove to and running downwind with it for over two days, he can't get any sun sights and keeps marking the chart with uncertain dead reckoning positions. Relying on dead reckoning myself because of storms and sight reductions and plotting that weren't working out the way they were supposed to, I found that his words made me feel slightly less hopelessly lost.

When the storm abates and the sun returns, he pulls out the sextant and resumes the business of navigating. Finding the island becomes a memorable highlight of his sailing career. "Bermuda popped up on the horizon right where it was supposed to," he writes. "The scene aboard was comic as the three of us jumped about screaming and shouting . . . celestial navigation can do strange things to people."

I found myself jumping up and down screaming with delight only because I'd headed south until coming within range of an RDF signal that broadcast for 150 miles. But I just knew that armed with his manual, I would one day find my own islands with the sextant. And I did. Over the next couple of years, the manual became very well worn, and one landfall after another was found with John's formula and words like *"declination"* and *"azimuth"* that he had demystified.

But the manual had nothing to say about which generation he belonged to, and I was so young at the time that advanced age was automatically associated with the wisdom and experience necessary to write a whole book on celestial navigation after rounding a cape. For all I knew, he could have followed right behind Slocum, or the Hiscocks. So every time I leafed through the pages and saw John's name, I'd imagine this crusty, grizzled, graybeard mariner battling the high seas and studying the almanac by the light of a swinging kerosene lantern.

Long after my trip on the 26-footer ended, I was still using John's words for reference when writing about celestial navigation, or for the few times I pulled out the sextant to bone up on my rusty skills. Each time, when skimming the introduction, I'd picture the same ancient mariner. Every once in a while, I'd run across his name as the expert author of an article in a sailing magazine and think idly, Wow. John Kretschmer. He's still around?

Time passed to the day that he and I were scheduled as presenters at the cruising seminar. When told that John would be there, I thought, Cool, I didn't even know he was still alive, and now I get to meet him. Then, Oh no, what can I add to the topic of sailing beside the likes of him? Then, Wow, I finally get to tell him that for more than half my life, his name has been as familiar to me as Chichester or Knox-Johnston, permanently engraved on my consciousness as the one responsible for teaching me how to navigate.

When I saw him walking up the dock for the first time, a young-looking, sandy-haired, clean-shaven, Teva-wearing guy with a ready laugh, that was the last thing I expected. My older and wiser teacher had only ten years on me. And when I told him what I couldn't tell David Lewis, or Ann Davison, how something he once wrote had inspired me along my way to keep going, he laughed in reply, though the infectious laugh lost some heartiness when I added I'd always assumed he was the same age as they were.

We immediately became friends, bonded by a mutual love for the sea and respect for each other's accomplishments, delighting in the stories and philosophical take on how the world of sailing has evolved in our lifetimes, long past the days of the old guard. You couldn't shut us up as we gabbed about everything from modern nautical gadgetry overkill to the best chicken breed to raise for meat.

Ever since, I've read his other books, *Flirting with Mermaids, At the Mercy of the Sea*, and *Cape Horn to Starboard*. He keeps sailing and writing nonstop, and we've continued talking and laughing as I've gotten to know him as a person more than a myth. He is still admirable—as a contemporary with whom the stories can flow, as well as a truly dedicated and accomplished seaman who has influenced the sailing life of many others. In the honored tradition of Conrad, Herreshoff, and Twain, all of whom are generously quoted throughout the pages, the storytelling in *Sailing a Serious Ocean* comes second only to listening to John in person.

In May 1985, when Tania Aebi was only eighteen years old, she cast off alone from the docks of South Street Seaport in Lower Manhattan and sailed 27,000 miles around the world on her 26-foot sloop Varuna. *Concerned about her lack of ambition, her father offered her this opportunity as an alternative to a college education, and she took him up on it. For the next two and a half years, with only a cat for company, she crossed the Caribbean, the South Pacific, the Indian Ocean, the Red Sea, the Mediterranean, and the North Atlantic, stopping in twenty-three countries along the way.*

She sailed through storms and calms, gathering stories, friendships, inspirational examples, and maturity along the way. She also learned a lot about setting a larger-than-life goal and being committed to following it through despite mechanical breakdowns, the death of her mother, loneliness, doubt, and fear. In November 1987, just barely twenty-one, Tania Aebi stepped back onto the cement shores of New York City, a solo circumnavigator. She spent the year after her return reliving the trip in words, writing her best-selling book Maiden Voyage, *the personal account that synthesized her modern-day odyssey and the dramatic childhood leading up to it.*

Aebi is a licensed sailor, and a mother, delivery captain, and writer. www.taniaaebi.com

Ferryman

"The stories of sea voyages, from The Odyssey *through Hakluyt, and into today, retain immediacy and freshness because they took place on the never-changing sea, and each one goes to the secret core of a man's joy. It is a pleasure found not only in the tale of adventures but in the certitude that here on the sea, a man can reaffirm his human animal self, by the power of his arms, his will and his skill in a direct encounter with a huge and impersonal element and to do so in close company with chosen companions."*

—William Snaith, *On the Wind's Way*

THE CABIN LOOKED like a crime scene. Bodies, books, clothes, tools, and assorted fruits and vegetables were scattered haphazardly, rearranging themselves with every wave. So much for that quaint idea that on a boat there's a place for everything and everything is in its place.

We were heading south, and the off-watch crew occupied every berth north of the bow and most of the cabin sole. They were desperately trying to catch a bit of sleep before their next call to duty. The red night-light in the galley flickered as undermanned electrons faltered against a flood of salt water pouring in through the leaky vent overhead. The light finally capitulated, but the eerie darkness did little to disguise where we were. Nothing can muffle the cacophony of a sailboat interior when the sea is raging. Conrad described a gale as "that thing of mighty sound," and as always, he was right on the mark.

It was November: Newport to Bermuda. It was bitterly cold, and winter seemed a lot closer than summer. In what was to become an annual rite, I had dubbed the trip the "Heavy-Weather Offshore Passage," and no one could accuse me of hype. Cresting walls of water arrived on deck with a complete lack of subtlety, shaking *Quetzal* to its core and making the entire boat shudder. Unused halyards clattered against the mast, reaching a crescendo in the strongest gusts. An overloaded sheet block groaned hoarsely trying to

1

control the tiny staysail. Locker doors flew open and then slammed shut as the boat rolled from gunwale to gunwale. Nobody was getting much sleep, except for me. I can always sleep, which according to my grandmother means I have a clean conscience. Unlike Conrad, my grandmother was not always right, although both shared a deep mistrust—even hatred—of the sea. Conrad because of its "unfathomable cruelty." My grandmother because it had tried to take her son from her during World War II.

My alarm sounded and put an abrupt end to a lovely dream. I rarely remember my dreams ashore but almost always do at sea. Something about sleeping in a washing machine allows better access to the subconscious. It was my watch. I wriggled most of the way out of my sleeping bag and the coffin-like pilot berth where I'd spent the last three hours. Then I decided to let gravity lend a hand. I should have known better. Newton was no sailor; gravity has its own laws at sea. Everything that can fall, will fall, and will continue to fall no matter how many times you stow the damn thing before you make landfall. I tried to anticipate the next lurch to port, but just as I made my move, an errant wave spanked the hull and we careened hard to starboard instead.

For a long second I was airborne with my sleeping bag draped around my knees, my arms flailing. Clutching the mast, I managed to land on my feet and somehow miss Chuck, who was sprawled across the sole with a wet sleeping bag pulled over his head. It was a remarkable landing, and I took that as a good sign. After thousands of midnight watches in the North Atlantic, you'd think this routine of getting up at all hours would grow old, that the magic would be snuffed out from sheer exhaustion if nothing else, that omens would turn to curses. But I am here to report that the magic of a night at sea is remarkably durable. I don't deny that given the slightest opportunity the ocean will rise up and test your resolve, challenging and occasionally shattering your nicely scripted notion of just who you think you are. But no other realm on our planet carves its initials as permanently into our brain's hard drive as the deep ocean, and I remember this night nine years ago, the first of many "heavy-weather" passages aboard *Quetzal*, like some might recall their wedding night.

As I struggled out of the sleeping bag and directly into my clammy foul-weather gear, I bounced off Mark. He was stuffed into the settee berth, suspended above the soggy sole by an overburdened lee cloth. He pretended not to notice my accidental hip check. He was someplace else, somewhere far away where the world was flat, stationary, quiet. I think he was holed up on a farm in Kansas, near the geographic center point of the country and as far from the sea as he could get. I would never have predicted that a few years later he'd cross the Atlantic with me as a stalwart member of the crew.

After finding a handhold, I slid butt by butt into the galley. I grabbed an orange, a pocket full of saltine crackers, a bottle of water, and my portable shortwave radio before stumbling headfirst into the cockpit. This process took two, maybe three minutes. I rarely tarry when it's my watch.

A blast of cold air shook the lingering image of my girlfriend from my brain. Unfortunately we were still charging before a gale in the North Atlantic and not ghosting along the Amalfi Coast, the setting of my rudely interrupted dream. Tadji, the aforementioned girlfriend, was nowhere in sight. Mike and Dirk were, and I greeted them with a smile. Their faces would never be described in a logbook entry, but they told a better story than the dreary weather and navigation details we typically scribbled down after each watch.

Mike had soft, bulging brown eyes turned down at the ends, curly black hair refusing to stay sheltered beneath his hood, a defiant moustache. He was cold but coping, happy to be out here, happy to be one of us (and would go on to become a frequent member of *Quetzal's* crew). Dirk, with bright, serious eyes, was competent but queasy, relieved to see me. My arrival meant that warmth and respite from the wind and seas were just down the companionway.

In sturdy, Dutch-accented English, Dirk delivered the watch report. "Winds still from the north-northeast, gusting to 40 knots, steady at 30 to 35, course around 170 degrees. Speed 7 knots steady. Running down the waves, well that's another story, sometimes 10 knots, sometimes 12 knots, sometimes more . . ." His voice trailed off.

Twelve knots. That explained the hooting and hollering I'd heard below. Although that speed translates into less than 15 miles per hour on land— dead crawling through a school zone in your car—at sea in a 47-foot sailboat, 12 knots puts you in a churn of adrenaline; it's right on the edge of control.

"Thirty-five knots is the definition of a gale, isn't it?" Dirk, the analytical one, asked. "Especially 35 knots apparent."

Only sailors would complicate something as simple as wind. We have two winds, true and apparent. Apparent wind factors in boat speed; it's the wind you feel on deck. True wind assumes you're not moving, which of course is rarely the case. Like a lot of so-called truisms, true wind is not a very useful measurement on a boat. Ours is very much an apparent world at sea.

"Dirk, I think gales are personal. You know one when you're in one, and each is different. It really doesn't matter if the wind is true or apparent; it's just blowing hard and you deal with it. But you're right, officially 35 knots sustained wind is a gale; at least that's what Admiral Beaufort tells us."

"Thought so," Dirk replied, satisfied that he had stood watch in a gale, another item to check off his bucket list. He was getting ready to cross an ocean on his own one day, and wanted to taste a gale while I was around to reassure him that everything was okay. As I write these words nine years later, Dirk recently e-mailed that he and his wife, Susan, had just made landfall in Scotland, completing a very nice North Atlantic crossing from Newfoundland aboard *Tide Head*, their Outbound 46 sloop.

As I came out on deck, I thanked Mike and Dirk and assured them that they were doing a fine job on their first offshore passage, and then I sent them below. Mike paused in the galley, snagged a cookie, and then poked his head back out the companionway hatch. "Need any help, Cap?" he asked dutifully, knowing and hoping that I didn't. By a quirk of crew size, I was afforded the luxury of a solo watch, and I cherished a little time to myself.

"No, I'm okay, Mike. I'll shout if I need you guys. Thanks."

"Sure? Do you want something to eat or drink? Dirk says he'll make tea."

"No, I'm fine, really. Just get some sleep, both of you. Thanks. And good watch."

The Atlantic had been corralled into a cave. Visibility was left to the imagination. Occasional foam streaks from cascading waves were the only horizontal references confirming the sanguine notion that our tiny section of the planet was, at least for practical purposes, flat and that we were still on top of it. We were in the Gulf Stream, and *Quetzal* was slaloming down waves spawned by the collision of wind and current. We were being hurled forward by the tiny staysail, a mere 300 square feet of canvas propelling a 30,000-pound boat with all the horsepower she needed. The mainsail was lashed to the boom, and the genoa was securely furled around the headstay. *Quetzal* was dressed down for heavy weather and felt right. The Swedes say, "There is no bad weather, just bad clothing," and the same might be said about boats. This was, if there is such a thing, a perfect gale. There was enough wind to nurture deep respect for the sea's power, but the large seas were still manageable, and I knew instinctively that the gale was not going to intensify.

The ride was thrilling, especially when we caught a breaking wave off the stern quarter. At that moment *Quetzal* would lift slowly, like a whale ruffling the surface just before breeching, and then surge forward surfing and squirming but still tracking true, leaving a trail of bioluminescence. When the wave finally overtook her, stranding her in the suddenly windless trough, she'd wallow for a split second and then dig her shoulders into the sea like a running back expecting contact after a nice gain. Soon the wind would return and the staysail would fill away. The mad rush of water over the rudder would restore steering control. Then she'd begin climbing another mountain of white ocean, and the roller coaster ride would start all over again.

I may have been captain of this enterprise, but I never doubted who was in charge. Neptune and I had worked out an arrangement years before. He laid out my job description in clear terms: Keep an eye on things and don't get too full of yourself. And I was on the job, doing what I do, what I've always done, it seems—sailing in deep water and keeping an eye on things.

But this passage was not about me. It was about my crew. They were an odd mix: an ice cream salesman, an engineer, a nurse, a small-business owner, and a peanut broker. Not an experienced sailor among them, but they all shared a passion to taste the ocean from the spray zone, just a few feet above the surface of the sea, the place where man and ocean get to know each other on very personal terms.

The folks who sail with me shake the world when they're ashore. But on that ugly night at sea, they felt refreshingly small. They knew intuitively that the ocean was no place for boasting. In a gale, it's a dark alley in a bad neighborhood; you have to look ahead and behind and be ready to react. They had come from all over the country and had never met one another before the passage. They had sought me out and paid a nice sum. Then they found their way to *Quetzal* and checked into my cramped and uncomfortable floating world. *(continued page 8)*

Standing Watch

As you probably suspect already, and will certainly know if you continue reading this book, I am not a skipper who blindly adheres to hard-and-fast rules at sea. In fact, for the most part I abhor them because successfully handling a small boat in a large ocean requires a flexible attitude and the wherewithal to change tactics as conditions dictate. You must assess the situation and take preemptive action, and if that doesn't work then try something else. That's how serious sailors cope with challenging weather and equipment failures. Following rigid rules can be more dangerous than helpful. I must confess, however, that I am a tyrant when it comes to standing your watch, and all my nice guy sensitivity vanishes if you don't show up on time.

When the watch system breaks down, everybody loses their rhythm, and, more importantly, they lose off-watch rest time and vital hours of sleep. Fatigue is a stealthy enemy at sea. This heartless attitude toward watchstanding is geared mostly toward larger crews, four or more, and I am a little more tolerant of watch adjustments with small crews. Sometimes you are feeling strong and connected to the wheel (or at least the autopilot controls) as the boat hurtles before the wind, and the mermaids are flirting with you, and the stars are telling you stories, and you just don't want to end your watch. That's a different situation. Some nights you know that your partner really needs sleep, and extending your watch is the right thing to do. Remember that you have to replenish the hours of missed sleep; they add up like unpaid credit card bills and almost always exact a toll, with interest. Keeping to the watch schedule almost always results in a happier passage.

Back to my sensitive ways. I feel strongly that watchkeeping should apply only to the evening hours. This book looks at bluewater sailing as an incredibly fulfilling way to live, as a preferred way to spend your precious time, and standing watch day and night can suddenly feel like you're punching a clock on an assembly line. There has to be time for whimsy and thought at sea, and there's no better environment on the planet for unfettered thinking *(continued next page)* than a boat at sea, and this should not be shoehorned into a naval system of discipline and around-the-clock watches. I believe all of this deeply. But just the same, don't be late for your evening watch.

On *Quetzal*, somebody is always in the cockpit when underway to keep an eye on things. I highly recommend napping during the day, and I stress the need for quiet hours either on deck or below, asking only that you check with the crew to make sure somebody else is happy enough to keep the watch. This system has worked brilliantly, especially when there are at least three people aboard, and it gives each day a sense of uniqueness. It works well for couples also, although sailing with just two people on long passages at some point almost always feels like you're on sentry duty, just passing at the guard gate of the companionway. Sailing with two can be exhausting and, as I elaborate later, may require a watch system tailored for each partner's sleep patterns. Sailing alone, of course, is another kettle of fish.

When we have a training passage crew aboard *Quetzal*, we usually have two-person watches that begin after dinner, or just when it's turning dark. In latitudes well north or south of the equator in their respective summers, sometimes it is not practical to begin a watch until 2100 or later; it's still light and hard to sleep. In the trade winds, especially in the winter months of either hemisphere, watch usually starts at 1900, as the hours of light and dark are nearly equal. We typically sail with five or six aboard, affording the luxury of three two-person watch teams, or two two-person teams and one solo watch. We usually start with three-hour watches, and often stretch it to four hours later in the passage. The accompanying table shows a typical watch in the winter trade winds both at the start of the passage and later in the trip.

TRADE WINDS WATCHSTANDING SCHEDULE

Early in the Passage

Watch A	1900–2200
Watch B	2200–0100
Watch C	0100–0400
Watch A	0400–0700

(Invariably someone is up with the sun, and the smell of fresh coffee brewing rouses other off-watch crew around the 0700 changeover.)

Later in the Passage

Watch A	1900–2300
Watch B	2300–0300
Watch C	0300–0700
Watch A	0700

I always rotate watches. By pushing the watches up each night, everybody has a different watch each night. For example, if Watch A had the 1900–2200 watch last night, then they will have the 2200–0100 tonight, Watch B will have the 0100–0400, and Watch C will have the first and last watches. This system keeps everybody from getting into a rut, and also allows some flexibility in swapping watch partners if that becomes necessary.

On long ocean passages, my crews always enjoy standing solo watches, and this makes the nights downright relaxing. Dividing the evening hours into six watches allows for an easy watch schedule of two hours on and then hours off. Again, the watch schedule always rotates forward. On a typical 18-day trade wind transatlantic passage, we might have two-person three-hour watches the first six days, two-person four-hour watches the next six days, and then wind up the passage with six days of two hours on, ten hours off solo watches.

With smaller crews, it is more common to stand solo watches. I have made several long passages with a three-person crew, and actually find this to be an ideal number on most boats. Exceptions might be on very small boats with cramped quarters and on large boats with heavy physical demands. We typically stand the same three hours on, six hours off schedule, and, depending upon the conditions and the quality of the self-steering, often extend the watch to four hours. The next person on watch is the standby person should the on-deck watch need an extra hand. The person just coming off watch should not be disturbed if possible; that six- or eight-hour stretch of uninterrupted rest and sleep is critical.

Sailing as a couple often requires a more personal watch schedule. While I usually try to maintain either a three-on, three-off, or four-on, four-off schedule, this can become exhausting, especially if hand steering is involved. My wife, Tadji, and I have developed a different watch that works well for us. Tadji has trouble sleeping on a boat in general, and especially trying to sleep at 1900 or even 2100 is just too early for her inner clock; she's a late-night person. She also does not like waking up at all hours to turn up for watch, and you can't blame her.

So to accommodate her sleep preferences, I usually make dinner, clean up, and then head to my bunk. Tadji stays up as long as she can, typically a little before or after midnight. Then she wakes me and I stay up until 0600–0700 and then wake her and hit the sack for a few hours. This system depends upon the first off-watch crew being able to sleep early in the evening; otherwise, if you are called to duty without having slept, the night seems endless. Fortunately I am a sound sleeper. I don't subscribe to the notion that the skipper sleeps with one eye and one ear open. That usually translates into a totally exhausted, cranky skipper prone to making bad decisions. When I am in my bunk, as my crewmembers listening to my snoring will attest, I sleep. This schedule has also worked well when I was making passages with my two young daughters. They would take the first watch and call me when they were sleepy.

Some had been dreaming about going to sea for years. For others it was a newfound passion. Chuck and Mark had read Patrick O'Brian, all twenty volumes, while Dirk pored over how-to books by Don Casey, Lin and Larry Pardey, and Nigel Calder. Mike was enchanted by the beautiful narratives of Bernard Moitessier. They were romantics, if you can call someone searching for something as simple as an uncluttered horizon a romantic. They wanted some sea stories of their own, to test themselves in a gale, for someone to assure them that it wasn't too late to launch a dream. They were searching for the sea, and, in the brutal honesty that flows through its currents, hoping to catch a reflection of themselves that they could live with. Conrad titled his sailing ship memoir *The Mirror of the Sea*, a perfect metaphor for the searching that takes place out there. Camus wrote, "After a certain age every man is responsible for his face." To thrive at sea, you must be responsible for who you are, not who you want to be.

Cautiously I poked my head above the spray dodger. We had the ocean to ourselves, at least the few hundred yards of it that I surveyed before retreating reflexively when a wave suddenly broke abeam. I was too late, and the wave soaked me. "Damn," I mumbled and then laughed. Where were we? It didn't matter. We were everywhere and nowhere, our position defined by dimly backlit digits on the GPS, a set of coordinates that meant nothing at that moment. Our world was 47 feet long and 13½ feet wide, period. In deep water, in a gale, with no land to worry about, the sea has but one position, one address. You're out there and you've always been out there. Yesterday and tomorrow merge in a conspiracy of wind and waves. You can't reach one and you can't remember the other.

And yes, the boat matters, it really matters. It's not just a slurry of fibers, toxic resins, stainless steel, and teak suspending you above the bottom of the sea; it's a vessel of hope. It's the Holy Grail. You talk to your boat, you reassure her, and she reassures you. You give her a slap on the side. You and the boat are in the thick of it together and you form a bond that strikes land people as weird, maybe even a little creepy, but what do they know anyway?

Before we had shoved off from posh Newport, we had made pacts with our private gods, utterly accepting of whatever came our way. That was the point of the passage, after all, to contend, to discover, to accept, and to endure. I wrote in my book *Flirting with Mermaids*, "I make landfalls for a living." That's a good line, and not a bad way to navigate through life. However, as I get older I have realized that making landfalls, even dicey ones, is the easy part of sailing. The tough part is making departures, shedding the shackles of society's expectations, kicking the addiction of electronic connections, subverting the guilt of our own obligations, and pushing off the dock physically and metaphorically. Most of the people who sail with me know that time is no longer their friend; their biological clocks are ticking. They savor the moments, even the unpleasant ones, with an understanding that they've reached a point in their lives where time is what matters most. They sense that our journey is circular, and with an almost childlike innocence they long to get back to a familiar place. T. S. Eliot describes the quest, "We shall not cease from exploration, and the end of all our exploring will be to arrive where we started and know the place for the first time."

Tucked back behind the dodger, I felt something heavy in my jacket pocket—my shortwave receiver. I was going to listen to the National Weather Service forecast when my watch started. Imagine that: nine years ago we still listened to weather reports on the radio. At the time, Internet weather, and the constant pursuit thereof, had not yet taken full possession of a sailor's life. I love weather, the good, the bad—even the truly ugly. You must love weather to be a sailor; it is a core part of the package. I am not a slave to forecasts, however, and I don't worship at the altar of satellite GRIB files. I don't dispute that GRIB (which stands for gridded information in binary form) models are very accurate, but the pursuit of weather information can border on obsession. The more you sail, the more you accept that fact that weather is also influenced by local phenomena, and forecasts can still be inaccurate. Your own observations are often just as important and usually more useful than the professional mumbo jumbo. Still, sailors go to great lengths to obtain weather information via radio and satellite and then doggedly believe it, even when the evidence blowing directly in their faces suggests otherwise (see Weather Information Sources on page 14). I have seen sailors desperately trying to download forecasts from their perch at the navigation station below, completely ignoring towering cumulus clouds shrinking the dark horizon abovedeck. Weather forecasts have become something of a self-fulfilling prophecy; you want to believe them, you want to trust them.

Having missed the National Weather Service forecast, I searched for the BBC instead. After scanning an array of religious channels, the World Service came in loud and clear. The announcer's voice, soft, sure, and beautifully accented, seemed out of place in our harsh environment. Was she Indian, or more likely Pakistani? I was sure she was beautiful. Plutarch, noted historian, essayist, and sexist, claimed, "When the candles are out, all women are fair." Sailors stranded on a boat with all men have been known to draw a similar corollary about all women ashore.

The first item concerned recent terrorist attacks in London. Why was I listening to this madness, ruining the splendid isolation of the passage? Only the "news" could make a North Atlantic gale seem sensible by comparison. Then the newscaster noted the violence erupting in Liberia, a deteriorating West African republic that at that moment seemed farther away than the invisible moon. Another burst of bloodshed in West Africa was, pathetically, hard to process, just another tragedy in a tragic land. But I listened, thankful for a voice in English not admonishing me to worry about the devil snatching my immortal soul. Once again, it seemed, rebel forces had reprised a perpetual civil war, seizing control of the country. Liberian president Charles Taylor, who, the announcer told me, had just been indicted by the International War Crimes Tribunal in The Hague, had fled Liberia and accepted asylum in nearby Nigeria. Wait a minute. What did she say? Not Charles Taylor, not him again. Not that son of a bitch. The man was stalking me, mocking me.

I had an immediate flashback. It was 12 years ago and I was back aboard *Isobell*, an Ocean 71 sloop. We were a couple days out of Newport and running before a North Atlantic gale. The coincidence was too obvious to ignore. *Isobell*'s delivery ranks as one of my more challenging passages in a history of challenging passages. With a crew of two, I had left Newport bound for Stockholm. There was nothing terribly unusual about that scenario. I made my living delivering boats across the Atlantic in those days. I was a hardworking sailor, delivering boats to far-flung quaysides. What made this crossing unique was that we left Newport on January 25, in the dead of winter. We had to chip ice off the rig and shovel snow off the deck the day we left. The Swedish owners were anxious to get their hands on their new boat, and they were willing to pay a hefty fee for a winter crossing. And I confess, the challenge intrigued the hell out of me.

Forty-eight hours out we were running before a brutal winter storm. According to a nearby Dutch freighter we had contacted on the VHF radio, the winds were Force 13, an announcement that surprised me because I thought the Beaufort wind scale topped out at Force 12, defined as hurricane force winds and above. Francis Beaufort was an Irish admiral in the Royal Navy who quantified wind strength and sea state in a simple 12-point scale in 1806, or so I had thought (see Beaufort Table on page 24). By anybody's definition, true or apparent, Force 12 or 13, hurricane or hurricane plus one, this storm was honking, maybe the worst storm I've ever encountered. You will read about this storm in detail in Chapter Eight, Storm Stories.

I was on watch, huddled in the cockpit beneath a makeshift pilothouse. I was amazed and thankful that the autopilot was able to steer a 40-ton boat in such wild conditions. It was a remarkable piece of equipment, and although it gobbled up amps like a starving elephant, we fed it happily and prayed to the patron saint of autopilots to keep it working. We had a handkerchief of a storm jib set and were making double-digit speeds. Life was surprisingly tolerable, and there was nothing to do but to hold on and try to stay warm. As I would do twelve years later en route to Bermuda, I fished the shortwave radio out of my pocket. Once again I had missed the weather broadcast and tuned in to the BBC World Service instead.

It was 1991 and Charles Taylor was an up-and-coming insurgent. With the quiet backing of the United States, he was staging a coup d'état, wresting control of the sad West African republic of Liberia that had been founded by former American slaves. Taylor's forces had laid siege to the capital, Monrovia, named for American president James Monroe but not exactly the seat of a democratic enterprise that its namesake might have envisioned. While I was battling a force too-much storm in the North Atlantic, Charles Taylor made his final push for power. The BBC report describing the takeover went something like this:

"The situation on the ground in Liberia is dangerous, and there are conflicting accounts of what has transpired. Unconfirmed sources have reported that the rebel forces of Mr. Charles Taylor now control the capital city, Monrovia, and that President Samuel Doe has taken flight. These sources report that Mr. Taylor's forces have occupied the presidential palace. They claim that Mr. Taylor's forces have stormed the presidential office, on the second floor of the palace, and thrown the presidential desk and presidential chair from a window."

Alone in the cockpit with the ocean raging around me, I laughed so hard that my sides ached. The report still ranks as my all-time favorite newscast. This was the greatest coup since the defenestration of Prague in 1618. Can't you picture it? That's just how I'll do it if I ever stage a coup. "I'm in charge now, so get that damned desk and chair outta here. Now!"

Scroll forward twelve years to just about the very same spot in the Atlantic. I felt a wave of melancholy wash over me. Charles Taylor's reign of terror was over, and I'd been there from the beginning. He was my dictator, my despot. I felt old and stodgy. In twelve years he'd managed to take over a country, pillage and plunder it, foment another coup in neighboring Sierra Leone, become persona non grata at the normally docile United Nations, and then escape into exile. What had I done during those same years?

The companionway hatch slid back and Chuck and Ron dropped into the cockpit. They clipped their harness tethers to the strong point on the bridge deck and announced that it was their watch. Ron surveyed the wilderness that is the ocean and whistled. "It doesn't get this dark in Georgia," he said, adding "but this sure is some mighty fine sailing." The weather was moderating, but we were still blasting along at near double-digit speeds.

Chuck used the short and long hooks on his tether like a mountaineer to work his way aft to the helm. He plopped behind the wheel just as *Quetzal* took off on a long surfing run. He was a good sailor and liked to steer. He flicked off the autopilot and took the helm. The grin on his boyish face cut the darkness like a torch.

"Wow, this is amazing. You can't see anything. We're just sailing into an abyss. You just have to trust that we're going to come out the other side."

I was still pondering the parallel careers of myself and Charles Taylor and was not quite ready to head below. I decided to join Chuck and Ron for their watch. The next three hours produced some of the fastest, most exhilarating sailing that *Quetzal* and I have experienced. The seas were still huge, every inch of twenty feet, but they were less angry, more organized, more to *Quetzal's* liking. It was a memorable watch as we sailed into the dawn, chatting, laughing, and at times awed by the raw power and naked beauty of the sea. With the soft light of another day pouring over the horizon, and nursing a steaming cup of coffee, I realized what I'd been doing for the last twelve years. And what I'd been doing the ten years before that too. And although I couldn't have known it, I would keep doing this for the next ten years, and am still doing it today.

I am a ferryman. I am Neptune's lackey, nothing more, and certainly nothing less. I never really fit in the so-called real world ashore, so I went to sea. I studied at Harvard south—Cape Horn—and then did graduate work ferrying sailboats all over the world and telling stories afterward. Today I ferry something more abstract—aspirations. I am a connection between sailing dreamers and bluewater, their conduit to the sea. They find me and we make passages, real passages; there's nothing virtual about what we do. I had come to realize that sailing with those who had not lost their sense of awe was what I was meant to do, and sharing hard-won opinions and shards of saltwater wisdom, all the while nurturing dreams of faraway places and fragile visions of personal freedom, was what I did best. Nietzsche wrote, "In every real man a child is hidden who wants to play." Man and woman, we

The crew of Queztal *in the cockpit on the way to Bermuda, on the first of many "heavy-weather" passages. The conditions have moderated, but it is still cool, still hat and glove weather. It's been a tough passage, but things are looking up. The cockpit enclosures are in place, including the aft panels, and they provide a lot of protection. (Left to right: Chuck, Mark, Dirk, Mike; not pictured, Ron.)*

Secure sea berths are critical for happy passagemaking, and few modern boats have them. Here you can see the port-side pilot berth, which is very secure on either tack because the wooden chainplate covers keep you in place. Below, the settee berth is quite comfortable when the lee cloth is in place. Lee cloths are much better than leeboards, which are hard to stow and hard to lie against. The lee cloth can be folded below the cushion when not in use.

all crave to rediscover the wonder of childhood, and every now and then the sea gives you a glimpse of it.

Ostensibly I teach my clients about passage planning, heavy-weather sailing, navigation, and the like, but mostly we just sail. We stand our watches, keep the boat moving, and spend a lot of time chatting. We talk about the ocean. We talk about boats. The cockpit becomes a confessional; it's difficult to lie at sea. Hilaire Belloc wrote, "The sea drives truth into a man like salt." We talk about life, we talk about love, we talk about books and movies, and then we talk about boats some more. The dreary protocols of politics and religion seem strangely irrelevant while philosophy is surprisingly trenchant. We cherish fair weather and contend with foul, and we never miss Captain's Hour. We hoot and holler when we make landfall. This is my job; this is what I do.

It's a good gig.

I still tell a lot of stories, and almost in spite of myself I have learned a few tricks along the way to make offshore sailing more manageable and enjoyable.

I share some of both in the pages that follow. The format is a mix of soft and hard sciences. I am a storyteller first and a teacher second. The narrative of each chapter is enhanced by a sidebar or two with what I hope you'll find is some useful information. The bulleted lists at the start of the chapters provide a brief overview of the chapter's contents. Sometimes I weave lessons into the stories. I write about specific boats that I think are well suited for offshore sailing and how to handle them in heavy weather. I am also not shy about serving up advice on outfitting, route planning, seamanship, navigation, safety, gear choices, and the nuances of life at sea. But if the book has any significance, it is because the people I have sailed with have taught me more than I could ever possibly teach them, and through their stories I hope you find inspiration to make your own voyages.

Weather Information Sources

My mother sailed most of the way around the world in the 1980s, and I am pretty sure that once she and her partner, Tim, sailed beyond the range of the NOAA VHF local weather broadcast out of Key West, they rarely if ever received another weather forecast. At least not many that they could understand. Foreign languages were not their strong suit. And what was the result of this cavalier disregard for the weather? They encountered one moderate gale in four years and 25,000 miles of sailing. Were they just incredibly lucky? I don't think so. They were patient. Oceanic weather patterns are dictated by seasons, and if you sail the right ocean at the right time of year, and don't sail at the margins of the season, you can usually avoid deep gales. Not always, of course, and especially not once you sail beyond the tropical trade wind zones. But in general this rule still holds true. That's why we still buy pilot charts, and over the long term they're reliable and a very useful planning tool. (See Pilot Charts on page 140.)

But we're not patient anymore, and besides, we live and sail in the information age. Who wants to look at boring climate-averaging charts when you can look at real-time wind and weather data beamed down from satellites? Although I am something of a Nothosaur (a swimming near-dinosaur) when it comes to incorporating technology aboard *Quetzal*, even I have been known to download GRIB weather files (see below) via my satellite phone when offshore. And, I confess, it is quite useful to know that the wind is either going to continue to blow from a certain direction, change direction, lose steam, or blow harder. I am not claiming that GRIB files obviate the need for other weather data and personal observations, but they're remarkably accurate and easy to interpret. And if you know the wind direction and how it's changing, you almost always know the weather too.

No matter how many antennas you have at the masthead or pointing skyward off the sleek arch raked off your stern, weather observation still starts with your eyes. All forecasts, including those wonderfully convenient digitally compressed files, are subject to errors caused by local anomalies. In particular, satellites are not good at recognizing disturbances caused by nearby land masses. They often miss land and sea breezes, and they can't spot dangerous katabatic downdrafts. You still need to pay attention to wind direction, wind shifts, wind speed fluctuations, sea surface changes, cloud patterns, and the good old barometer, which is still vital to predicting what's in store for your small stretch of ocean.

When it comes to obtaining weather information from other sources, there's a logical sequence that most boaters, including offshore sailors, should follow.

The local NOAA/NWS VHF weather radio forecast broadcast on Channels WX 1 to 7, on frequencies 162.4 to 162.55, is the place to start. These forecasts cover local areas, usually up to 60 miles offshore, and are quite reliable for up to a couple of days. The National Weather Service is the part of NOAA responsible for marine weather, and it also broadcasts offshore and high seas forecasts at specific times each day via HF radio. The offshore forecasts are for U.S. and Caribbean offshore waters beyond the reach of VHF range, while the high seas forecasts cover the world. You can obtain these voice forecasts via either shortwave receiver, or preferably with an HF single-sideband receiver. The NOAA website, www.noaa.gov, lists all the available broadcasts, times, frequencies, and channels. Voice forecasts are also in writing on the site, along with other useful data including real-time buoy reports, current and Gulf Stream information, tidal information, and tropical storm updates. The NOAA website will restore your faith in government agencies.

This leads us to what was once and may still be the most important weather information source for offshore sailing, the venerable weather radio fax, usually just called weather fax. These weather charts, also available on the NOAA site, www.noaa.gov/fax/marine.shtml, are divided into regions and categories and broadcast at different times throughout the day. You can find weather charts that show wind and wave analysis, sea surface charts that show weather systems, or upper air charts that tend to show broad weather movement. In the old days you needed an SSB HF radio and a weather facsimile machine to print these charts. Now it's possible, and more common, to use an HF radio with a weather fax software package, and download faxes to a laptop for viewing. If you want to understand weather and predict what the atmosphere's next move is and how it will impact you, then nothing is more valuable than a real-time weather fax chart. Check the NOAA site for specific broadcast times.

Navtex (navigational telex) is information received by stand-alone units delivered in text format for vessels sailing up to 200 to *(continued next page)*

400 miles offshore. These were once quite popular on offshore sailboats because of their simplicity as they automatically recorded weather updates. We all like to see pictures these days, and because navtex has limited range, it has, for the most part, been replaced by more effective satellite-based weather sources.

This of course leads us to satellite weather—specifically, GRIB files. GRIB stands for gridded information in binary form. Essentially GRIBS are computer-generated weather forecast data files that are compressed to allow more information to be transmitted efficiently. These files can be attached as texts to e-mails, allowing them to be sent either via satellite phones or via HF SSB receivers, which makes them extremely useful to offshore sailors. The amount of information available is astonishing, and the forecasts, extending usually up to a week, are the most accurate I've ever used, especially if you limit the forecast window to three days or less. GRIB files show not only wind direction and speed but wave height and direction, temperature, visibility, surface pressure, and just about every weather variable a sailor might need. They're extremely user-friendly. You don't need much of a background in meteorology to interpret them. Most importantly, they are updated in three- or six-hour increments and are easily extended forward for simple forecasting.

Before discussing specific GRIB file service providers and the equipment needed to obtain the files on board, I should note that most sailors, even trans-ocean sailors, get a lot of their GRIB files through wi-fi. Anywhere you can pick up wi-fi with a cell phone, tablet, or computer, you can pick up GRIB files almost effortlessly, and many of the files are free for the taking. Without wi-fi you can also download GRIB files if you have phone service and a data plan. This can be expensive, but the GRIB apps load quickly, and for many sailors it's worth the cost, and is usually still less than satellite phone time. So if you are sitting in Newport contemplating a passage to Bermuda, a five- to six-day run for most boats, you can study the GRIB files for five days out, print them out, and be on your way. In the course of a world cruise, you will need to update the information from on board, and that's quite doable as well.

To obtain GRIB files at sea, you need either an HF SSB receiver or a satellite phone, a GRIB viewer software package available from a variety of sources, and a laptop, tablet, or in some cases just a phone. Because the data is provided through e-mail, you will also need to establish a service with either saildocs. com, globalmarinenet.com, or other Internet services; some services are available free of charge. On *Quetzal*, I use my iridium handheld sat phone to e-mail one of several GRIB providers, usually UGRIB. I'll then wait to receive a return e-mail with the GRIB files attached and ready to be viewed on my old Dell laptop.

Sailors disagree over whether online GRIB files offered free provide the same degree of accuracy as the other sites that require payments or subscriptions. I admit I tend to use the free sites, and have found the data to be accurate and reliable.

My favorite free sites are:

www.grib.us
www.passageweather.com
www.weatheronline.co.uk
www.windfinder.com
www.windguru.com

There are several websites that charge, usually after a free trial period, for access to GRIB files and other weather-related services, including routing and detailed forecasts. Two that I have used are:

www.predictwind.com
www.ocens.com

two

Is There Such a Thing? | A Heavy-Weather
Passage | Shipmate Overboard

A Rogue-ish Wave

"In the moments between crests there was the wild slope of water roaring toward us, then the blast from the gale at the top of the crest and the long fall down the roaring lee into the steep shadow of the next sea. The powerful surge and pitch of our sternway put such a strain on the rudderpost I feared we might lose it. There comes a time when a man would have to be a complete fool not to realize that his fate hangs on a particle of time."

—Charles Borden, *Sea Quest*

ALTHOUGH I HAVE BEEN KNOWN to plead for Neptune's mercy during the darkest moments of a ferocious storm, I am essentially a fundamentalist when it comes to science. I am a devotee of deductive reasoning and an unabashed supporter of the scientific method. Still, I confess that I am just a tiny bit suspect of the current theory that fleets of rogue waves are marauding across oceans like Mongolian hordes, taking aim at helpless vessels and rearing up from otherwise unruffled seas to flatten them like flounder. It seems that every destructive wave is at once labeled "rogue" just as every boating accident occurs in "shark-infested waters."

I have spent a good portion of the last thirty years plying the ocean in various small sailboats. I have crisscrossed the Atlantic, made my way to Cape Horn and back, and sailed thousands of miles in the Pacific. I've slogged through countless gales and some severe storms, and even survived two hurricanes. And maybe I have encountered rogue waves—maybe, probably, almost certainly, but I can't be sure. While some nasty walls of water have definitely rocked my world, most of the monstrous combers I've known were the cancerous offspring of deep ocean storms. I know that this type of inductive reasoning is usually faulty, as if my experience alone proves that rogues are rare, but you'd have to think that I am a good candidate for getting clobbered by savage yet random waves.

Scientific data, especially satellite remote sensing, have revealed that rogue waves are more common than previously thought and, despite my misgivings, might explain many mysterious ship disappearances. In *The Power of the Sea*, my friend Bruce Parker writes, "Rogue waves are terrifying." But he offers assurances that "We are close to being able to predict when they'll occur." I hope he's right, but I am not sure a prediction model would have helped us avoid one particular wave on a storm-tossed North Atlantic two Novembers ago. I am sure, however, that one wave, a man among boys, most definitely a *rogue-ish* wave, came within a razor's edge of destroying my ability to take people to sea and permanently altering the primal connection to the ocean that has defined my life.

We were bound from Nova Scotia for Fort Lauderdale by way of Bermuda. A series of southerly gales and a fast-moving hurricane had persuaded us to delay our departure. My training passages dictate a tight schedule that doesn't always wash with the vagaries of the North Atlantic. Frustrated and anxious to get underway, I was painfully aware that we would have to skip the Bermuda landfall. *Quetzal* was hunkered down, lashed to the commercial fishing dock in Shelburne, near the southwestern tip of Nova Scotia, with enough lines to rig a three-masted barque. A Force 11 nor'easter was forecast to rake the Canadian Maritimes, and Shelburne was in the crosshairs of the storm's projected route.

Slashing, horizontal streaks of rain peppered the decks like warning shots preceding the strongest gusts. *Quetzal* heeled 30 degrees one way and then the other. The anemometer had blown off the masthead, so we couldn't record the wind strength. There were seven of us aboard and we were snug below in the main saloon. I made a hearty spaghetti dinner, and we calmed our nerves with a couple of bottles of red wine. The pitch of the wind's fury was freakishly beautiful. I have an almost morbid fascination with nature at its angriest—it seems to temporarily shake the hubris out of me and leaves me feeling vulnerable and very much alive.

The wind dropped at some point in the night, and at first light we extricated ourselves from a web of cordage and got underway. Once again the forecast was not favorable for heading south, but everybody was in favor of sailing someplace, anyplace—and we were all weary of being shackled by satellite prognostications. This was the "heavy-weather passage," after all. So we headed west, toward Cape Cod, which lay 270 miles and two days of hard sailing away. Our new plan was to regroup on the Cape and snag the first decent weather window to sail directly to Fort Lauderdale.

When a southwest gale greeted us just off Georges Bank, we decided to heave-to. Giorgio, Kevin, and Ric tied the third reef in the main, and the rest of us hoisted and trimmed the staysail. Deep-keeled and low-slung, *Quetzal* heaves-to naturally, and eight hours later we were underway, racing another nor'easter to the coast. We won, but not by much, and as the storm raged we anchored near Provincetown, near the very tip of Cape Cod as it arches back toward the mainland, the very first spot the Pilgrims landed. We stood watch all night, and miraculously the anchor held. Two small Coast Guard cutters in nearby Chatham were not as lucky. They were stove in by breaking waves and had to be rescued by other Coast Guard vessels. The next morning we had a favorable wind at last, an Arctic blast dead out of the north. We set a course south for the first time in a week.

We shot past Martha's Vineyard into the offshore waters south of New England. With just a poled-out headsail, we routinely punched out double digits on the GPS. The sailing was exhilarating, and I was in no mood to slow down. We had an appointment with the great Atlantic conveyor, the Gulf Stream. But the Stream is not just an ocean current; it is a barrier, a chastity belt when approached from the north in heavy weather, and you breach it at your own peril.

We were aiming for the narrowest band of the current, a 45-mile swath of cobalt sea, approximately 300 miles off the coast of Maryland. I had chosen this conduit carefully because the Gulf Stream *(continued page 25)*

Thoughts on Waves

The question I am asked most frequently when we're at sea is, "So, how big are these waves?" The people asking are rarely satisfied because I invariably suggest they're smaller than the crew thinks they are. Maybe I am just trying to convince myself that the seas are not as large as they seem, or maybe I am trying to appear humble before the overwhelming forces of nature.

Since the voyage of Odysseus, the ocean has never suffered hubris from those who ply her surface, and I've learned to keep a low profile at sea. My standard answer is usually something like, "I don't know, four feet to six feet, maybe six feet to eight feet with a few bigger ones every now and then." Of course I am often wrong.

As small-boat sailors, waves impact our lives more than any other natural element. Yes, even more than wind, and yet waves are misunderstood and almost always over-exaggerated by inexperienced sailors. Veteran passagemakers tend to understate wave size, determined not to let wave heights, which are very difficult to accurately determine from the deck of a sailboat, dominate the conversation. There's something that's not quite socially correct for an experienced sailor to wax or worry about wave heights, even though we're thinking the exact same thing as new sailors: "These waves are huge!"

Advanced wave theory and the chaotic principles of fluid dynamics that try to corral them are incredibly complex (and fascinating). There are some simplified ratios and long-standing references that help sailors understand waves and their impact on our tiny, floating worlds. First, we need a brief introduction to waves, how they form, how we define them and measure them, and what those measurements mean.

Surface waves are formed by wind blowing over the ocean and transferring some of the wind energy to the water. There are three types of waves: *ripples, seas,* and *swells. Ripples* are annoyingly easy to understand, and their only purpose is to exasperate sailors and leave us whistling for wind so larger waves can form. *Seas* are those larger waves, actually component waves of many different durations, directions, and heights. These confused components are the reason it is difficult to follow a single wave because it always seems to merge into other waves and lose its identity. *Swells* are longer wind-driven surface waves that are more symmetrical and whose energy can travel vast distances. Swells have often moved hundreds or even thousands of miles away from the original wind source that spawned them. I leave tidal waves and tsunami waves out of the discussion for now.

What we are trying to determine when sailing is not how high a single wave is, but "how high are these seas," the average height of the waves.

Waves are determined by three basic criteria: *wind speed*, usually measured in knots; how long the wind has blown, or its *duration*; and finally, how much distance there is between where you are and where the wind is blowing from, or *fetch*. These factors, and how great they are, allow us to measure waves. Waves can then be defined by

- their *height*, the distance from the trough (lowest point of the wave) to the crest (highest point)
- their *length*, the distance from crest to crest
- their *period*, the time between crests.

Steepness is the angle between the crest and trough and determines whether a wave breaks.

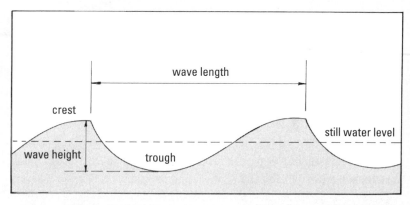

The anatomy of a wave.   *(continued next page)*

Because waves vary in shape and size, we need to make some assumptions to come up with an average wave height. The *significant wave height* is the average of the highest one-third of the waves. While this is not always easy to observe, with practice you can become fairly accurate. I use the boat, my height, and the horizon as reference points. With the boat in the trough, if the wave just obscures the horizon then I add the freeboard to 6 feet and have a decent measurement. Doing this several times usually results in a fairly consistent measurement. With bigger waves, I have used the 10-foot radar mast on the stern. With larger waves still, I reference them to the mainmast.

Once you have determined the significant wave height, and based on simple ratios using your significant wave height as the number 1, you can then calculate

- the average wave height (0.64 : 1),
- the highest 10 percent of the waves (1.29 : 1), and
- the highest waves (1.87 : 1).

For example, let's assume you determine the significant wave height to be 8 feet. Then the average wave height (8 × 0.64) is 5 feet; the highest 10 percent of the waves (8 × 1.29) are roughly 10 feet; and the highest wave (8 × 1.87) that you might encounter is theoretically 15 feet, give or take. Now let's go back and look at how wind speed, duration, and fetch determine a wave's full development. The accompanying table, which corresponds to the Beaufort scale (see page 24), shows how these factors will determine wave period, length, and height, rounded to the nearest foot. These are typical figures for comparison and clearly demonstrate how dramatically waves build as the factors increase.

HOW WIND AND WAVES INTERACT

Beaufort Force	Wind Speed (knots)	Duration (hours)	Fetch (NM)	Period (seconds)	Length Height (feet)	Mean Height (feet)	10%
Force 4	11–16	5	24	4	154	2	4
Force 5	17–21	9	65	8	305	4	9
Force 6	22–27	15	140	10	502	8	17
Force 7	28–33	24	290	12	787	15	29
Force 8	34–40	37	510	15	1,132	23	46
Force 9	41–47	52	960	18	1,607	36	73
Force 10	48–55	73	1,510	21	2,214	52	105

This table should give you all the incentive you need to limit your exposure to storm conditions by adopting aggressive forereaching strategies that take you away from the direction of the storm and thereby reduce the fetch. This is discussed at length throughout the book.

We can also calculate the speed in knots of the wave period, or simply how fast a wave is traveling, by employing the same formula that we use to determine a boat's theoretical hull speed:

$1.34 \times \sqrt{}$ of the wavelength.

This table is a quick reference for short and moderate wave periods. For larger period speeds, use the above table. Simply take the square root of the wavelength and multiply it by 1.34.

> 5-foot wavelength travels at 3 knots
> 10-foot wavelength travels at 4 knots
> 15-foot wavelength travels at 5 knots
> 20-foot wavelength travels at 6 knots
> 30-foot wavelength travels at 7 knots
> 40-foot wavelength travels at 8.5 knots
> 50-foot wavelength travels at 10 knots

Breaking waves are the most dangerous waves for sailors. Breaking waves are not whitecaps, which are the result of fully developed waves simply dispersing excess energy. Waves break when the base of the wave can no longer support its top. When the steepness angle of a wave becomes too great, it breaks, such as when a wave hits shallows. In a way, waves overrun themselves; we've all seen this at the beach. This can also be a factor in ocean sailing when large seas and swells suddenly encounter banks or shallow areas, causing the waves to become unsustainably steep. I recounted an incident like this in my book *At the Mercy of the Sea*. Huge seas spawned by Hurricane Lenny ran into the relative shallows of the Saba Bank, in the eastern Caribbean. The breaking waves that resulted became weapons of mass destruction, and my friend Carl Wake and his gallant boat, *La Vie En Rose*, did not survive.

Ocean waves also break when they collide with other ocean currents. The Gulf Stream in the North Atlantic and the Agulhas Current off the Cape of Good Hope in the Indian Ocean are infamous for creating huge breaking seas when they set against strong, or storm force, contrary winds.

The steepness angle is represented as a ratio of height to length. At 1:14 or less, waves become unstable and break. Another way to look at this is that when the wavelength becomes less than seven times the wave height, waves will break.

Of course simply going online and checking a variety of websites that provide real-time wave information can eliminate these calculations. One of the best sites is NOAA's National Buoy Data Center, http://www.ndbc.noaa.gov/. Just click on any of the hundreds of buoys and you will instantly have the significant wave height, dominant wave period, and wave direction. You will also find the wind speed and direction, barometric pressure, air and   *(continued next page)* sea temperature, and dew point. Of course this assumes that you have Internet access, which of course is not always the case at sea.

Finally, the venerable Beaufort scale, developed by Irish admiral Francis Beaufort of the Royal Navy in 1805 and officially called the Beaufort Wind Force Scale, is still an accurate and reliable way to gauge offshore conditions based on wind speed.

BEAUFORT WIND SCALE

Beaufort Force	Wind (Knots)	Appearance of Wind	Sea State	Land Conditions
0	Less than 1	Calm	Sea surface smooth and mirror-like	Calm, smoke rises vertically
1	1–3	Light Air	Scaly ripples, no foam crests	Smoke drift indicates wind direction, still wind vanes
2	4–6	Light Breeze	Small wavelets, crests glassy, no breaking	Wind felt on face, leaves rustle, vanes begin to move
3	7–10	Gentle Breeze	Large wavelets, crests begin to break, scattered whitecaps	Leaves and small twigs constantly moving, light flags extended
4	11–16	Moderate Breeze	Small waves 1–4 ft., becoming longer, numerous whitecaps	Dust, leaves, and loose paper lifted, small tree branches move
5	17–21	Fresh Breeze	Moderate waves 4–8 ft. taking longer form, many whitecaps, some spray	Small trees in leaf begin to sway
6	22–27	Strong Breeze	Larger waves 8–13 ft., whitecaps common, more spray	Larger tree branches moving, whistling in wires
7	28–33	Near Gale	Sea heaps up, waves 13–19 ft., white foam streaks off breakers	Whole trees moving, resistance felt walking against wind

Beaufort Force	Wind (Knots)	Appearance of Wind	Sea State	Land Conditions
8	34–40	Gale	Moderately high 18–25 ft. waves of greater length, edges of crests begin to break into spindrift, foam blown in streaks	Twigs breaking off trees, generally impedes progress
9	41–47	Strong Gale	High waves 23–32 ft., sea begins to roll, dense streaks of foam, spray may reduce visibility	Slight structural damage occurs, slate blows off roofs
10	48–55	Storm	Very high waves 29–41 ft. with overhanging crests, sea white with densely blown foam, heavy rolling, lowered visibility	Seldom experienced on land, trees broken or uprooted, "considerable structural damage"
11	56–63	Violent Storm	Exceptionally high waves 37–52 ft., foam patches cover sea, visibility more reduced	
12	64+	Hurricane	Air filled with foam, waves over 45 ft., sea completely white with driving spray, visibility greatly reduced	

not only shifts position as it rambles toward the old world but varies in width as well. At a bulge just east of our waypoint, the current was more than a hundred miles wide. The wind was clocking to the northeast, which meant that wind and current would be on a direct collision course. The Atlantic was already roiled, having been stirred by a week of gales and a meandering hurricane. It didn't take a marine physicist to predict that the conditions in the Gulf Stream were going to be brutal, and the wind shift was only going to make things worse. Naturally I wanted to limit our exposure and cross the Stream as quickly as possible. Aiming for the narrowest band of current seemed to make perfect sense. I was about to realize the magnitude of that mistake.

Another rugged passage in the North Atlantic, this one Quetzal's *first crossing. Note that the dodger panel has been blown out. A marauding wave plowed right through the panel, soaking the crew. The whisker pole in this photo, lashed to stanchions, no longer rides on deck. These days it is mounted on a separate track on the mast, ready to be deployed via a two-part block and tackle.*

Ric and Diane were on watch as we approached the northern edge of the Gulf Stream. Daylight was just creeping above the horizon. Within minutes the conditions changed from moderately rough to extremely rough. Ric, although relatively inexperienced as a helmsman, especially in heavy weather, was doing a fine job of steering *Quetzal* down the face of steep and occasionally breaking seas. Diane was sitting in the cockpit, facing aft and watching Ric and the huge waves piling up astern. Both were harnessed to the boat. They were cold and tired but seemed strangely satisfied and looking forward to the end of their watch in less than an hour. Ric and Diane had been making plans to buy a cruising boat, ditch their land lives, and take up full-time cruising. They had signed aboard for this exact moment, to get a taste of heavy weather and learn how to cope with a cruel sea.

The ride had become noticeably different, and even from below I knew that *Quetzal* was in a danger zone. I was anxious to get on deck. I slid the companionway back and felt the rush of warm air, a signature of the Gulf Stream. I slammed the hatch behind me and stepped into the cockpit.

I heard the wave before I saw it. It crested with a deep-throated roar. I ratcheted my head up and saw the monster curling above the stern. It occupied most of my field of vision—it was the largest wave I had ever seen. It was a moment of complete clarity, and time slowed as the wave began to break. I knew we were going to be crushed, and I wondered, coldly, objectively, if we would survive. I instinctively clutched the support rail on the side of the companionway and shouted, "Hold on."

A torrent of salt water swallowed us in a frothy rush. The bimini and solar panel frame crashed down on Ric, flattening him behind the wheel. *Quetzal* skidded out of control. At the base of the wave she began to list hard to starboard. She was going over; the mast was in the water. "Hold on, hold on, hold on," I screamed stupidly, as if they could do anything else. Bracing for a broach and full roll, I pinned myself against the coachroof.

But *Quetzal* didn't go over, didn't broach. Somehow she regained her footing, straightened up, then dug her deep keel into the hissing foam and refused to budge.

I was stunned and enormously relieved to see Diane. She was right where she'd been before the wave hit. What force, what power, what magic had held her in place? She looked at me with an expression that I'll never forget. She

Me on the foredeck, preparing to tie in the third reef on a rough passage. I am wearing my safety harness, and I'm clipped to the jackline on deck. Jacklines on Quetzal are 1-inch polyester canvas webbing. They run inside the shrouds from the cockpit to the stemhead fitting. They should be removed when the boat is not underway because UV shortens their life dramatically. Although I am working on the low side, I made my way forward on the high side, the safe side.

was bewildered but not afraid, as if she knew she'd just experienced something that would frame the rest of her life. Ric was also okay, although he was unable to move, pinned down by debris. He even managed a smile. I briefly wondered how the crew below had fared.

But time was not standing still; it just seemed that way. *Quetzal* was wallowing. Another wave broke across her beam and flowed through the cockpit. It was not a massive wave but it didn't matter. It swept Diane away.

I watched with horror and stunned disbelief as the wave carried her aft. I leaped after her. She was already most of the way off the boat when the backs of her legs snagged the upper lifeline. A split second later I had a death grip on her thighs. I tried to drag her back into the boat, but I couldn't overcome the force of the water. Ric, who had to watch this appalling spectacle helplessly, reached out for her as he desperately tried to free himself.

I screamed at Diane. "Get back in this boat. You're not going anywhere."

But I didn't believe it. Pulling with all my strength, I tried to lift her back aboard. But I failed. My world was crashing. For nearly a decade *Quetzal* and I had carried new sailors across calm and calamitous seas. But now the future was suspended by a lifeline and a couple of shackles, a particle of time. I knew that if Diane was washed away, I was going with her, and it would all be over.

Once again it seemed like time stopped. Even today I can close my eyes and see Diane peering out from her hood pulled tight around her face. I can see the water rushing by the boat, trying to pull her away. I can hear myself screaming at her and at the ocean.

But Diane would turn out to be the lucky one that day, as you will find out in Chapter Ten.

Sailboat-Speak

Every activity has a lingo, but few can match the esoteric vocabulary that hardcore sailors use to describe boats. When writing about sailboats, we often mix aesthetics and technical terms in the same sentence. We further complicate matters by using anthropomorphisms; boats are definitely not inanimate objects, and I always find it slightly offensive when a boat is called "it" instead of "she." In describing an old Allied Seawind II, I wrote in a review, "The profile shows a pronounced sheer emphasized by a plucky bowsprit and a low-slung deckhouse. She is definitely a bluewater boat."

A non-sailor would have no idea what I was talking about. Even a moderately experienced sailor would probably have a hard time drawing a mental picture from that description. Below is a glossary of sorts. It's not meant to be an all-encompassing sailing dictionary, just a guide to help you understand some of the specific, seemingly arcane words and phrases that I use to describe sailboats, how they're constructed, and a few of their less obviously named components. Terms in bold within a definition are other important words of the sailor.

Aft Cockpit Boat. A boat with the tiller, wheel or wheels, located in the after section of the boat, usually near the stern. As opposed to a **center-cockpit boat**, in which the helm is located more toward the center, or **amidships**.

After Body. The aft, or behind section, of a boat or hull.

Athwartships. A reference point that lies at a right angle to the centerline of the boat.

Balanced Rudder. Technically a rudder that carries roughly 10 percent of its area forward of its pivot point.

Ballast. Weight, in modern sailboats either lead or iron, mounted low in the vessel, almost always in the keel to increase stability. There are two types of ballast, **internal** and **external**.

A boat with *internal ballast* has the weight, usually cast pieces of lead or iron shot, placed inside the keel cavity, mixed in a slurry of resins and then fiberglassed over. The advantage of internal ballast is that there are no bolts to leak or be damaged in a hard grounding, and, short of the keel being completely delaminated, the keel cannot fall off. Internal ballast is also referred to as **encapsulated**.

External ballast implies that the keel is a separate component that is fastened to the bottom of the hull. This type of ballast is also referred to as a **bolted-on** keel. External ballast is usually fastened to some form of a keel **stub**, which is a structural member of the hull designed to support the external ballast. The advantage of external ballast is that the metal of the keel takes the impact in a grounding instead of the fiberglass that surrounds the keel cavity.

Bilge. The area above the keel and below the cabin sole where water is trapped and removed by means of a bilge pump. However, I often describe a boat as being **slack in the bilges** or **broad in the bilges**, and this applies to the shape of the hull between the topsides and the bottom.

Bobstay. A wire, and occasionally a length of chain, that runs from the stem to the outboard end of the bowsprit.

Boomkin. A spar aft of the stern designed to support a backstay or sheet. Used primarily on ketch or yawl rigs.

Bowsprit. A spar forward of the bow that supports the forestay.

Bridge Deck. An area in the cockpit that fronts the companionway. Offshore boats should have a bridge deck as it prevents water from sloshing below when the cockpit gets swamped. Can also be an important structural member. *(continued next page)*

Bulb Keel. A fin keel with a bulb, either of iron or lead, placed near the lower section of the keel for increased stability. Often used on boats with shoal draft.

Bulkhead. Any vertical part in a boat, akin to a wall in a house.

Bulwark. A raised part of the topsides, above the deck, that forms a rail or support.

Camber. The side-to-side, or **athwartship**, curve of the deck.

Canoe Stern. A rounded stern and transom, also called a **double-ender**. Long or short canoe sterns depend on the amount of overhang.

Center of Effort (CE). The center point of the sail area.

Center of Lateral Resistance (CLR). The center point of the underwater plane.

Centerboard. A relatively heavy device that is housed in a trunk on the bottom of the keel and lowered for more lateral resistance and lift. Found on shoal draft boats with a long keel.

Chine. A hard edge in the hull section, usually found on metal, particularly steel, boats.

Clipper Bow. A bow entry, taken from the clipper ships, that has a reverse S curve and leads to a bowsprit.

Club. The boom on a jib or staysail, which is then called **club-footed**.

Coachroof. Also variously called trunk cabin and deckhouse, it is the part of the hull that encloses the cabin and is raised above the deck. **Low-slung**, **wedge deck**, and **flush** are particularly low coachroofs; in the case of flush, a deck without a noticeable coachroof.

Coaming. The upper sides of the cockpit, often wood or finished with wood trim, and also the side of the coachroof.

Companionway. Entry or access to the cabin from the cockpit. Offshore sailboats should have a moderate-sized companionway that can be well secured with **washboards** for heavy-weather sailing.

Compression Post. A support, usually but not always a stainless tube, that supports a deck-stepped mast from belowdecks.

Cored Hull. A type of construction that employs a core material, usually balsa or foam, that is sandwiched between two layers of fiberglass. Cores reduce weight and add strength. They can delaminate and cause structural problems, although this is rare. Cored decks are commonplace, cored hulls less so, especially on heavily built offshore boats.

Counter Stern. A stern with an aft slope from where it's lifted above the waterline. As opposed to a **reverse stern**, or **reverse transom**.

Cutwater. The leading edge of the stem, and a very nice term that is not used much anymore.

Deadlight, **Portlight**, and **Porthole.** Confusing terms used by sailboat reviewers like me, with a convoluted etymology. Generally, deadlights are fixed ports, portlights are opening ports, and portholes are either, but the term is a bit out of date and is rarely used in sailboat-speak.

Delamination. A material breakdown, but sailors use the term most often referring to a core material that has lost its stiffness, usually due to getting wet. Delamination can also occur from a lack of structural support.

Dorade Vent. A vent that extends off the deck, allowing air to pass below and, in theory at least, not water. These vents don't always work as advertised. First used on the famous Sparkman & Stephens-designed ocean racer *Dorade*, hence the name.

Draft. The distance from the waterline to the bottom of the keel, or the depth of water that is required for a boat to float. **Deep, moderate,** and **shoal draft** are self-explanatory but also relative, especially to a boat's LOA (length overall).

Entry. The point of a bow where it enters the water. Usually described as a shape—fine, narrow, broad, and so forth.

Extrusions. Metal, almost always aluminum (on small inshore sailboats they can be plastic), pieces that slide over the headstay and allow a sail to be hoisted and dropped by means of a **luff tape**, in the case of a racing boat. Or, as I describe more often, they rotate around the headstay by means of a furling drum, allowing the sail to be furled. Sometimes called **foils**.

Fin Keel. A fin-shaped keel section that is detached from the rudder and provides lateral resistance and generates lift. There are several variations of fin keels. I sometimes write about a "powerful" fin keel, which more accurately might be described as a "long fin keel instead of a full keel." Keels are incredibly complex and can have straight leading and trailing edges, or they might be swept back. Chord length, the length of a keel measured fore and aft, divided by span, or depth, indicates whether a keel has a high or low aspect. Most cruising boats that I like have moderate- to low-aspect fin keels. Keels are built as foils, with designers using various foil-shape specs from NACA (National Advisory Committee for Aeronautics). Other variations of fin keels include wing keels, and shoal draft keels like the Scheel keel, named after designer Henry Scheel.

Flare. The forward part of the hull that curves outward. More common in powerboats.

Floors. Athwartship frames that provide structural support for the hull. Well-built boats have laminated floors as opposed to molded liners that take their place.

Forefoot. The forward section of the hull below the waterline, from the stem to the leading edge of the keel. I have used the term cutaway forefoot, which implies that the forefoot has been reduced in area and most likely runs aft to meet a fin keel or modified full keel.   *(continued next page)*

Fractional Rig. When the forestay does not extend all the way to the top of the mast, instead attaching to the mast below the masthead. Measurements are in fractions: a forestay that attaches ¾ of the way up the mast is a ¾ rig.

Freeboard. The distance measured from the deck edge to the waterline.

Full and By. A term I never use but should because it's lovely. Sailing close to the wind with all sails set and drawing.

Full Keel. A long keel with an attached rudder. This is the most traditional keel shape, derived from ancient times, and still very capable as a keel shape for oceangoing sailboats. A modified full keel has a cutaway forefoot, and sometimes a cutaway section just forward of the rudder. Developed by designer Ted Brewer, the aft cutout is called the Brewer Bite.

Gelcoat. A brand that became a trade name. A flexible polyester resin that served two purposes: it allowed a boat to be released from the mold and it provided a smooth and shiny finish.

Ground Tackle. The anchor, chain, rode, et cetera.

Gunkhole. A shallow, out-of-the-way anchorage. Gunkholing is exploring such places at a leisurely pace and often used as the objective of a shoal draft boat.

Gunwale. The outer railing of a boat, where the deck and topsides meet; pronounced "gunnel." The phrase "from gunwale to gunwale" implies that the boat is rolling miserably.

Heel. Yes, it is the angular inclination of a boat, but it is also the lower part of the mast and rudder.

Heeling Arm. The vertical distance between the CE **(center of effort)** and the CLR **(center of lateral resistance)**.

Hull Speed. The theoretical maximum speed of a non-planing hull. Found by multiplying 1.34 by the square root of the LWL (length at waterline).

Joinerwork. Fine woodwork in a boat, especially in the cabin. Some Taiwan-built boats, like *Quetzal*, have exceptionally nice joinerwork.

Keel. See **fin keel** or **full keel**.

Knees. Triangular-shaped members to support the hull and deck. Chainplates are sometimes secured to the knees.

Lazarette. A storage locker, or lockers, in the stern area.

Longitudinal Stringers. Framing that runs fore and aft, usually foam with fiberglass or gelcoat over them. They stiffen flat sections of the hull and are a sign of good construction.

Mast Partners. The structural area supporting where the mast goes through the deck.

Mast Step. A structural member that supports the heel or base of the mast in the bottom of the boat.

Molded Liners. Fiberglass pieces that are molded independent of the hull and deck and then tabbed to the hull to provide layout arrangements and, more importantly, to support the hull. This type of construction relies on the bonding of the liner to the hull and can be problematic. Few serious boats rely on molded liners for their structural integrity.

Osmosis. Blisters that develop between layers of fiberglass. A problem that was considered severe in the 1980s and 1990s, it was generally thought to be caused by inferior polyester resins. Vinylester and epoxy resins have since dramatically reduced the problem. Also, many consider the "pox" epidemic to have been overblown.

Overhangs. The parts of the bow and stern that extend beyond the waterline. Measured as the difference between the LWL and the LOA.

Pilothouse (PH). A part of the cabin trunk that extends over the cockpit and is raised. The pilothouse technically should enclose the helm, although this is not always the case on sailboats. **Hard dodgers** are sometimes confused with pilothouses.

Pitch. The motion, particularly up and down, of a boat in the fore and aft direction.

Preventer. A line running forward from the boom to a strong point on deck to prevent an accidental jibe. It is better to mount the preventer as aft as possible on the boom and run it as far forward as practical; this allows for a soft jibe, which is easiest on the boom, sail, and deck.

Profile. The side view of the boa, as seen from amidships. Often the view presented in boat diagrams.

Raised Deck. A deck without a distinct cabin trunk, used on small boats like the Cal 25, to create room below.

Rudderstock. The shank of the rudder that extends up through the hull to the steering mechanism.

Running Backstays. Usually called **runners**, temporary backstays to support the jib or staysail. Only the weather runner is deployed, and they are exchanged as part of the process of tacking.

Scantlings. The structural dimensions of a boat.

Section. Cross section of a hull design. Many designers work with ten sections, sometimes called stations.

Sheer, Sheer Line. The curve of the deck line, most obviously observed in profile, and measured from bow to stern. Traditional boats typically have pronounced sheer, modern boats less so. Sheer is one of the design features that makes sailboats beautiful.

Side Deck. The space between the coachroof coaming and the gunwale.

Skeg. An extension of the hull in front of the rudder and supporting the rudder. I use the phrase skeg-hung rudder and prefer it to a spade rudder for serious sailboats.

Spade Rudder. A rudder supported only by its **rudderstock**. It is not supported by the hull or by means of a skeg.   *(continued next page)*

Split Rig. A rig with more than one mast. In modern sailboats, usually a ketch rig, sometimes a yawl.

Stability. There are different types of stability, but it is usually measured as the moment or force required to return a boat to upright after it has been knocked down.

Stem/Stemhead Fitting. The stem is the part of the hull between the waterline and the forward most part of the deck. The stemhead fitting is mounted on deck and supports the forestay and often incorporates rollers for the ground tackle.

Strut. A frame or appendage that supports the propeller shaft.

Tabbing. A layer of fiberglass that bonds wooden bulkheads or furniture facings to the hull.

Transom. The stern section, the furthest aft athwartship surface and usually where the name and hailing port are marked. Many modern boats have opened up the transom to provide easy access to the water via a **stern step**, or **swim step**.

Tumblehome. The outward curvature of the hull between the deck and waterline.

Underbody. The shape of the hull, keel, and rudder below the waterline.

Washboards. Horizontal pieces, usually made of wood, that fit together to close off the main companionway.

Whisker Pole. A spar used to hold out the clew of a headsail when reaching or running.

three

Oceangoing Sailboats | Buying a Sailboat | Owning
a Sailboat | Naming a Sailboat

Quetzal and Other Sailboat Obsessions

"For boats, even the uglier ones, are among the loveliest creations of man's hands, and though owning them brings a train of debts, hangnails, bruises, bad frights, and all kinds of worries not experienced by those who content themselves with the more practical vices, the relation between a man and his boat is as personal and intimate as the relation between husband and wife."

—Desmond Holdridge, *Northern Lights*

"The desire to build a house is the tired wish of a man content thenceforward with a single anchorage. The desire to build a boat is the desire of youth, unwilling yet to accept the idea of a final resting place."

—Arthur Ransome from *Racundra's First Cruise*, 1923

"The other great nexus of metaphors and feeling is the ship itself. No human invention, with all its associated crafts in building and handling, has an older history—or has received more love."

—John Fowles, *Shipwreck*

A FERRYMAN NEEDS A FERRY, and while *Quetzal*, my well-traveled and much-ballyhooed 47-foot cutter, is certainly the main character in this book, she has to share the stage with many different boats. I have sailed more than fifty different kinds of sailboats at least a thousand miles, and have logged somewhere around 300,000 bluewater miles. I say "somewhere" because I have lost track. I just keep sailing year after year and can't seem to stop, and it seems absurd to keep tallying miles. I am not sure that miles matter very much because they define sailing as the distance between landfalls, as if land's edge somehow defines the ocean and our relationship with it, and that's patently false. Time at sea seems a more valuable measure, especially time without the burden of looming landfall. One thing I know for sure is that sailboats, and the unquenchable desire to steer them toward the deep-blue waters of the planet, is a passion that never dims.

I can't help myself. I love sailboats. No other man-made object blends design, craftsmanship, passion, and pure optimism the way a sailboat does. With a good sailboat, anything is possible. Even when I am ashore, I am usually thinking about boats. Like many people reading this book, I have an inner radar that triggers a warning alarm when a sailboat is nearby. The sight of a mast, a hull, the broken remains of a rusted-out iron keel, anywhere, even propped in a field far from the sea, will force me to detour and check it out. Rummaging around a boat that will never feel the pitch of the sea again makes me melancholy, and I am compelled to find out what happened. I know there is a story among the sprung planks and rotting frames.

I get anxious during those rare times when I am traveling inland. Like a lemming on its way to a cliff, I work my way toward the sea. When the coast appears, I am profoundly relieved. My pulse quickens when I near a harbor or catch a glimpse of a distant sail curved by the wind. I am always scurrying for a vantage point to overlook a marina or, better yet, boats swinging to their anchors. I have climbed cactus-covered hills and balanced on perilous rocky perches just to see my boat lying at anchor below. It's fair to say I am obsessed with sailboats, but I don't apologize. E. B. White was writing about himself, but he could have been describing me when he wrote, "If a man is to be obsessed by something, a boat is as good as anything, perhaps a bit better than most."

When I am not sailing (which is how I have made the bulk of my living my entire adult life), or writing books and magazine articles about sailing, or lecturing about my voyages, or working on my boat, or scheming future voyages, or scanning the horizon for glimpses of boats, I occasionally conduct workshops on all manner of sailing subjects. It's another way to make money talking about one of the few things I know a lot about, and another way to keep the real world, and a real job, at bay. One of my most popular weekend workshops is "How to Buy a Cruising Boat."

An intriguing group of people, from inexperienced dreamers to those on the threshold of serious cruising, gather at my Fort Lauderdale house looking for enlightenment, or at least some honest and trustworthy advice to help steer them toward the right boat. No boats are for sale. The weekend is devoted to evaluating cruising boats, with no hidden agenda, finder's fees, or brokers lurking behind the aloe plants in the backyard waiting to pounce with their business cards. The workshops are informal, informative, and a lot of hard work for those attending and for me, but it's work I love.

We discuss design and construction features and how they translate when it comes to meeting the demands of ocean sailing. Sailing terminology is esoteric and can be confusing to even experienced sailors. Like the folks in my workshops, you are about to be subjected to an array of terms describing keel and rudder shapes, hull forms, construction materials, engineering concepts, and more, and I apologize in advance. If I lose you along the way, check the glossary at the end of Chapter Two, which should help you make sense of my sailor-speak. We slice through the hyperbole of magazine ads and talk about practical matters like financing, and the truth about some surveyors and other experts who prey on the buyer. I tell my clients to reign in their emotions and zero in on the right boat calmly, rationally, and methodically.

We usually inspect at least ten boats during the weekend, ranging from finely outfitted world cruisers to reluctantly afloat hulks. We look in the bilges, note whether the ballast is internal or external, check how the bulkheads are tabbed to the hull, and note signs of leaking. The boats are scattered around Fort Lauderdale, and as we drive from one boat to the next we discuss the pros and cons of the previous boat. I remind the group to focus on the practical aspects of a boat: is it well designed, well built, and, most importantly, well suited for their cruising plans? I serve up clever axioms like "design always trumps construction," "form floats function," and my mantra, "a good bottom is hard to find." We also discuss whether a boat will hold its value when it's time to sell.

This is solid, mature advice, right? I have to confess, it is a bit of a sham. Sure, I know a lot about boats and can tell you whether the hull shape of a boat will make it pound in a seaway, how well the hull and deck are joined, if the rig will stand up to a blow, and what year a certain manufacturer switched to more blister-resistant resins. But when I look back at the boats I've owned over the years and how I purchased them, I know that I'm a charlatan for espousing this sensible approach to finding a sailboat.

You can't separate emotion from buying a sailboat, and why should you? Designer and wit R. D. "Pete" Culler writes, "Boats, like whiskey, are all good," and I wholeheartedly agree. I am a boat drunk, and although I willingly admit my problem, I doubt I'll ever recover. There's no 12-step plan for me. I am an addict, content to wallow aimlessly in any pathetic boatyard. I have owned an eclectic group of sailboats over the years, and their only common denominator is that I have loved them all. I understand why sailboats are considered feminine in most cultures. They're lovely and seductive, but beyond that they also do all the heavy lifting, the real work of voyaging. We sailors are just along for the ride. It's the boat that matters when the ocean gets angry.

Desmond Holdridge, author of the classic *Northern Lights*, describes his first boat, a doughty little wooden schooner, like this: "I thought her the finest thing that had ever floated. I thought that with her I could go anywhere in the world. I thought a great many things about her, most of them pure illusion."

I have the same sentiments about my first boat, a 1966 Bristol 27 sloop. Designed by prolific Swedish-born naval architect Carl Alberg, she was a proper little cruising boat with a long keel, an attached rudder, slack bilges, and a classic 1960s swoopy sheerline. Dependable Alberg designs were as ubiquitous as shag carpeting and wood-grain Formica in those early days of fiberglass boatbuilding. She had a proud bearing in the water and was handsome in a humble Scandinavian way. She was also heavy, overbuilt, and painfully slow—the predictable result of a stubby waterline and barely 300 square feet of sail area for horsepower.

Today we use a variety of ratios to predict sailing characteristics. Two ratios commonly used are sail area/displacement (SA/D), and displacement/length (D/L) (waterline). The Bristol 27 SA/D is 15.5 and its D/L is 382.

To put these metrics in perspective, consider:

SA/D 15 and below are heavy motorsailers
SA/D 16–17 are bluewater cruisers
SA/D 18–19 are performance cruisers
SA/D 20 and above are ocean racing boats
D/L of 100 or less are ultralights and multihulls
D/L 100–200 are ocean racing boats
D/L 200–250 are performance cruisers
D/L 250–300 are bluewater cruisers
D/L 300 and up are heavy cruisers

You can see that by any measure, the Bristol 27 was not going to win many races.

SA/D AND D/L RATIOS FOR SOME FAVORITE KRETSCHMER BOATS

	SA/D	D/L
Bristol 27	15.5	382
Contessa 32	15.5	306
Westsail 32	13.89	435
Nicholson 35	17.92	365
Pretorian 35	14.79	217
Jeanneau Ginn Fizz 37	21.76	253
Tayana 37	16.57	359
Shannon 38	16.72	333
Bristol 40	15.39	376

	SA/D	D/L
Valiant 40	15.46	255
Hallberg Rassy 42	15.04	258
Mason 43	14.49	366
Outbound 44	18.44	189
Peterson 44	14.39	232
Kaufman 47	17.5	209
Hylas 47	15.77	290
Hylas 49	16.6	232
Gulfstar 50	13.35	250
Sundeer 60	17.5	80

I didn't care; she was the only serious boat I could afford when I purchased her thirty plus years ago from a shadowy Detroit fish broker. She was named, appropriately, *Lobster Mobster*. At age twenty-one, that name rattled my idealism. I scrubbed it off and tempered the gods' wrath by renaming her *Jeanne*, after my mother, who had given me most of the money to buy the boat. Looking back I now realize that *Lobster Mobster*, with a menacing red lobster claw on the transom, had a certain take-no-prisoners verve that I just didn't comprehend at the time. I shipped her by truck from Michigan to the Florida Keys and moved aboard.

Lurching from one sandbar to the next, I eventually learned how to sail and, thankfully, to navigate. *Jeanne*'s best attribute was that she endured my inexperienced assaults and abuses without complaining or leaking.

After a couple of years I sold *Jeanne* and decided that I needed a larger boat. I had a vague idea that somehow I might be able to make money with a boat through chartering and teaching, and I also wanted more space for the extended cruising I hoped to do.

My next boat was a Jeanneau Gin Fizz sloop named *L'Ouranous*, an about-face from stodgy *Jeanne*. Built in 1978 and 37 feet 6 inches overall, she was sleek and cosmopolitan, or that's how she struck me then. Today when I see old Gin Fizzes, they seem a bit clunky. But the same can be said about a lot of us, so I'll stick to my first impression. Our Gin Fizz was for sale in Fort Lauderdale, fresh from an Atlantic crossing. She was also just about everything I didn't want in a boat, with a jaunty bolted-on fin keel, a paltry, partial skeg to protect the rudder, excessive beam, and a flat hull shape that promised to pound your fillings out in a seaway. Her cockpit was, by my standards then, dangerously large, and the small cabin aft of the helm seemed absurd. She was just too modern for my tastes. I was still reading books by Eric Hiscock and Hal Roth, and if these curmudgeonly gurus didn't trust modern designs, why would I?

The yacht broker selling the boat was starving and desperately needed a deal. Those were tough times in the early 1980s, and I was his only potential customer. I'm pretty sure the Gin Fizz was his only listing. He kept calling, sending me pictures and updated listing sheets, and finally, just to get him off my back and maybe because I felt sorry for him, I went and looked at the boat.

Ooh la la! I was charmed like a boy's first visit to Les Deux Magots in the Latin Quarter. I was a young Hemingway, and *L'Ouranous* was so French, so foreign, so filled with intrigue that she would undoubtedly give me stories to write about. In those faraway days before French builders came to dominate worldwide sailboat production, the Gin Fizz was truly exotic, a European rarity in the United States. When I pushed open the companionway and dropped into the dark mahogany-trimmed interior, I was seduced. The cabin smelled of the unfiltered tobacco of European cigarettes, and the aroma made a suburban Michigan kid feel sophisticated. I sat at the navigation station and the world seemed within reach. Visions of St. Tropez and

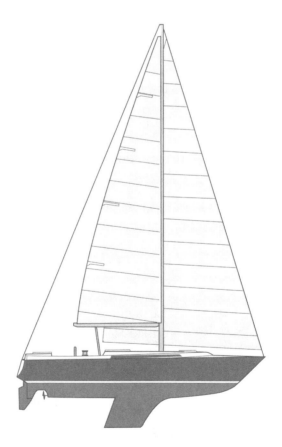

Sail plan and hull profile of Jeanneau's Gin Fizz. (Joe Comeau)

(Left) Epoch, *a Jeanneau Gin Fizz, at anchor off Dinner Key, Miami. (Right)* Epoch *on the hard in St. Augustine, me looking wiped out on the lawn chair below after painting the bottom. Note the hull shape and beer bottle.*

Tahiti floated in my brain. There were neatly folded charts of the Bay of Biscay, the Canary Islands, Guadeloupe, and St. Martin. The scribbled positions and course lines made my heart race—*L'Ouranous*, just a few years old, had already been "out there." My practical concerns were swept overboard. What did Hal Roth really know anyway? I bought her, changed her name to *Epoch*, and sailed her to Bermuda, the Caribbean, Panama, and back to Florida. My mother later sailed her most of the way around the world.

Without realizing it at the time, we had stumbled onto a very good boat with the Gin Fizz. Although it was just an off-the-shelf production boat, Jeanneau was then, and still is today, a quality builder. My mother sold the boat to a family hoping to cruise the Caribbean, but the close confines of boat living quickly snuffed out that dream. The young man they sold it to proceeded to sail it around the world again, and the chap he sold it to sailed it to New Zealand. Sailors all over the world have realized that these old boats from the 1970s are still excellent values, and this year alone I have seen Gin Fizzes refitted for serious cruising in Antigua, Costa Rica, and all over the Mediterranean. And one more note about the Gin Fizz: Laura Dekker, the Dutch young lady who recently became the youngest person to circumnavigate, sailed a jazzed-up 1977 Jeanneau Gin Fizz on her epic voyage.

The next boat that came into my life was *Gigi*, the legendary Contessa 32 sloop that carried me across the Atlantic and around Cape Horn. I have written extensively about *Gigi*, and the Contessa 32 in general, and readers know that it's the boat that I hold closest to my heart. It just may be the best fiberglass production boat of all time, certainly the most beautiful. But then again, I am a tad biased. My friend, partner, antagonist, benefactor, and mentor, Ty Techera, owned her, but he'd tell you she was as much mine as his. Sailing well beyond our talents, *Gigi* looked after two bumbling but game midwesterners and escorted us to the bottom of the world and back. She turns up throughout these pages, both as a benchmark boat and as an unflinching character in a few stories. My first book, *Cape Horn to Starboard*, recently republished, lavishes praise on this winsome collaboration between designer David Sadler and legendary builder Jeremy Rogers.

I also owned another diminutive British cruiser, a Varne 27, a coquette of a boat designed by Duncan Stuart. She was rakish and deceptively seaworthy with a sweet hull shape, a bold swept-back fin keel, and a skeg-hung rudder. But she was ridiculously small and impractical for serious cruising. She was one of the few boats afloat that made the Contessa 32 seem spacious. I bought her from an irascible Irishman who owned and operated a Fort Lauderdale boatyard. He had repossessed the abandoned boat and just wanted it out of his yard.

The timing was critical. I was being pressured by a girlfriend to buy a house and settle down and needed to act quickly. "How much do you want for the boat," I asked. "How much do you have," he answered, realizing at once that I was not a man of means. When I told him, he said, "That's what I want." What a relief—I had a boat and no money left for a down payment on a house.

Once again I had to change the name. How could I ply the oceans in a boat named *Rattlesnake*? Her former owner, a South African I never met, must have had some anger and trust issues. Hoping to assuage the gods one more time, I stayed with the animal theme, and *Rattlesnake* became *Stormy Petrel*. I have always admired the flittery pelagic petrels, and it seemed an appropriate name for this bantam boat. I had grand plans to sail her back to England, her motherland, where the boat was well respected. My plans were ambitious. I envisioned a crossing via the Arctic, and then, after writing a book about the trip, hoped to sell her for a nice profit. But the voyage never materialized, and I eventually passed her on to my brothers up in Michigan, where she languished on Lake St. Clair.

Although I was delivering boats professionally, and was rarely ashore, I felt naked and vulnerable without a boat of my own. Still, my next boat purchase is difficult to explain. There was no sensible reason to buy *Lone Star*. A home-built Bruce Roberts Offshore 44 ketch, she was made of steel, and it showed. Although she was just ten years old, her hull plates were wrinkled, her chines were wavy, she was streaked with rust, and her makeshift interior was straight out of a Home Depot. But there was something about her, something beyond the shabby cosmetics, something admirable in her sturdy bearing. She felt like a small ship, and I knew she could take just about anything the ocean tossed her way. For some idiotic reason, I wanted a steel boat. Blame Bernard Moitessier.

Although perfectly capable fiberglass production boats had given me no reason for pause, I seemed to have had a philosophical conversion of sorts, at least concerning my own boat. I saw myself in a different light, more an explorer than a sailor, and I wanted a boat to match my new image. I wanted a rough-edged boat, one that would be at home lying alongside sporadically planked wharves in the developing world and one that would send a clear anti-yacht message when I dropped the hook in a crowded Caribbean anchorage or eased stern-to in a Mediterranean quay. I wanted a boat for expedition-style sailing. I wanted a boat that Bernard Moitessier would understand and respect.

Moitessier, you may recall, was the famed French singlehanded sailor and author. But he was more than that; he was a philosopher with a pipeline straight to my soul. He wrote in his book *The Long Way*: "My real log is written in the sea and sky; the sails talking with the rain and stars amid the sounds of the sea, the silences full of secret things between my boat and me." *Lone Star* was my philosophical statement. I wanted to have secrets only she and I knew.

I just didn't expect them to be spelled out in blood and rust.

Bruce Roberts has designed some hideous-looking boats and some handsome, capable ones, and you can't blame him for some of the atrocious homebuilt hulks that carry his name. The Offshore 44 was definitely one of his better designs, with a soft sheerline, a powerful fin keel, and full skeg underbody, moderate and well-balanced proportions, and a sensible ketch rig. The fact that the owner of *Lone Star* was desperate to pay off an IRS debt, and willing to take a pittance for the boat, made it easier for me to take the plunge. I am not a Texan, and *Lone Star*—like *Lobster Mobster*, *L'Ouranous*, and *Rattlesnake* before her—had to be changed. After forging a compromise with a now ex-wife, we changed the name to *Fortuna*, the Roman goddess of luck and fortune whose symbol was a ship's wheel. I had some of the former and very little of the latter during the ten years I owned *Fortuna*.

Neil Young had it right when he sang "rust never sleeps." Day after day *Fortuna* quietly but persistently disintegrated, oxidizing and corroding before my eyes, doing her best to mutate from a boat into a cloud of iron pyrite that would sink back to mother earth waiting to embrace her at the bottom of the sea. I kept the rust at bay long enough to sail her to the Caribbean and Central America and to get a taste of the chartering and expedition sailing business, but a long-planned family circumnavigation never materialized. I was too busy sailing other people's boats to sail my own, and my life changed with *Fortuna* forlornly tied to a dock. Eventually, I sold her.

I've never owned a Hylas 49, but I have logged close to 60,000 miles aboard various models, equivalent to two circumnavigations. (There's that mileage measurement again; it's hard to escape it in our quantitative world.) I've been through several severe storms and have the ultimate respect for this classic Sparkman & Stephens design. Evolved from the Stevens 47 (see page 100), the Hylas 49 is a blend of comfort and seaworthiness not found in many boats. The deep hull shape never pounds, the long fin keel tracks well in big seas, and the fiberglass construction is robust. For years I was the chief delivery

Fortuna.

My steel boat Fortuna, *a center-cockpit Roberts Offshore 44 ketch, in Fort Lauderdale.*

skipper for Hylas Yachts, and I sailed frequently with Tony Siebert, the inspiration behind the Hylas 49. Tony owned a Hylas 47, and while he loved the way the boat sailed, he knew it could be a lot more comfortable. Although he never received official credit for the 49, it was filled with his ideas.

Gradually my role changed, and instead of delivering new boats down to the Virgin Islands charter fleet, I developed a relationship with two Hylas owners and became their de facto skipper. This new arrangement of scheduled

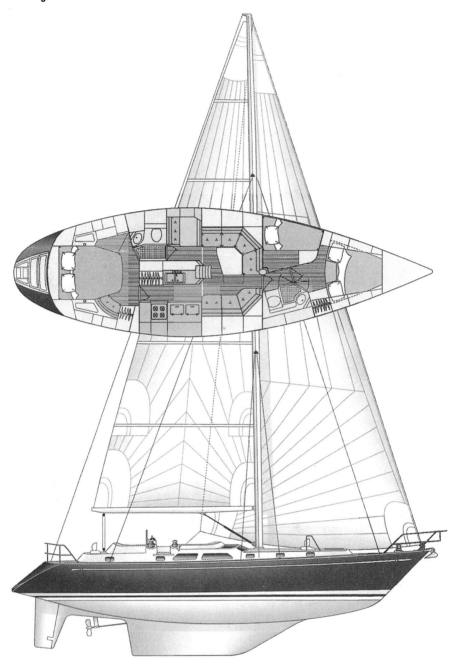

The Hylas 49 hull shape, with a longer fin keel, fuller sections, and a short waterline, is dated, but it is very seaworthy. The Hylas 49 has a SA/D of 16.6, a D/L of 232, and a B/D of 45. By comparison, Quetzal's SA/D is 17.5, D/L is 209, and B/D is 36. Not surprisingly the Hylas is a bit slower and needs more breeze to make way, but ultimately it is amazingly stable and seaworthy.

passages worked well for me because I was weaning myself away from being a full-time delivery skipper. I had two young daughters and a faltering marriage. The girls needed me, and I needed them. For the first time in my adult life, I needed some semblance of a schedule. For five years I delivered a Hylas 49 from New York to the Virgin Islands in the late fall, then up to Fort Lauderdale in the spring, then back to New York in the summer. I completed this private Bermuda Triangle with the owner, George, a self-made man, a brilliant engineer, a good sailor, and a truly amazing chef.

Although each leg was usually longer than a week, George and I often sailed without other crew. And while I would spend most of the day on deck, he would stay below, cooking and fixing anything that wasn't in perfect condition. A typical dinner might feature osso bucco from aged veal, rosemary-seasoned potatoes, a fresh gorgonzola salad, and a bottle of St. Emilion Bordeaux. This was a life I had surprisingly little trouble adjusting to.

Just how good a boat is a Hylas 49? We never missed a meal, no matter the conditions. Even in gales we would rig up the cockpit enclosures, set up the teak table, and dine in as much style as you can when you have to hold everything in place. I doubt George knows what a valuable lesson he taught me, but I have always managed to produce a good meal at sea ever since. A boat is not an excuse for a poor meal.

Another Hylas 49 owner, Henry, helped me launch my training passage business. For years I had been taking passengers along on deliveries, offering experience and training for a nominal fee, usually a contribution toward provisions. Henry helped me see that I was sitting on a good business opportunity. And being an astute businessman, he made me an offer that worked well for both of us. He wanted his boat in the Chesapeake Bay in the summer and the Caribbean in the winter. I offered berths on these passages, and just like that John Kretschmer Sailing was born. *Super Chief* was the perfect boat for my nascent business. I did not have boat expenses to worry about, and, more importantly, I knew that the Hylas 49 could stand up to the ocean's moodiness and mistakes from inexperienced sailors while maintaining a tight schedule.

My first paying passage aboard *Super Chief* was from Antigua back to Annapolis, and I assembled an interesting crew. My dear friend Bob Pingel, who writes the "Boat Doctor" column for *Sailing* magazine, signed aboard as my mate. He was joined by Glen, an amusing entrepreneur from Texas who had made a reluctant fortune with an online dating service. A third man, John, was an aspiring cruiser, and Bob and I nicknamed him the "common man." He was extremely handsome but seemed oblivious to the fact. On the flight down from Miami, the flight attendants tarried in the aisle by his seat, smiling, flirting, all the while offering him extra this and that. But he didn't seem to notice. He was an incredibly kind fellow who worked in a warehouse, dreamed of cruising full time in his S2 36, and adored his wife. "I am just a common man," he told us.

We met our last crewmember, Craig from Ontario, at the airport in St. John's, Antigua. I had never met Craig before, so I asked him on the phone when he signed up for the passage what he looked like so I might spot him in a crowd. He described himself, and then, with a slight laugh, added, "My wife says I look a little like George Clooney."

Bob and I went to the airport to meet him, and when Bob asked what he looked like, I said, "George Clooney." A few minutes later a crowd gathered as a dashing man and a beautiful woman exited the terminal. The guy had on designer sunglasses and an expensive leather jacket, and there was something of an entourage around them. He looked a lot like George Clooney. Wow, I thought to myself, Craig from Ontario is a heavy hitter, and he really does look like George Clooney. Pushing my way through the crowd, I shouted, "Craig, Craig, it's John, John Kretschmer." The woman looked concerned, and the man sneered at me with contempt. The entourage quickly sealed them off, and they strode away to a waiting limousine. I think it was George Clooney, and apparently he didn't like being called Craig.

An hour later we found Craig in the bar. He'd gotten in early and thought we'd forgotten about him. Naturally we nicknamed him George and kidded him about what his wife was thinking about at night.

The passage north was slow, with fickle winds punctuated by violent thunderstorms. The sturdy Hylas 49, with a soft ride in a seaway and the heft to ride out squalls without panicked sail shortening, was an ideal learning platform. The crew mastered celestial navigation, learned how to coax a boat across an inconsistent stretch of ocean called the "horse latitudes," enjoyed my cooking, and endured many sea stories. And I had a great time as the master of ceremonies. It was obvious to me that this was the direction I would be sailing in the future.

Henry decided to sell *Super Chief* just about the time my marriage collapsed. I still owned *Fortuna* and moved aboard with my two young daughters as they split their time between Mom and Dad. My older daughter, Nari, had a special kinship with *Fortuna* and a secret talisman. Although just five years old, she often came along to the boatyard during one of *Fortuna*'s many refits. The repairs were serious (new hull plating), and I worked with a welder for the better part of a month. I didn't know that the welder had affixed a heart to the bow just below the cove strip in Nari's honor.

Although the girls and I loved living aboard, *Fortuna* was not the boat for my sail training business, so I put her up for sale. I priced it for a quick sale (still it was far more than I had paid), and soon a plumber from Long Island, New York, was keenly interested. Fortunately he was part of the cult;

he wanted a steel boat, and no amount of common sense was going to talk him out of it.

He flew down to Fort Lauderdale and inspected the boat. He was entranced, talking about the "big picture." Good thing, because many of *Fortuna*'s details were not pretty. I felt guilty as it became obvious that he was actually going to buy the boat. I began to point out areas of corrosion and rust that I had recently disguised with a fresh coat of paint. Finally he waved his hand to stop me, and in his thick New York accent said, "John, I'm a plumber for god's sake, I know rust when I see it. Would you shut up and let me fall in love with your goddamned boat?"

We agreed on a price, went sailing on a windy December day, and he bought the old girl. I later learned that my girls had tried to sabotage the deal by hiding behind bushes and pelting him with coconut seeds when he showed up for the closing.

Suddenly I was boatless and miserable. The girls and I moved into an apartment, and I began to look for another boat in earnest. I spent hours on yachtworld.com, studying listing after listing. I knew what I wanted, and I knew what I didn't want. I wanted a boat that was ready to sail from day one, not a project boat and the false promise of saving money. *Fortuna* had been a fixer-upper, and I promised myself I would not go down that knuckle-busting, spirit-zapping, pocket-draining path again. I wanted a boat that I could sail anywhere with complete confidence; it had to be a true bluewater passagemaker, like the Hylas 49. I wanted a boat that would accommodate paying passengers in comfort. I did not want a tub. I wanted a beautiful boat between 40 and 50 feet, something eminently seaworthy but also nimble and fast. I wanted a bigger Contessa 32 and a sleeker Hylas 49. And I wanted all of this in a boat that had to cost less than $100,000. Unfortunately I had a lot more wants than dollars, and my broker friends assured me that my dream boat did not exist within the constraints of my budget.

I was undaunted. I knew that this time I needed to buy just the right boat. I would find it, and maybe, if I got lucky, it might be my last. I lusted after a sleek Finnish-built Swan, a clean, older 47 preferably, but a nice 44 would suffice. My rough-and-ready steel boat days were behind me, and I was definitely ready to return to the yachting scene, anxious to trade the dreamy philosophy of Bernard Moitessier for the steady draftsmanship of Olin Stephens and the spare but sturdy craftsmanship of a Scandinavian boatbuilder.

It seemed a propitious time to snag an old Swan. They had long been among my favorite boats, and I had delivered enough of them to appreciate their brilliant engineering, superb performance, seaworthiness, and handsome lines. They had also fallen out of fashion by this time, 2003, as newer, roomier boats like Oysters and Hylases were becoming popular with well-heeled cruisers. The racing crowd scoffed at the Swan's moderate proportions, teak decks, long overhangs, and bulky spars. Extreme designs were in, and Swans, particularly the older ones, were well-rounded boats. But out of fashion or not, they were still priced out of my league, way out of my league. Even beat-up, 30-year-old 44s were bringing $150,000 or more, and the cheapest 47 was more than twice what I might realistically spend. Sadly I looked elsewhere.

I was vaguely interested in a Jeanneau Sun Magic 44, and also looked at a Beneteau First 456. And while these former Admiral's Cup boats are both proven and underappreciated designs in the United States, I wanted more boat, something special, some nautical chutzpah.

A Robert Perry-designed Passport 47 came to my attention, but the two-stateroom layout was not ideal, and the boat was likely beyond my means. I made an offer on a sleek Wauquiez Centurion 45 lying in Annapolis, but my price was dismissed out of hand by an indignant Italian owner who had sailed it across the Atlantic. Believe it or not I was tempted by a very handsome custom-made Dutch steel boat in Miami, but I came to my senses on the drive back to Fort Lauderdale.

That night in the dreary white-walled apartment, with the girls asleep and a bottle of red wine leaking on my desk, I returned to yachtworld.com with a purpose—to find a damned boat before I went crazy. I had bumped my upper price limit to $139,000, a chimerical haze no doubt produced by the nice Malbec. I'd find more money somewhere, somehow. Scrolling through the listings like a detective, I finally spotted it: a 1985 Kaufman 47.

I had always admired Mike Kaufman's designs, especially his collaboration with Rob Ladd on the Skye 51 and 54. I instinctively knew that this boat had fallen through the cracks. Who else besides me would be interested in a Kaufman 47? Who else had even heard of it? I remembered reading a review when it was first launched, and I even remembered its nickname, "Taiwan Swan."

I read the listing carefully. There was not much equipment, but I didn't care about that. Nothing is older than old gear on a sailboat, and the lack of equipment was actually a positive. I was more interested in the miserable blurry pictures and the tiny interior plan drawing. I enlarged them and studied them intently. The pictures confirmed what I already knew: the boat had the hull shape I was looking for—low and lean, almost ridiculously low, with a longish fin keel and a large rudder mounted well aft and tucked safely behind a substantial full skeg. The entry was knife like, and the wedge-shaped cabin trunk looked very much like a Swan. The interior plan revealed three equal staterooms and two pilot berths in the main saloon. My hands were sweating as I punched the keys. I was excited. I had found my boat. But how would I ever afford it?

Lusting over the photos like some folks stare at dating profiles, I eventually realized exactly where the boat was. Although the listing did not note a current location and mentioned a broker in Norfolk, Virginia, I knew the boat was in Washburn's boatyard in Solomons Island, Maryland, right across the creek from where my sister Liz and brother-in-law Trevor own and operate a marina. The next morning I called Trevor and, after a bit of small talk, got to the point. "Can you see Washburn's from your office?" I asked impatiently.

"Hold on, I'll check. Why, by the way, do you care if I can see Washburn's?"

"There's a boat I'm interested in, a Kaufman 47. It's on the hard, black bottom paint, red boot stripe. Do you see it?"

"Sorry, John, I can't see it, but I can drive over there later today and take a look if you'd like."

"That would be great, Trevor. I'm really stoked about this boat even though I probably can't afford it. It's called *Madrigal*. Call me as soon as you get back."

"Don't worry, John. Nobody is going to steal this boat away from you. It's snowing like mad here today and most roads are closed."

I have great respect for Trevor's opinion about anything that floats. South African by birth, he attended the Merchant Marine Academy in Cape Town and afterward served as first mate and navigator aboard passenger liners sailing from the Indian Ocean to the Mediterranean. He saved enough money to purchase *Wandering Star*, an Endurance 37 cutter that he sailed around the world singlehandedly. He met my sister Liz in Australia on his second circumnavigation, and they eventually fetched up in Maryland after sailing together across the Indian Ocean, around the Cape of Good Hope, and across the Atlantic Ocean. Through hard work and business acumen they've become managing partners of Spring Cove Marina, one of the nicest facilities on the Chesapeake Bay.

Trevor called back a few hours later.

"The boat looks nice, John. Looks like a Swan, actually, but with a nicer interior. It has a beautiful hull shape. It obviously hasn't been sailed in a long time, but it's generally clean. Also, you might be interested to know it's in the part of the yard where St. Mary's College keeps their donated boats. They have a big-time sailing program and they raise money by taking boats in donation and selling them. That may be good news, or it may not. I know the coach, a guy named Mike Ironmonger. Do you want his number?"

You bet I did. I thanked Trevor and began mulling the possibilities. I knew from past experience as a delivery skipper that donated boats often could be had for a song. It all depended on the donor's tax status. I nervously called the number Trevor gave me.

"Ironmonger" came the reply without any small talk.

"Hi, is this Mike Ironmonger?" I asked stupidly, as if there might be two Ironmongers at St. Mary's College.

"Sure is. What can I do for you?"

"My name is John Kretschmer and I was—"

"Did you say John Kretschmer?" He said it in a way that made me nervous, as if I owed him money or had dated his daughter.

"The author of *Flirting with Mermaids* John Kretschmer?"

I sighed with relief.

"Yes, that John Kretschmer," I said. "I'm calling about the Kaufman 47 you have for sale."

"Great to talk to you. That's one of my favorite books. And the Kaufman is a great boat. Are you interested in buying it?"

Before I could respond he continued.

"If you are, your timing couldn't be better because we really need to sell it. We just cancelled the listing with the broker in Virginia, so I can deal with you directly. Have you seen it?"

The good vibes were coming through the phone line. I pictured myself at the helm, driving the boat on a screaming reach. Wait, John. Hang on, brother. It's time for a reality check. The price was still $139,000.

"No, I haven't seen it yet, but my brother-in-law Trevor has."

"Trevor's a great guy," Ironmonger assured me. He seemed to be in a good mood.

I agreed with his assessment of Trevor and then got back to business.

"When you say that you have to sell the boat, does that mean the price is negotiable?"

"We've already dropped the price down from $179,000, but yes, it is certainly negotiable. The boat is going to go cheap."

"Just how cheap is cheap, if you don't mind me asking."

Ironmonger paused for dramatic effect and then said quietly as if someone might overhear us.

"I can't say for sure—the Board of Trustees has the final say—but I'd guess $100,000 will buy it. Just don't tell them you heard that from me."

Two days later I picked up a rental car at Baltimore Washington International Airport and sped south toward Solomons Island. I reluctantly slowed down as snow and sleet blanketed the road. But I didn't let the weather stop me, and I plowed recklessly through another supposedly rare Southern Maryland snowstorm.

I drove straight to the yard, parked the car, and trudged through six inches of snow. I spotted the boat from a hundred yards and stopped to admire the lines. It might have been Michelangelo's *David*. It was beautiful, powerful, perfection in fiberglass and snow. So much for being a rational boat-buying expert. I knew right then that I would find a way to buy the boat even if I had to rob a bank or sell one of the kids. I was in complete lust, another one of those things that make land people uneasy around us. I hurried to the boat, rummaged a ladder, and climbed aboard.

Ironmonger had told me he would be out of town, but he said the boat would be unlocked. I surveyed the cockpit and forced myself to endure the

Quetzal *(then* Madrigal*) when I first saw her in the snow. (Top) My first view of her, a beautiful hull shape. (Bottom) The companionway and cockpit, covered in snow. A crazy day to fall in love with a boat.*

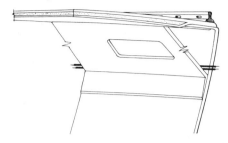

A unique hull-to-deck joint features a structural truss that not only stiffens both the hull and deck, but through cutouts allows easy access to wiring conduits and through-hull fittings, including stanchions, cleats, and hull-to-deck fasteners. It is also a handy storage area.

The cabin sole-to-hull bond is structural, a good and bad feature. The good: it makes the whole boat stiffer and prevents bilge water from running into lockers. The bad: it limits access to the hull beneath the sole.

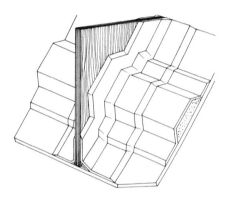

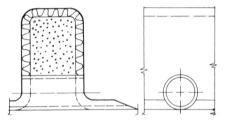

The solid fiberglass hull is stiffened with closely spaced, full-length longitudinal foam stringers. These stringers encapsulate the bulkheads, which are isolated from the hull by fiberglass sections.

Drainage is critical, especially in low-freeboard boats like Quetzal that ship plenty of water aboard. Making sure the floors have limber holes is vital, but the limber holes need to be isolated from the foam.

cold and trudge around the deck before pushing the companionway back and dropping below. The boat was dry, and the teak interior was inviting. Trevor was right, it was in good shape; in fact, the interior looked almost new.

I spent a few hours poking around the boat, looking in all the lockers and checking the plumbing, wiring, and other systems. By the time I popped back on deck, the snow had stopped and the sun was flirting with making an appearance. I cleared the snow from the helm seat and sat behind the massive wheel. I pictured the boat on the ocean. I had a very good idea how she would sail; I could feel it in the seat of my pants. I was not quite as sure how I would actually find the money to buy her.

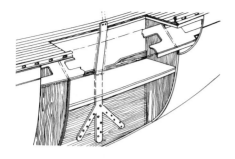

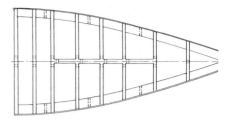

A structural grid made up of athwartship floors and longitudinals is the strongest way to build a bluewater hull.

The chainplates are massive stainless steel channels, bolted to a specific fore-and-aft chainplate bulkhead, which is then supported by two widely spaced fore-and-aft bulkheads, distributing the load throughout the hull.

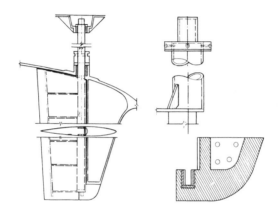

The rudder structure is protected by the skeg but designed to stand alone if the skeg should become damaged. The stainless steel rudder stock and bronze quadrant are robust.

After a quick visit with Liz and Trevor, I flew home. Sitting at my desk in our cramped apartment, I took an honest look at my finances, the result of which is always depressing. I am not much of an accountant, and the $100,000 figure was more hypothetical than a hard number. It didn't take a lot of calculating to see that the most I could possibly pay was $80,000, and that would not leave much to refit the boat for bluewater. I was about to find out just how desperate St. Mary's College was. I took a deep breath and called Ironmonger.

"So what did you think of the boat?" He was excited; he could smell a sale.

"I liked it. It's close to what I want, but it doesn't have a lot of gear." I was lying, and trying to sound unenthused.

"Well, what do you expect for $100,000?"

"I guess I expected a bit more, I have to say." It was killing me to lie like this, and I couldn't sustain the ruse. "Look, Mike," I said, "here's the thing. I want the boat, I really do, and I'm willing to make you an 'as is where is' offer."

"I'm not sure I like the sound of this," he chimed in.

I blundered on. "You know I'm just a poor writer and delivery captain, and, well, I can offer you $70,000 right now, no sea trial, no survey, no hassle. I'll just send a check by overnight mail."

Ironmonger was silent. Then he finally spoke. "Kretschmer, that's half of what we're asking." He sounded more incredulous than angry. "I'm going to burn my copy of *Flirting with Mermaids*!" It took me a second to realize it was a joke. "Okay," he continued, "fax me an official offer and I will present it to the board, but don't hold your breath expecting them to take it."

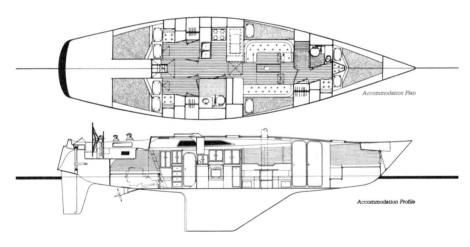

Accommodation Plan

Accommodation Profile

Very fine entry, with a nice bow overhang but still relatively long LWL. An LOA of 47 feet and LWL of 40 feet 2 inches translates into an overhang ratio of 14 percent, which I think is about right. Note that the overhang is entirely in the bow. The boat will make a nice initial entry through most waves and, by carrying the beam and waterline aft, will perform well when reaching with a following sea. The rudder is large and positioned well aft for excellent downwind steering. The forefoot has a modest degree of flatness, especially compared with the Contessa 32 (see page 89), and will occasionally pound when punching upwind into a seaway. The engine has a V-drive transmission to save room and make the two aft cabins possible, and is a compromise I can live with. Note the angle at which the shaft exits the hull, certainly not ideal for motoring efficiently.

The interior plan (above) works for me because the boat has six excellent sea berths. But in reality the three cabins are all a bit tight. The forward head is small, and the saloon is quite compact for a 47-foot boat. The U-shaped galley is great, with lots of counter space, and I have turned out hot meals in the roughest of conditions.

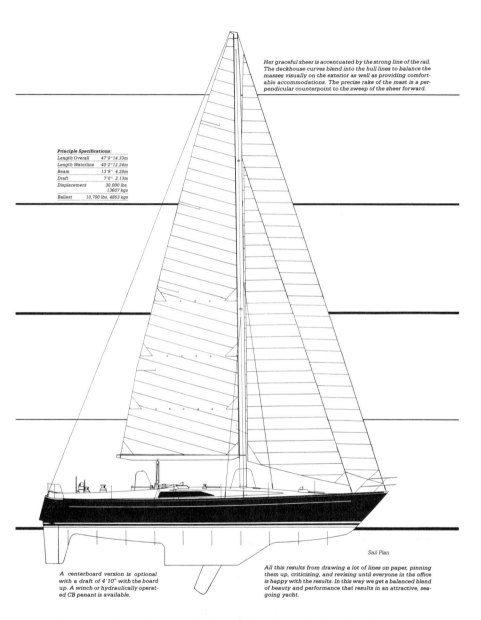

Her graceful sheer is accentuated by the strong line of the rail. The deckhouse curves blend into the hull lines to balance the masses visually on the exterior as well as providing comfortable accommodations. The precise rake of the mast is a perpendicular counterpoint to the sweep of the sheer forward.

Principle Specifications:

Length Overall	47'0" 14.33m
Length Waterline	40'2" 12.24m
Beam	13'9" 4.20m
Draft	7'0" 2.13m
Displacement	30,000 lbs, 13607 kgs
Ballast	10,700 lbs, 4853 kgs

Sail Plan

A centerboard version is optional with a draft of 4'10" with the board up. A winch or hydraulically operated CB penant is available.

All this results from drawing a lot of lines on paper, pinning them up, criticizing, and revising until everyone in the office is happy with the results. In this way we get a balanced blend of beauty and performance that results in an attractive, seagoing yacht.

Note the short boom on the sail plan of the Kaufman 47 (from the manufacturer's brochure) with the ¾ boom sheeting arrangement. This boom and high-aspect mast is a carryover from the IOR rating rule. Mid-boom sheeting angles load the boom and make it hard to sheet, but it is a compromise I accept, and it's definitely better than having the mainsheet run across the cockpit. Not only does this make it hard to move around the cockpit or go below, it makes it very difficult to rig a spray dodger. The sail plan calls for the boat to be sailed as a cutter, yet most are more efficiently sailed as sloops and use the staysail primarily for heavy weather.

I faxed an offer and held my breath. He called me back the next morning. "Kretschmer, you are a lucky man. I can't believe it. The board is willing to sell you the boat for $85,000, as is where is. That's an amazing deal."

"*Welllllll*," I said, as I wondered what to say next. "It looks like we're getting closer."

"Closer! What do you mean?"

"I think we can work things out, but I have to talk to my financial guy and I'll get back to you soon."

"Don't wait too long. At this price the boat will sell."

My financial guy was my ten-year-old daughter, Narianna. "What do you think about this deal, baby? It looks like we're close to getting a new boat to live on."

She was still smarting over the sale of *Fortuna* and didn't offer much advice. "I don't know, Daddy. It sounds like a lot of money," she said and returned to her book about Queen Elizabeth.

I called Ironmonger. "I talked to my financial guy and he says it sounds like a lot of money. I can go to $75,000, same deal, as is where is. What do you say?"

"I might actually burn your book now," he said without much humor. "Send in a revised offer and I'll present it."

Ironmonger did not call back. He let me stew, and for two long days I felt like I had played too strong a hand. He must have found someone else to buy the boat at that price. All I had done was do the dirty work for some other lucky buyer. Damn. I was sorely tempted to call him, but I resisted, knowing that I had to stay firm. Despite my angst I still had a gut feeling that I was going to end up with the boat, and you always know these things.

Finally he called. "Kretschmer, you know St. Mary's is a small college, and supporting the athletic program takes a lot of money. Right?"

"Right," I agreed, not sure where he was headed.

"Well, if you don't go to $80,000, we're going to have to fire one of our coaches. Any suggestions which one I should let go?"

"Don't do that," I said laughing, "$80,000 it is."

I had a new boat, and for the first time it was a boat that wasn't a compromise. I bought it because I wanted it, not because it was a good deal or simply because I could afford it. No nagging second thoughts haunted me as I sent the biggest check I'd ever written. Off it went in a Fed Ex envelope.

I don't believe in fate or pre-destiny, but I must confess that finding this boat challenged my convictions. Once again I had to change the name, which by this time, four boats later, I considered an act that ensured good luck. Besides, for someone who sings as atrociously as I do, it seemed almost criminal to go to sea in a boat named *Madrigal*.   *(continued page 72)*

25 Sailboats for a Serious Ocean: An Eclectic List and Some Thoughts

Here is a range of sailboats from 32 feet to 57 feet that are all capable of making successful ocean passages. This is not a comprehensive list by any means, but rather a brief introduction to some of the many different models available for serious sailing. What is unique about this list is that it focuses on used boats that represent sound values in today's soft market. Bluewater sailing is not just a rich person's pursuit. In fact, I am certain that offshore sailing is returning to its more humble origins, and boats that are out there traveling the world are shrinking back to normal proportions. Once again you see cruisers in boats less than 40 feet. And though you'll find this list to be international, every boat listed is also available in the North American market.

CONTESSA 32. A classic, incredibly well-proven boat that is close to my heart. As readers know, I sailed *Gigi* across the Atlantic and around Cape Horn. Arguably the most-loved production boat of all time in England, David Sadler's design is noted for extreme seaworthiness and the sweetest motion afloat. Also noted for its small living space and being very wet on deck. First launched in 1971, somewhere around nine hundred have been built, most by legendary builder Jeremy Rogers in Lymington, England. However, eighty-seven were built in Canada by J J Taylor & Sons, and these boats are tailored for the North American market. Changes include wheel steering, a taller rig, and a cored deck. Both English- and Canadian-built boats routinely show up for sale in North America.

Price Range: From $25,000 for a 40-year-old model in rough condition to more than $200,000 for a new, custom-made boat. Most boats are in the $45,000 range. Similar Boats: Wauquiez Centurion 32, She 33, S&S 34

PACIFIC SEACRAFT 34. A deceptively capable and well-proven design by venerable naval architect Bill Crealock. The hull shape blends tradition with what was at the time it was launched (1984) a more modern long fin keel and full skeg underbody. It's a study in moderation and drawn with a keen eye for staying on good terms with Neptune. It is a capable offshore boat. Construction has a better reputation than it probably deserves, but the overall low-slung design makes it work. Pacific Seacraft was a top-rated builder for many years before going bankrupt in 2007. After years of being quite expensive, older 34s have became quasi-affordable. Steven Brodie in Washington, North Carolina, bought the company and the molds.

Price Range: Under $100,000 for boats built before 1990, to $150,000 for late-model 34s. Similar Boats: Crealock 37, Cabo Rico 34

PRETORIEN 35. Designed by Holman and Pye, among the all-time best cruising boat designers, though sadly not well known to most   *(continued next page)*

American sailors. Designed in 1979, this boat combines the elements of a modern hull form with sound compromises that have served offshore sailors well—skeg-hung rudder, fine entry, moderate sections, and seaworthy cockpit. Built by Henri Wauquiez, it's one of those boats that's becoming a cult classic, helped no doubt by the popularity of Hal Roth's book, *How to Sail Around the World*. Roth chose a Pretorien for his last cruising boat. The boat is extremely well constructed with full-length stringers and superb tabbing. This nimble fin-keel cruiser may seem expensive at first glance, but the more you probe, the more the value becomes apparent. Approximately 170 were built before production stopped in 1986.

Price Range: From around $50,000 for an early boat to $80,000 for a later model. Similar Boats: CS 36, Hood 38

CAPE DORY/ROBINHOOD 36. No list of serious sailboats would be complete without a Carl Alberg design. He designed many boats, and the Cape Dory 36, which later morphed into the Robinhood 36, is a fine example of a capable blue-water cruiser. I am not a fan of full-keel boats in general, but the moderate proportions of the CD 36, with its handsome sheer, balanced rig, and stout construction, easily persuaded me to include this boat in the book. Well proven and widely available, it's a good choice for serious sailing. Cape Dories, like Pacific Seacraft, were expensive when first built but now, more than thirty years later, are affordable.

Price Range: An early-1980s model in good condition can be purchased for $60,000. A later Robinhood version built after the year 2000 will cost more than $100,000. Similar Boats: Alberg 37, Cabo Rico 38, Allied 36

VALIANT/ESPRIT 37. This is a great-looking boat designed by Robert Perry, whose designs are well represented in my collection, and every collection, of serious sailboats. It may seem sacrilegious to include the Esprit 37 in this list and the not the better-known Valiant 40 (which is included in the list of "Old-But-Proven Classics That Can Still Cross Oceans" on page 96), but I like the 37 better, and it is *my* list after all. Sometimes called the Nordic 37, and later known as the Valiant 39, this hull shape is fast enough and very seaworthy, a nice equation of factors. The size is easily managed by a couple and is ideal for singlehanding. It's a no-nonsense passsagemaker, well built and very easy on the eyes. It is not luxurious or overly spacious below, but the layout is well suited to ocean traveling.

Price Range: When you find an Esprit on the market, it seems to sell for around $60,000. Similar Boats: Valiant 40, Pacific Seacraft 37, Rafiki 37

PROUT SNOWGOOSE 37 CATAMARAN. Okay, monohull sailors, come to terms with the fact that cats are not only here today, they've been here and have been crossing oceans for decades. This is particularly true of Prouts, and especially the legendary Snowgoose. While not as roomy or as sexy as most of today's wide-load cruising cats, the solid, nimble Snowgoose has been everywhere, from Cape Horn to Greenland. A solid bridge deck and a traditionally stayed cutter rig make the Snowgoose safer and more manageable, especially in heavy weather. When a Snowgoose in good condition turns up on the market, it does not linger. Savvy cruisers realize these boats are great values.

Price Range: An older Snowgoose can be had for $50,000, while the new Elite models from the 1990s usually go for just over $100,000. Similar Boats: Prout Snowgoose 35, Fountaine Pajot Louisiane 37

ALAJUELA 38. The pedigree of this boat traces an arc through Colin Archer and William Atkins, the success of the Westsail 32, and finally to Don Chapman and Alajuela Yachts in Southern California. Three things are true about the Alajuela 38—it's beautiful, it's surprisingly fast, and it's well loved by a cult following. And yes, did I mention it's beautiful? Some have called the A 38 a refined Westsail 32. That's not quite right. Sure, it's a double-ender, but it is a different animal. It's lean and graceful, not stout and pugnacious. Don't get me wrong, I love the Westsail 32, truly, but the Alajuela will sail circles around it. Well constructed, most 38s have aged well. But remember they are old boats; many were launched in the 1970s. Always interesting boats on the used market—and that's not always a good thing. Some were sold as kit boats, which means that they were finished and fitted out by the owners, and these boats tend to undermine value. Of course, that also means that there are some steals out there; just be wary. So much for not liking full-keel boats with big bowsprits. I don't like them, but I love the Alajuela 38.

Price Range: Mid 1970s models sell in the $50,000 range. Some fully restored boats are closer to $100,000 but may be worth it. Similar Boats: Freya 39, Tayana 37

PRIVILEGE 39. This is the serious, affordable bluewater catamaran first launched in 1988. These boats are out there, everywhere. They are roomier and more modern than the Snowgoose. Originally developed by famous singlehander Philippe Jeantot, the Eric LeFevre-designed boats were intended for serious sailing from the get-go. They are not glorified charter boats and feature mostly solid bridge decks, solid hulls below the waterline, cutter rigs, and smaller cockpits. Although plenty went into charter service, many did not, and it is not unusual to find models well fitted out for cruising. In fact, many have circumnavigated. The Privilege 39 is, in a very odd twist, akin to a modern-day Westsail 32 for French cruising families. They buy one, sail it around the world or across the Atlantic twice, and then sell it to the next cruising family.

Price Range: Older, first-generation Jeantot Marine 39s can be found for less than $175,000, which in the cruising catamaran world makes them a bargain. Similar Boats: Prout 39, Manta 42

FREYA 39. This is one of my favorite boats on the list. Designed by Trygve Halvorsen, the Freya 39 is famous in Australia, where it was first built. A flush-decked double-ender, it is still the only boat to win three   *(continued next page)* straight Sydney-Hobart races, in 1963, 1964, and 1965. It's fast, really fast for a long-keel boat, and very seaworthy. It is, in some ways, the Contessa 32 of Australia, a much-loved boat. Jim Gannon in Northern California built it as a semi-production fiberglass boat in the late 1970s and early 1980s. While some Freyas were completely finished and fitted out, others were sold as kits. The hull construction was first rate. There are not many around, and there are also steel and wooden Freyas out there, so again, be wary. Deals that seem too good to be true usually are. Pam Wall and her late husband, Andy, sailed their Freya around the world and then back and forth across the Atlantic. I've seen Freyas in Horta, Corfu, Ireland, and Tahiti in the last couple of years.

Price Range: This is very hard to gauge because a poorly finished kit boat might sell for $35,000, while a beautifully finished Jim Gannon boat can easily sell for more than $100,000. Similar Boats: Corbin 39, Fair Weather Mariner 39

PASSPORT 40. Another Bob Perry design. The Passport 40 has the seakeeping traits of the Valiant 40, but it's faster downwind and a lot more comfortable below. The boat is ideal for a couple or a small family. It's easily handled, tracks true in a seaway, and doesn't beat up the crew. It is also beautifully fitted out below, and the interior with the Pullman cabin is just about perfectly laid out for a cruising couple with room for occasional guests. The cutter rig usually includes a mobile cutter stay so it can be sailed more nimbly as a sloop. There are some issues, Taiwan issues, but not too many. The hull is solid fiberglass and heavily laid up. The first hull came off the ways in 1980, and the boat remained in production until 1991, with nearly two hundred boats sold. The Passport 40 is a definite deep ocean boat, and one of my favorites. And I am not alone because prices have been creeping up as folks realize that the 40 is a world-class boat selling for a fraction of newer, less-capable boats.

Price Range: Older models sell for around $120,000, and later models in good condition are in the $140,000 to $150,000 range. Similar Boats: Valiant 40, Nordic 40, Nassau/Tatoosh 40

CALIBER 40. Designed by Mike McCreary, the Caliber 40 does not fit neatly into categories, and that's why I like it. Think of it as a Sabre with a chip on its shoulder, a bit more meat in the hull form, and better tankage. It has a nice hull shape, yes, but it's been flattened a bit forward and aft. It looks perfect in profile, less so looking aft from the bow. Still, I like the shape and the compromises it makes. It has a great interior. I'd sail one around the world, and a few already have. Expensive yes, but prices are dropping. The long-range cruiser (LRC) models are designed expressly for serious sailing. Sadly, Caliber is no longer producing boats, but the 40 had a long and successful production run.

Price Range: Pre 2000 boats can purchased for less than $200,000; later models, especially the LRC models, usually carry asking prices of about $200,000. Similar Boats: Tartan 4100, Sabre 42, Island Packet 40

BABA 40. Oh boy, here he is again, my friend Bob Perry. And here's another full-keel boat—well, sort of. A close inspection of the hull shape shows quite a bit of nuance. Yes, the rudder is attached to the keel, but the forefoot is truly cut away. The hull has a lovely sheer. The rig is powerful, and this boat moves nicely, especially on a reach. And it's beautiful. Form and function, hmm. I think a beautiful sailboat often is a capable sailboat, but I guess it all depends on how you define function. Built by Ta Shing, arguably the best Taiwan yard through the years, the Baba 40 and its various offshoots, including the Panda and Tashiba, are out there, from the Mediterranean to the South Pacific and beyond. The actual Baba 40 had a short two-year production run, but more than 110 boats were built between 1980 and 1982.

Price Range: $130,000 should be plenty to buy a nice, clean, well-equipped Baba 40. Similar Boats: Tayana 42, Tayana 37

HALLBERG RASSY 42. If I had to say what is the most common boat that I encounter all over the world—the most common "quality" cruising boat, that is—I'd say, without hesitation, the various models of Hallberg Rassy. These robust, practical Swedish cruisers are everywhere. The 42 is instantly recognizable with a broad cove stripe, moderately high freeboard, and comfortable center-cockpit design. The hull shape features a long fin keel and a partial skeg before the rudder. A newer version, the MK II, was designed by German Frers and launched in 1991 and was in production for more than a decade. The actual production runs of most HR models are surprising since nearly two hundred MK II 42s were built. Yes, these boats are expensive, but they are brilliantly designed for crossing oceans and living comfortably once you arrive. And they hold their value well, which makes the expensive part less of a negative.

Price Range: MK I models range from $40,000 to $175,000, MK II from $200,000 to $300,000. Like all quality used boats, you must view these prices in comparison with those of new boats, which would typically cost at least four to five times as much. Similar Boats: Contest 43, Hylas 44

TASWELL 43. This is one of the top-quality boats on the list. Designed by Bill Dixon and built by Ta Shing, it's a gorgeous boat. The hull shape shows a large fin and full skeg, but like the Caliber some sections are flattened a bit for better interior floor volume, a compromise most cruisers are happy to make. They might curse for a while pounding upwind between Guadeloupe and Antigua, but when they nose up to the wall in English Harbor the lovely interior below will make them forget all the noise. And this is not to say that this boat is a pounder, far from it, but just more so than some of the other boats on the list. But the interior, particularly the finish, is stunning, and the two-cabin layout is very livable. The cutter rig is versatile and powerful, and the sailing and deck gear are top quality. I can make a legitimate argument that the Taiwanese firm Ta Shing evolved into the finest sailboat builder in the world in the late 1980s and early 1990s. The 43 was launched in 1987 and had a short three-year production run.   *(continued next page)*

Price Range: Taswell 43 prices are hard to predict but typically fall between $150,000 for a well-used model to around $200,000 for a boat in great shape. Similar Boats: Oyster 435, Bristol 45.5

HYLAS 44. This is the first of three Hylas models on the list, so indulge me. I can't help it. Much of the book is focused on how boats stand up in heavy weather, and I have vast experience aboard Hylases. I was their main delivery skipper for years and also helped in the development of the 49. The 44 is a sweet boat. It's not as heavy as the other models, and it's actually fairly nimble. Designed by German Frers, it gets its stability from a near 50 percent ballast displacement ratio and very soft lines. It has a great ride in a seaway. Built by Queen Long in Taiwan, it has solid and fairly conservative construction. I sailed a 44 through Hurricane Bob years ago (you will read about that in Chapter Eight), and I also endured a fierce North Atlantic gale on a delivery up to Newport, Rhode Island. The biggest negative on the boat is the small cockpit, but the comfortable accommodations are a tradeoff that many are willing to make. The Hylas 44 hit the market in 1985 and was replaced by the Hylas 45.5 in 1993. Many boats were originally in the fleet of Caribbean Yacht Charters, but despite this limitation they're highly sought after used boats.

Price Range: Like the Passport 40, used Hylas 44s keep creeping up in price; they range from $150,000 to $200,000. Similar Boats: Hallberg Rassy 42, Peterson 44, Morgan 44

NORSEMAN 447. Yes, another Bob Perry design makes the list, and it's one of his most handsome boats. The 447 is well recognized as a great cruising boat, and many have circumnavigated. It was offered in both center- and aft-cockpit arrangements. While the center-cockpit model is more popular, I prefer the aft, but that's just me. I like to see the arc of both sails when I steer—crazy, I know. Solidly built by Ta Shing (do you notice a certain trend here between designers and builders?). I met a couple last year in Grenada who had done three circumnavigations in their 447, and their story of riding out a monster monsoon in the Indian Ocean is a testament to a terrific boat. Launched in 1980, the boat was available new until 1986.

Price Range: Prices vary depending on models; center cockpits are pricier, but in general 447s range from $150,000 to $200,000. Similar Boats: Mason 44, Nordic 44

BENETEAU FIRST 456. This is a great sailing boat, very well engineered and built, and often misunderstood. This sleek cruiser shares only a name with today's Beneteaus and little else. One of the original First Series designed for the Admiral's Cup, this is a fast, seaworthy boat that can stand up to a blow. My friend Steve Maseda, an accomplished sailor, has sailed his boat all over the Atlantic and once through a big blow off Hatteras a few years ago. I have logged a lot of miles aboard, too, and love the way the boat handles. Just last weekend we had 25 to 30 knot winds in the Gulf Stream on the way to the Bahamas and had no problems at all. Steve's solent rig—a double headsail sloop, as Perry calls it—works brilliantly. If only there was a way to rig up a spray dodger! These boats were in production for only a few years in the mid 1980s, but plenty were built so they're an excellent value.

Price Range: $90,000 for a tired model to $140,000 for one recently refitted. Similar Boats: Jeanneau Sun Magic 44, C&C 44

OUTBOUND44/46. An almost new boat! I like the Outbounds a lot. My friends Dirk and Susan De Haan (from Chapter One) crossed the North Atlantic from Newfoundland to Scotland last summer in their 46. They were slammed by a fierce five-day gale, and the boat stood up to the pounding, although they had issues with some gear choices. A Carl Schumacher design, this boat was designed as a performance cruiser. It has a fairly modern underbody, but it's not twitchy at all and can carry loads too. The design premise was to build a boat with a solid glass hull that would still be legitimately fast. The shape is flatter and faster than most of the boats on this list, and it is important not to load the ends. The standard sail plan is a solent stay, or double-headsail sloop. Outbound Yachts, which produced one of the first boats to come out of mainland China, is also one of the few modern success stories in the sailboat industry. Approximately fifty boats have been launched in the first eight years of production, which shows how success has been redefined by very small production runs.

Price Range: Outbounds are rarely for sale, and when they hit the market they don't last. Expect to pay at least $250,000 for one of the earliest models. Similar Boats: J/46, Morris 45, Saga 43

HYLAS 46. I thought about swapping this out for the Swan 46, also a Frers design. But I kept the Hylas for two reasons. First, a capable and very livable center-cockpit, it hits the target for what most cruisers are looking for today. And second, I have a good story in Chapter Eight about surviving Hurricane Mitch in a 46. That was one heck of a blow, and the 46 handled it well. Like all Hylas models, the 46 is built like a rock with first-rate gear. The design is definitely more modern than that of the other Hylases on the list, the 44 and 49. The 46 is faster than either of those boats, but it doesn't always have the softest ride. I have plenty of offshore miles on this model and wouldn't hesitate to take it anywhere. It was launched in 1996 to replace the venerable 44 and the short-lived 45.5 models.

Price Range: The numbers listed here are not going to support my claims that offshore sailing is not just the province of the rich. 46s range from the low $200,000s to more than $400,000 for a late-model boat ready to circumnavigate. Similar Boats: Tartan 4600, Hallberg Rassy 43 MK III

SWAN 47. It's about time I add a Sparkman & Stephens (S&S) design to the list, and nothing could be more appropriate than an old Swan. I chose the 47 because I love it and because my Kaufman 47, *Quetzal*, is very similar. Between 1974 and 1979, seventy Swan 47s were launched. And I just saw one, a perfectly restored model, in Palma de Mallorca. The owner was *(continued next page)* not around, but I drooled over the boat. Flush decked, or more accurately wedge decked, the 47 is a powerfully designed and built boat. The spar section is massive, the rigging robust, and the fittings symphonies of stainless. Some cruisers may find the awkward bridge deck/cockpit arrangement off-putting, but it is all about sailing with the Swan 47. The boat is very close winded—it is an S&S design, after all—but also reaches well and really powers up under a big chute. Swans age very well because of the intelligent and solid original construction. Plus there's a certain cachet that only a Swan offers, and more and more of these older classics have been converted into full-time cruising boats.

Price Range: Sadly, you will still have to shell out at least $200,000 to buy an old 47, and almost $300,000 to purchase a nice one. Similar Boats: Kaufman 47, Wauquiez Centurion 47, Baltic 46

TAYANA 48. Yes, here's another Bob Perry design. I can't help it, the man has been the dominant force in serious ocean cruising boats since the 1970s. This boat came to the list by way of my friends Andy and Melissa. Young, successful, and intrepid, they decided to sail around the world. Only problem was they didn't know how to sail, and they were definitely not what you'd call "hands on." They bought a lovely 48 and took off. They soon realized that all the bells and whistles on board were more of a nuisance than a help, and they almost gave up early on. But the boat was sound and seaworthy and they pressed on. Today they are in Sri Lanka, about two-thirds of the way around. They give their boat, Spectacle, a lot of credit. The 48 is a bit of a chunky cruiser, maybe not Perry's best-looking design but certainly one of his most capable and comfortable boats. Ta Yang, the company that builds Tayanas, evolved over the years, and early defining models like the 37 and 42 seem quite quaint when compared to the 48, which was launched in 1992. A beamy, center-cockpit design, the 48 carries a generous rig designed for trade wind conditions, which is a nice way of saying that it's not much of a light-air performer. The interior features three private cabins and enough elbow room to hold a dance competition.

Price Range: Although ostensibly still in production, a mid 1990s model in good condition will cost between $230,000 and $300,000. Similar Boats: Tayana 47, Sunward 48

HYLAS 49. The Hylas 49 is one of my all-time favorite boats, period. The 49 puts the S in serious. It is amazingly seaworthy. I have logged more than 50,000 offshore miles aboard a variety of 49s and have weathered some serious blows. And yet it is also very comfortable below with three private staterooms. The 49 evolved from both the Stevens 47 and the Hylas 47, which I've written about a lot. It improved on most of the unfriendly features of those boats but kept the incredibly ocean-friendly hull shape. Built by Queen Long in Taiwan, it's solid. And because it is still in production, it is continually being improved. Today's boats include a fair bit of Kevlar in the layups, for example. Also, the 49 maintains its value because Hylas is still viable. This is a terrific bluewater boat—as long as you don't try to sleep in the centerline queen berth in a gale. The Hylas 49 version of this 1979 original design was launched in 1995. This is the boat that my wife, Tadji, always picks when we play the game "so if money was no object, what boat would you choose?"

Price Range: If you're lucky and handy, you can find a Hylas 49 for less than $300,000, but expect to pay more. Similar Boats: Stevens 47, Hylas 47, Oyster 485

AMEL SUPER MARAMU 53/54. These are among the most accomplished cruisers afloat, and very much in demand. For many years Amel built just one model, and if you want a new one you can expect to wait a couple of years, even in these trying times. Fortunately there are plenty of used boats to consider. If you're not familiar with the Super Maramu, as they are called, you will either love it or hate it when you see it. Standard features include a fixed dodger over the cockpit, roller-furling sails, faux teak decks, and incredible engine access from the cockpit. While the hull shape is certainly seakindly, and the ketch rig reasonably fast, it's the clever design features that distinguish the Amel. From built-in leeboards to ingenious tank tenders to a wine locker in the bilge, these boats are meant for serious cruising and pleasant living. Like the Hallberg Rassys, Amels are seen all over the world. I am not sure I want one, but I sure do respect them.

Price Range: From the low $200,000s for an early 1990s model to near $500,000 for a later model, these boats have a huge range. There are Super Maramus for sale all over the world, so it's worth traveling to find the right boat. Similar Boats: Outbound 52, Hallberg Rassy 53

SUNDEER 56/60. I am not sure I agree with all of Steve Dashew's design premises, but nobody is as relentlessly innovative. And nobody puts his boats to the test like Dashew. He hates to sail slowly, and although he never admits a mistake, I admire his fresh thinking. His Deerfoot series began the trend toward true performance cruising, performance as defined by double-digit speeds and 200-mile-plus days. The Sundeer 56/60 and the 64 are his idea of production boats. Seventeen boats, most of them 60s, were launched from Tillotson Pearson's plant (TPI Composites) in Rhode Island. They were designed to be efficient two-person cruisers, fast and comfortable but not meant for carrying a lot of people. The easily balanced hull shapes move well without flying a lot of canvas, and many have completed circumnavigations and high-latitude cruises. While the boat is fast upwind, the flat, narrow forefoot will pound in a seaway. Of course you expect this when you crack off and let speed make your velocity made good (VMG) more efficient anyway. The Sundeer/Deerfoot concept intrigues, and they've proved themselves where it counts, at sea. However, the reality of cruising in a boat this large means you will be spending twice as much as the family plugging along in their Passport 40.

Price Range: Expect to pay between $400,000 and $500,000 for a Sundeer 60. Similar Boats: Deerfoot 62 *(continued next page)*

BOWMAN 57. The Bowman is one of the most capable and accomplished fiberglass boats ever built. It's the anti-Sundeer. Think of it as a Contessa 32 on steroids: it's a tough, capable boat that doesn't seem 57 feet long. Only the Ocean 71 has a track record as impressive. Just look at the hull shape: sweet, powerful, and deep. I recently talked with Roger Swanson, the Blue Water Medal winner and owner of *Flying Cloud*, a 1975 57. Swanson has sailed around the world three times, around Cape Horn three times, to Antarctica, and on his third try through the fabled Northwest Passage. He's an amazing sailor, and *Flying Cloud* is one tough boat. Yet it's also beautiful. Interestingly, few sailors want boats like this today. They are not roomy in the way a modern 57-footer is, and certainly not as user-friendly. But if you want a boat that can sail anywhere anytime, and you're dreaming of serious passages, these British-built boats designed by Holman and Pye just may be the best value out there.

Price Range: Older, tired 57s occasionally drop to around $200,000, while newer, well-equipped models can easily cost double that. Similar Boats: Ocean 60, Camper Nicholson 58

Icebergs can be beautiful but terrifying. One of the realities of global warming is that more glacial melt in the polar oceans means more icebergs. This is one reason to carry good radar, although the really dangerous bergs, the smaller growlers and bergy bits, are not good radar targets. Despite the threat of icebergs, more sailors than ever are venturing to high latitudes. Remember, as you move north in the summer, the light increases, until at some latitudes there is very little darkness at all. You just have to keep a good lookout. Also, ice reports are very accurate these days. Environment Canada publishes daily iceberg updates at weatheroffice.gc.ca.

Quetzal motoring for a close look at an iceberg spotted in the Strait of Belle Isle, between Newfoundland and Labrador.

Five Questions to Ask Yourself *Before* Buying a Bluewater Boat

When the time comes to purchase the boat that will take them to sea, many sailors are bewildered, awash with questions, and desperate for straight talk. People often track me down and ask whether a Pacific Seacraft 37 is really better than an Island Packet 38, or if a cutter is necessary, or should they consider a ketch? Is a boat that nobody has heard of worth considering? Will it have resale value? Should they rule out a metal hull just because I don't recommend it? How old is too old for a fiberglass boat, and are all production boats off the list?

And while advice from so-called experts like me can be helpful (it can also be biased and confusing), the most important questions should be addressed to yourself. Here are a few questions that you need to answer honestly if you want to find the right boat.   *(continued next page)*

Do You Need a Bluewater Boat?

This is not a trick question, just the most important question to ask yourself. Most people assume that a bluewater boat is safer than a boat designed for coastal cruising, so it makes sense to err on the side of safety, right? Not necessarily. The surest way to answer this question is to make a list, in order of preference, of three areas you'd like to cruise. If you live on the East Coast of the United States and your top cruising grounds are the Chesapeake Bay, the Florida Keys, and the Bahamas, you don't necessarily need a bluewater boat. If they're New England, the Bahamas, and the eastern Caribbean, you don't necessarily need a bluewater boat. If they're the eastern Caribbean, the Mediterranean, and the South Pacific, you need a bluewater boat. You get the idea. If you don't plan to cross an ocean, or multiple oceans, the extra cost, comfort limitations, and lack of light-air performance of most oceangoing boats are probably not worth it. Remember the formula—even serious cruisers spend ten days in port for every day at sea. Be honest. If you dream of crossing an ocean, and not just making an occasional passage to and from a cruising ground, you need a bluewater boat.

Who is Going Sailing with You?

Don't laugh; this is a serious question. Is the dream of cruising yours alone but you're selling it to a reluctant partner? Does your partner dream of being at sea, or at anchor in a protected harbor? Are small kids part of the equation? If they are, do they want to go cruising? How experienced are you and your crew? Have you ever been in a storm? Have you ever been hove-to in a gale? An honest evaluation of who is going to be aboard and their enthusiasm and experience levels will help you choose the right boat. The less experience you have, the better boat you need, to a point. If you don't have a lot of experience, you need a boat that will look after the crew in rough going. This kind of boat I describe in the list of 25 boats, and in the list of 10 old sea dog boats on pages 59 and 96.

This boat is well designed, well built, and simply and intelligently outfitted, has soft motion in a seaway, and can heave-to in a gale and forereach in a storm. Ironically, experience will lead you to choosing these boats, but you really need a good boat when you don't have experience. The Contessa 32 was an incredibly forgiving boat, perfect for a young neophyte bluewater sailor like me. A sweet motion will make reluctant crewmembers happier than will private cabins and massive main saloons with flat screen TVs.

Can You Fit All the Possessions You Need for Happy Traveling in the Trunk of Your Car? How About Inside an SUV? Or Do You Need a U-Haul Truck?

Regardless of the boat, be it a Hylas 56 or a 28-foot Bristol Channel cutter, at some level cruising, especially bluewater cruising, devolves into camping on the water. It's noble to choose a small, cozy boat after you convince yourself that you are ready to leave your worldly goods and obligations behind. However, if you are a stuff person, a gear person—this is not an indictment—then you might not be happy in a minimalist setting. You are unlikely to undergo a personality change when you go to sea. If you want to bring tools, and books, and gadgets, then factor where they will go in the boat you buy. There's no guilt over deciding that you need a bigger boat than you originally thought, or that you need to spend a bit more money to find a boat that matches your style. Going cruising is part of the equation. Being happy as you cruise is the other part.

Have You Purchased Fixer-Upper Houses, Cars, or Boats Before?
If you have, and you enjoy the process of turning a wreck into a work of art, then consider buying a boat that needs work. If you don't enjoy this process, if you don't have skills with tools, be honest. If you don't have experience seeing a construction project through to a successful conclusion, don't buy a fixer-upper boat at any price. More cruising dreams are delayed, and ultimately shattered, by the false potential of saving money on the front end. Boats, even seemingly well-put-together boats, are devious, and they can break your heart. Boats that need major retrofits can be downright evil. Even a well-found cruising boat generally requires an additional 20 to 25 percent investment beyond the purchase price, and four to six months before it's refreshed and ready for your bluewater dreams. Major retrofit projects can easily double the price of a boat. Also, remember that rosy project timetable sketched out on a cocktail napkin at the bar after you just closed on the boat? Expect it to double, or triple. As you can tell, I am not a fan of large retrofit projects. I have never known one that was finished on time and on budget. If your desire is to get to sea, your time is too valuable to waste. Leave the boatbuilding to the pros and find a boat that is ready to go.

Name Five Features—Beyond a Solid, Seaworthy Hull Design—That You Really Want in a Boat
Do you prefer a cutter or double headsail sloop rig? Good sea berths or comfortable in-port berths, natural light and good ventilation below, private cabins for each member of the crew/family, a galley that you can actually cook in at sea? Armed with this list, you can begin to weed out some potential candidates, and you'll find it's almost a relief to cross boats off the list. Along the way, as you inspect and hopefully sail different boats, you will invariably compromise on some of these features. Private cabins may not be necessary, and some sloops can be converted to cutters. Having parameters to focus your search for a boat helps the process dramatically.

Running wing-and-wing, or sometimes called wing-on-wing, is not my favorite point of sail. I would usually prefer to set the asymmetrical spinnaker. Sometimes, especially when the conditions are light to moderate and you are running dead downwind, nothing is more efficient than this rig. Note the whisker pole preventer lines and the main boom preventer, which is running forward to the midships cleat. Boom preventers must be run forward, not directly to the deck, and the farther forward the better. I often run the boom preventer to the forward cleats. Avoid point-loading the boom and the deck by running a preventer line directly to the rail. The forward preventers, which should be three-strand nylon for maximum stretch, allow for a soft jibe.

Finding a new name was not easy. I wanted to call the boat *Zorba*, after my favorite character from my favorite author, Nikos Kazantzakis. But Zorba was flatly rejected by both members of the new-name panel, my two daughters. Nari particularly disliked it.

"First, Daddy, you can't name a boat after a man. It's just not right. And besides, Zorba sounds like a cheesy Greek restaurant, not a beautiful boat."

I argued that plenty of famous sailboats had male names, including Moitessier's *Joshua*. But the cheesy Greek restaurant argument was harder to refute, and they both finally voted it down on the grounds that it was a stupid name for a boat. *Seahorse* was nominated, but we all agreed that it sounded too Texan, and Nikki explained that "horses belong on land." Nari, who knows her old man very well, nominated *Quetzal*. A beautiful bird of the Central American rain forest, the quetzal was the sacred bird of the Maya. It is also on the verge of extinction because it is one of the few creatures that will not stand for captivity. It has to be free or it dies. The metaphor was a bit obvious but well suited for me, and *Quetzal* passed unanimously.

Quetzal, *sailing as a cutter, on a close reach in the lee of Guadeloupe, making an easy 7 knots. Note that while the genoa is roller-furled, the staysail is hanked on. Because the staysail is often flown during heavy weather, I like the bulletproof system of stout bronze piston hanks. You can also see the lightweight carbon-fiber Forespar radar pole astern. The life raft, packed in a valise, is mounted just inside the stern rail when underway—a good location for quick deployment. The valise is also much easier to stow than a hard canister, and I always pack the life raft below when I leave the boat.*

What Boats Are Really Out There

Boats That Contributed to the SSCA Bulletins

The 10,000-member-strong Seven Seas Cruising Association is an organization of world cruisers devoted to providing timely and pertinent information about the state of cruising. The association's bulletin has been a bible for serious cruisers for many years. Each contributor notes both their boat and location, and then provides details ranging from where to anchor, local officials, thoughts on gear, and other esoteric bits and pieces about the cruising life. The SSCA remains as fresh today as when it began sixty years ago. My mother was a contributor to the bulletin during her circumnavigation in the 1980s. I have been a member off and on over the years, and have also twice been the keynote speaker (their term) at their main gam in Melbourne, Florida. The SSCA motto, "Leave a clean wake," is the true ideal of cruising.

I have used only boats that are actually cruising for the data compiled here. I am specifically interested in what kind of boat is mentioned, how long it is, and what kind of rig it has.

Data has been compiled from three two-year periods: 2002–03, 2006–07, and 2011–12. Overall I logged 277 boats, which is a decent sample. The data reflect the state of the economy in one way: there were almost twice as many bulletin contributions during the 2006–07 boom years than during either of the other periods when times were not quite as prosperous, to put it gently. While it would be logical to assume that the boom years would have seen a shift to bigger cruising boats, the data suggest otherwise. All three periods, which cover the last decade of cruising, point to the same "average" cruising boat: a 42-foot fiberglass monohull with a cutter rig. Although there were definitely more boats cruising in 2006–7, the ratio between those 36 feet and under and those 50 feet and over stayed about the same, around 15 percent of the total for all three years. The great majority of boats, around 68 percent, fall between 37 feet and 49 feet, which of course makes sense. The data also clearly show that while there are plenty of expensive boats out cruising, there are even more inexpensive boats plying the oceans of the world.

Multihulls are definitely becoming more popular cruising boats, going from 5 percent in 2002–03, to 7 percent in 2006–07, to 22 percent in 2011–12. Metal boats are still in the minority, averaging about 4 percent through the decade. Only a handful of wooden boats made the list. Also, cutters continue to dominate the data, representing 45 percent of the boats. This figure is a bit misleading because the majority of serious cruising boats realize the benefits of a staysail and have some means of deploying a staysail stay and staysail, making them, in effect, slutters, a sloop/cutter hybrid but usually referred to as a cutter.

The three tables list all the different boats. Here is a summary:

2002–03	2006–07	2011–12
75 boats	134 boats	69 boats
Average LOA 42'	Average LOA 42'	Average LOA 42'

BOATS THAT CONTRIBUTED TO SEVEN SEAS CRUISING ASSOCIATION BULLETIN 2002–03

36' and Under

25' Cal 25	35' Niagara Sloop
28' Bristol Channel Cutter	36' Custom Cutter
31' Wylie Cutter	36' Union Cutter
33' Hans Christian Cutter	36' Van de Stadt Cutter
34' Roberts Sloop	36' Catalina Sloop
34' Beneteau Sloop	36' Bayfield Cutter
34' Rogers Catamaran	

37' to 42'

37' Irwin Cutter	40' Bristol Sloop
37' Najad Sloop	40' Island Packet Cutter
37' Pacific Seacraft Cutter	40' Acapulco Cutter
37' Beneteau Sloop	40' Valiant Cutter
37' Tayana Cutter	41' Formosa Ketch
37' Tartan Sloop	41' Scepter Cutter
37' Valiant Esprit Cutter	41' Amel Sharki Ketch
38' Sabre Sloop	42' Tayana Vancouver Cutter
38' Hans Christian Cutter	42' Pearson Ketch
38' Bently Cutter	42' Westsail Cutter
39' Prout Catamaran	42' J Sloop
39' Hallberg Rassy Sloop	42' Passport Cutter
40' Passport Cutter	

43' to 49'

43' Taswell Cutter	45' Cabo Rico Cutter
43' Ovni Cutter	45' Custom Cutter
43' Oyster Sloop	46' Cross Trimaran
43' Polaris Cutter	46' Hylas Sloop
43' Camper Nicholson Ketch	46' Brewer Cutter
44' Roberts Offshore Ketch	46' Peterson Cutter
44' F & C Ketch	46' Liberty Cutter
44' Custom Brewer Cutter	47' Stevens Cutter
44' CSY Cutter	47' Vagabond Ketch
44' Island Packet Cutter	48' Swan Sloop
44' Beneteau Sloop	48' Amel Ketch
45' Norseman 447 Cutter	49' Morgan Ketch
45' Slater Ketch	49' Hylas
45' Custom Steel Cutter	

(continued next page)

50' and Up

50' Alden Cutter	53' Amel Ketch
50' Kanter Steel Sloop	53' Oyster Cutter
50' Najad Cutter	56' Sundeer Sloop
50' Custom Cutter	56' Custom Cutter
52' Morrelli Catamaran	84' Palmer Johnson Ketch

Summary: Average LOA 42', 50% Cutter Rig, 96% Fiberglass, 95% Monohull

BOATS OUT THERE CRUISING, SSCA BULLETINS, 2006–07

36' and Under

Seabird Yawl 25	Crealock PS 34
Vancouver 27	Roberts 34
Catalina 27	Bristol 34
Albin 27	Cal 35
Columbia 28	Island Packet 35
Bristol Channel Cutter 28	Custom 35
Americat 30 Cat	Vancouver 36
Baba 30	Gulf Star 36
Hans Christian 33	Van de Stadt 36
Mason 33	Mao Tao 36

37' to 42'

Beneteau 37	Privilege 39 Cat
Crealock 37 Yawl	Naut 40
Jeanneau 37	Endeavor 40
Alberg 37	Maxi 40
Lagoon 37 Cat	Ocean Cruising 40
Pacific Seacraft 37	Island Packet 40
Lidgard 38	Mariner 40
Alajuela 38	Admiral 40 Cat
Cheoy Lee 38	Acupulco 40
Catalina 38	Passport 40
Morgan 382	Pacific Seacraft 40
Columbia 38	Cape George 40
Hans Christian 38	Spindrift 40
Trident 38	Van de Stadt 40
Sabre 38	Camper Nicholson 40
Corbin 39	Sceptre 41
Amel Sharki 39	Lord Nelson 41
Moen 39	Islander Freeport 41
Freya 39	Custom 41 Tri

Morgan 41
Coronado 41
Catalina 41 Cat
Valiant 42
Brewer 42
Whitby 42
Vagabond 42

Pearson 42
Pearson 424
Passport 42
Tayana 42
Golden Wave 42
Westsail 42

43' to 49'

Spindrift 43
Westsail 43
Hans Christian 43
Beneteau 43
Young Sun 43
Fastback 43 Cat
Morgan 43
Cape North 43
Slocum 43 Pilot House
Nauticat 43
Paine 43
Oyster 43
Shannon 43
Lavranos 43
Dix 43
Saga 43
Gozzard 44
Beneteau 44
CSY 44
Ovni 44
Reliance 44
Nordic 44

Norseman 447
Hardin 45
Cabo Rico 45
Liberty 45
Prout 45 Cat
Custom 45 Steel
Bowman 45
Hallberg Rassy 46
Cross 46 Tri
Amer Santorini 46
Hylas 46
Jeanneau 47
Gulf Star 47
Swan 47
Wauquiez 47
Suncoast 48
Celestial 48
Island Packet 485
Hallberg Rassy 49
Caliber 49
Najad 49

50' and Up

Alden 50
Schumacher 50
Columbia 50
Stevens 50
Dumas 50
Gulfstar 50
Aleutian Ketch 51
Formosa 51
Prout 52 Cat
Knight and Gannon 52

Gulfstar 53
Kanter 53
Roberts 53
Hylas 54
Farr 56 Pilot House
Custom Schooner 56
Bowman 57
Camper Nicholson 60
Deerfoot 74

(continued next page)

BOATS THAT CONTRIBUTED TO THE SSCA BULLETINS IN 2011–12

42' and Under

27' Vancouver	39' Shucker
32' Ontario	39' Privilege Cat
32' Westsail Cutter	40' Hallberg Rassy
32' Challenger	40' Leopard Cat
32' Steel Custom	40' Garden, One Off
33' Gemini 105 Cat	40' Jeanneau
33' Hans Christian Cutter	41' Fraser Cutter
33' Mason Cutter	41' Tartan
34' Pacific Seacraft Cutter	41' Sceptre
35' Alberg	41' Amel
35' Custom Swedish	42' Westsail Cutter
37' Tayana Cutter	42' Oyster
37' Tayana PH Cutter	42' Tayana Cutter
38' Jeanneau Gin Fizz Ketch	42' Baltic DP
38' Island Packet	42' Ontario
38' Cabo Rico	42' Corbi
39' Corbin	42' Brewer
39' Camper Nicholson Ketch	42' PDQ Cat
39' Amel Sharki	

43' to 49'

43' Slocum Cutter	45' Liberty Cutter
43' Saga	45' Omega
43' Fastback	46' Morgan
43' Custom Cutter	46' Najad
44' Brewer	46' Cross Cat
44' Peterson	47' Caliber
44' CSY	47' Ferrel Cat
44' CSY PH	49' Najad
45' Bristol	49' Liberty
45' Kronos Cat	

50' and Up

50' Beneteau Oceanus	53' Amel Super Maramu
50' Able Apogee	54' Irwin
50' Custom Cat	54' Moody
50' Alden	58' Tayana
50' Crowther Cat	67' Garden Custom
52' Tayana	74' Deerfoot
53' Custom Cat	

four

Launching Jitters | Buying/Flying a Life Raft |
Designing a Sailboat | Herreshoff, Perry, Kaufman,
and Other Designers | Production Sailboats | Design
Features of a Bluewater Sailboat

Launchings

"When the caulking was finished, two coats of copper paint were slapped on the bottom, two of white lead on the topsides and bulwarks. The rudder was then shipped and painted and on the following day the Spray *was launched. As she rode at her ancient, rust eaten anchor, she sat on the water like a Swan."*
—Joshua Slocum, *Sailing Alone Around the World*

THE TRAVELIFT LUMBERED to a stop just before the haulout well at Spring Cove Marina. *Quetzal* was dangling above the tarmac, a prostrate position in which no boat should long tarry. Standing amidships, I backed away as far as possible without falling into the creek. I wanted to admire her powerful underbody one more time, knowing that once she entered the water I wouldn't see below the boot stripe again for a year or more, at least not without a mask and snorkel. What's below the water is where confidence arises, and with the ambitious sailing schedule I had planned, there would soon come a day when I would need that deep fin keel to track true and that large rudder to respond to my frantic urgings.

There was just enough ambient motion for *Quetzal* to sway slightly in the slings, reminding me of a trapped dolphin about to be released into deep water. When Alan, the yard manager, finished daubing bottom paint on the bare spots where the boat had been supported on jack stands, Donny, the long-time lift operator at Spring Cove, eased ahead and then pushed the lever forward. *Quetzal* headed south toward the water, and I shuddered. The process of moving beautiful boats suspended in the web of huge spider-like machines makes me nervous. It was launching day and I had conflicting emotions.

Sailors are always launching things: boats, voyages, expeditions, dreams, even stories; it's the perfect nautical metaphor. I should have been excited. I was about to begin—or I should say launch—the next phase of my offshore sail training business aboard my own boat, and the boat of my dreams at that. In a few weeks I was bound for Bermuda; then, with another crew,

79

we would sail north to New England. After a summer of cruising with my daughters, we would shove off on the heavy-weather passage that you read about in Chapter One, Newport to Bermuda. I was even planning an Atlantic crossing after short winter and spring trips to the Bahamas and the Florida Keys. Further, most of the passages were booked, and *Quetzal* was in excellent condition. I had stretched my meager dollars and managed to add new running rigging, a spray dodger, several new through-hull fittings, a smattering of new electronics, a rebuilt feathering propeller, solar panels, and a fresh coat of antifouling paint. But I had gone from being euphoric at buying the boat to being unsettled as I prepared to finally sail her.

Was I nervous about the upcoming passages? Had I been too hasty in scheduling working trips so quickly after launching a boat I had never sailed? Not really. I make passages for a living, and as a longtime delivery skipper I specialized in hasty passages. More than once I flew to Europe to pick up a boat and pushed off to cross an ocean within twenty-four hours. My personal life was in turmoil, but that's a constant state of affairs for me, so that wasn't it either. Maybe it was the memory of a recent expedition gone all wrong, just the week before actually, that was fresh in my mind and still troubling me.

I had flown to England to give a talk to the Contessa 32 Class Association. It was twenty years after we had rounded Cape Horn in *Gigi*, and most Americans sailors had long since forgotten our passage, and my book about the voyage (*Cape Horn to Starboard*) was out of print. But both were still fondly remembered in the United Kingdom. In fact, before the book was republished, beat-up copies of the original sold for more than fifty dollars on Amazon.co.uk.

But this affection had very little to do with me. The Contessa 32 is the best-loved fiberglass sailboat in England, legendary for its seaworthiness and sleek good looks, and English sailors remembered me as an upstart American who escorted their masterpiece on an epic voyage. There was little doubt that *Gigi* was the star in this drama, and I was just along for the ride. Actually, that seemed about right.

The event took place at the Royal Southampton Yacht Club, and I had to scrounge a tie and jacket at the last moment just to get in the door. Sailing association meetings are bastions of cronyism and inside jokes. Members who crashed and burned during a hard jibe in a big regatta or went aground during the annual club cruise are subjected to good-humored ridicule. You know the stories; we've heard them and told them. But this meeting seemed longer than most. Even Contessa's founding father, my dear friend Jeremy Rogers, looked weary as one speaker after another droned on. The efficient waiter topped up my wine glass with each new topic, like the social committee chairman weighing in on the latest fund-raising initiative, and the selling of official Contessa ties. By the time I was finally introduced and I staggered to the podium, I was drunk.

I give a lot of talks and speak to sailors at clubs, association meetings, bookstores, and boat shows all over the world. My shtick is well honed. However, buoyed by the cask of red wine I had consumed, it was a little too honed, and I veered off topic and launched into a far-ranging speech about life, love, and how the pursuit of the perfect boat mirrored the pursuit of the perfect life. I quoted Camus, Mark Twain, E. B. White, Bernard Moitessier, my mother, and my saggy-armed third grade teacher Mrs. Deemer, something that I am sure had never been done before. I combined all the lectures I usually give into one confused discourse that eventually got back to sailing our little Contessa 32 around Cape Horn. Fortunately most of the crowd was also drunk. Apparently grateful that I had at last stopped talking, they erupted into applause. The party continued, more booze was served, and I tried to slip away. An older gent, in a bow tie and tweed jacket, tracked me down and escorted me back to the bar.

"Nice talk, young man," he said, clutching my elbow and pressing his ruddy face close to mine. "But I must say I just can't abide that horrid American accent."

The next morning I rose early and, despite an obdurate headache, hurried off to Pumpkin Marine, a large discount marine chandlery in nearby Portsmouth. I was on a mission to buy a new life raft. Life rafts are standard fare aboard most European yachts, and, despite a weak dollar, they were still much less expensive in England than in the United States. For some odd reason Americans think life rafts are necessary for serious cruising boats only, as if the sea is interested in scuttling only worthy vessels. Due to this curious logic, I was able to buy a six-person double-floor offshore raft in the UK for just less than $2,000, about half the price of a similar model in the United States. A bargain like this, in those halcyon pre-Facebook days, could be shared only by spending a big chunk of the savings at the bar, running up a tab to make sure other sailors knew just how savvy I was.

I was flying back to Baltimore, and *Quetzal*'s maiden voyage was scheduled just days after my return. Before leaving for England, I had inquired with American Airlines to make sure that it was possible to bring the life raft back with me.

"If I buy a life raft that has a filled CO_2 cylinder," I asked, speaking slowly and clearly and emphasizing CO_2, "will I be able to bring it back on the plane as part of my checked baggage?"

I was assured that every passenger was allowed one CO_2 parcel as long as it was checked. "You're certain about this?" I asked again, adding, "It has CO_2, you know compressed carbon dioxide." The voice at the other end was trying not to sound perturbed with my patronizing tone. "Sir, the regulations are quite clear, one CO_2 parcel per person. Have a nice trip."

The raft was in a soft valise, not a hard canister. The valise was more convenient to stash safely below when I was away from the boat, and easier to use on another boat if I needed to take it along on a delivery. Importantly, it could be stowed in the cockpit while underway, making it accessible and quickly deployable in an emergency.

One of the lessons I learned while writing *At the Mercy of the Sea*, the story of my friend Carl Wake's tragic encounter with Hurricane Lenny, was that it made no sense to mount a life raft in a cradle on deck. In their final moments, Carl and his rescued crew, Steve Rigby, could not reach their life raft. Indeed, their last known words were, "We are going to make one last attempt to get to the raft." It was only twenty feet away, stored on deck just forward of the mast, but it might as well have been perched at the top of the mast or stashed in Carl's garage back in Florida. Lethal walls of water swept the deck of Carl's 42-foot cutter, making it impossible for either of them to go forward. During the height of the storm, with the blown spume blotting out the world, they were not even sure if the life raft was still there, twenty feet away. If the life raft had been in the cockpit or mounted on the stern, things might have been different. The only survivor in the story (he was on another boat) managed to cling to a life raft for thirty-six hours before being rescued.

My new life raft was in stock, and the clerk and I hefted it to the cash register. Before swiping my credit card, I decided, just to be safe, to call again and confirm that I would be able to bring it on the plane with me. The American Airlines rep, a pleasant Englishwoman named Allison, repeated the same information I'd been told in the States: "Every passenger is allowed one CO_2 item in their checked baggage." I purchased the raft and sped off toward Heathrow, running late. I returned the car, tracked down a baggage trolley, and wheeled my huge parcel to the checkout counter. With a 65-pound box, I was prepared to pay an overweight baggage fee.

"What's in the box, sir?" the attendant asked as I lifted it onto the conveyor belt.

"A life raft."

"Oh dear, I am sorry, but you can't take that on the airplane." She seemed scandalized that I would even attempt such a thing.

Unfazed, I informed her that I had already checked with the airlines and that I had been assured that I could check the raft. "I am allowed one CO_2 parcel," I informed her knowingly and resisted the urge to wink at her.

She looked at my ticket and avoided eye contact.

"Sorry, Mr. Kretschmer, you must have been given the wrong information. You can't bring it on the plane."

I remained calm. "Miss, I checked with Alison just a few hours ago," as if she must know Alison in the main American Airlines office, "and she informed me that I could check one CO_2 parcel. Call Alison. She'll tell you."

"I really am sorry, but she gave you the wrong information."

So much for staying calm. I was starting to sweat and politely but firmly asked the attendant if could see her supervisor. People in line behind me looked impatient. I was clogging the check-in works. The manager turned up promptly.

"What's all the fuss about here?" His can-do attitude struck me as canned, a fresh graduate of the customer service academy where he'd mastered the art of pleasantly saying no.

"Well, sir, I have a life raft here, and it has to come on the plane with me, and if you will check your own regulations you'll see that I am allowed one CO_2 parcel. I confirmed that with Alison on the phone this morning."

"Well, Mr.—"

"Kretschmer."

"Yes, Mr. Kretschmer, I am sorry, but there are no life rafts allowed on the plane. Alison, whoever she is, was mistaken."

His tone was cordial, but there was absolutely no room for compromise. And he wasn't impressed with Alison, who, it seemed to me, was being treated rudely by her co-workers. My look of despair earned a small measure of sympathy.

"I shouldn't do this, but take a look at this memo from the FAA. That's your regulators, not ours, by the way."

He handed me a sheet of official looking paper. Under the heading CO_2, it stated that each person was allowed one small item in their checked bags, then in huge block letters it continued with EXCEPTIONS, and the first item on the list was LIFE RAFTS.

"And furthermore, Mr. Kretschmer, we can't be responsible for that parcel. You will have to take it over to the air cargo terminal on your own. And they're not open until tomorrow. Sorry, I really am. Our staff upstairs can help you reschedule your flight. Best of luck to you. Next person please."

He was dismissing me, waving to the next person in line to step up to the counter and treating my life raft like toxic waste.

"Wait a minute," I pleaded. "There has to be another solution." Less than three years after the 9/11 terrorist attacks, it was a touchy matter to get angry in an airport. I tried not to sound shrill. Then I remembered that I'd once heard that the pilot had the final word as to what ultimately went on the plane. It was a long shot.

"Can you ask the pilot?"

The manager was exasperated, but he said he would and I moved off to the side, a troublesome traveler with dangerous cargo. Mumbling to myself that I'd rather sail across an ocean than fly, I was almost resigned to rescheduling my flight and shipping the life raft back to the States. But then the perky manager reappeared.

"The pilot said you can bring the raft on the plane, but he wants to have the CO_2 canister in the cockpit. He's a sailor, by the way."

My happiness was half a sentence long. "That's great . . ."

"Wait, no it's not. That's impossible. It's all sealed up and ready to use in an emergency at sea. The canister is not removable."

"Mr. Kretschmer, please. That's the best I can offer you. The flight leaves in thirty minutes. I suggest you make your decision quickly."

I felt strangely alone despite the vastness of the bustling terminal. For a moment the echoes subsided and I could hear my own thoughts clearly. A sense of despair settled over me as I decided to at least investigate what might be involved in removing the CO_2 canister. I cut away the duct tape that I'd wrapped around the box, which looked like a mummy, and ripped it open. Then I pulled out the valise and carefully unthreaded the thin nylon line holding it together. The raft was inside another waterproof plastic bag.

Reaching along the side of the bag, I gingerly probed for the canister. I nudged it, really, just barely touched it when KaBoom—Psss—. The life raft began to inflate! I had launched my brand-new life-raft in the middle of one of the world's busiest airports.

The hissing raft unfolded like a monster, a yellow and black Michelin Man knocking over little rope line dividers and nearby suitcases. People screamed and ran for cover. I am sure they thought a bomb had gone off or was about to. Within seconds two police officers had me pinned to the wall and a third had an automatic rifle pressed against my temple.

"Don't shoot him," the American Airlines manager cried out, and for the first time I agreed with him. The Bobbies quickly realized that I was not a life raft–wielding terrorist, just a pathetic, cheap sailor. They let me down, and actually apologized for scaring the hell out of me. Then we all laughed at the bizarre scene. The life raft, still hissing, had assumed its final, fully inflated shape. It looked like a lunar module alight in Terminal 3. People from all over the airport came to gape at it. The manager clapped me on the back. "Well, I guess you don't have a CO_2 problem anymore. Come on, let's get you on that plane."

I searched for the release valves and began forcing air out of the raft. It was a struggle. Life rafts are not designed to deflate easily. Soon fellow travelers starting helping, pouncing on the raft trying to flatten it. My new life raft had become an airport bounce house. I had to stop one well-meaning woman in high heels from stepping viciously on the tubes. With about half the air out, I rolled it up, threw it over my shoulder, and ran toward my gate with the American Airlines manager leading the way. He was now my best friend and, like a fearless pulling guard, he cleared a path through the crowds.

Ironically, after all the fuss, we sidestepped security and made it to the gate with minutes to spare. I shook the manager's hand and boarded the plane. As I schlepped the unwieldy folds of vinyl and PVC fabric along the narrow aisle, one passenger remarked, "You don't trust the little yellow life rafts on the plane, so you bring your own?"

My attempt to be a savvy, money-saving international traveler had been a disaster. So much for bragging rights at the bar. By the time I had the raft repacked and the CO_2 bottle recharged, I could have purchased it at West Marine in the States for just about the same price and saved all the trouble. But then again, what's the story worth?

As *Quetzal* touched the water, my sister Liz, Trevor, and I hopped aboard. Trevor, with a steady hand, uncorked the champagne. Liz splashed the bow and exclaimed, "May the gods bless *Quetzal* and all who sail in her." It was a perfect launching.

With *Quetzal* and I both back in our natural realms, I felt a lot better. It was the launching that I had been worried about after all, and with the boat floating of her own free will I had a frisson of well-being and a clear vision of where I was headed. I was going to sea, in my own boat, on my own terms. I would sail where and when I wanted, and I would share my expertise, opinions, and stories with those who found their way to me and signed aboard *Quetzal*. I had a plan that just so happened to mesh with my dreams. That's a definition of happiness.

After a quick motor around the harbor, I eased the boat into a slip. I had an appointment with designer Mike Kaufman, whom I had hired to survey the boat while I was in England, and now I hoped to pick his mind in person. He knew more about the boat than anyone else. Yacht designers are great sources of information when writing boat reviews. They aren't as defensive about their boats as builders, maybe because they can always blame the builder if the boat doesn't live up to expectations. Designers are usually insightful, refreshingly honest, and available. Over the years I have called many yacht designers out of the blue, including Lyle Hess, Chuck Paine, Doug Peterson, Bill Crealock, and Gary Mull, to discuss one of their designs. My colleague at *Sailing* magazine, Bob Perry, always has something provocative to say about his own designs and others. Sadly, one reason designers are so readily available these days is because there is so little new design work to be had. The late Lyle Hess told me he was thrilled when I called to discuss one of his designs that I was reviewing. He wasn't sure if his phone still worked.

Mike Kaufman fit the stereotype in all but one way: he was busy. By combining marine surveying with new powerboat designs, he had all the work he wanted. When he turned up at *Quetzal*, he had just come from surveying the tall ship *Pride of Baltimore II*, which was a memorial to the *Pride of Baltimore I*, which tragically sank in a white squall off Puerto Rico in 1986. Kaufman, with obvious civic pride, assured me that the new *Pride* was in sound condition.

Settled in the cockpit of *Quetzal*, he looked around admiringly at his handiwork. He gave me a copy of the original Kaufman 47 brochure, with beautiful pictures of *Quetzal*, which was then called *Madrigal*, taken eighteen years before on the Chesapeake Bay. He told me how the project came about.

Kha Shing, a prominent Taiwanese powerboat builder at the time (in the mid 1980s), wanted to build sailboats. "They approached my partner Rob Ladd and me," Kaufman explained. "They told us that to be a prestigious builder, they needed to build sailboats as well as powerboats. Of course Rob and I agreed. They wanted us to design a boat. They didn't care what it looked like; it just had to be a sailboat."

Kaufman and Ladd went to work. They used their popular Skye 51, an incredibly sleek performance cruiser also built in Taiwan, as a benchmark of sorts. They decided that the boat would have three equal staterooms to appeal to the growing charter market. Originally it was supposed to be 46 feet, but it ended up at 47. At this point Alan Morgan, a successful British yacht dealer who had been importing and customizing boats from Taiwan since the early 1970s, agreed to market the boat in Europe, but he wanted a "Taiwan Swan." He really loved the old S&S Swan 47, and he urged Kaufman and Ladd to make the boat as similar to the Swan 47 as possible.

In the middle of the design, Rob Ladd left the project and went to Florida to work for the importer of the Skye 51 and 54. Kaufman soldiered on and ended up drawing a boat that hit the mark, a synthesis of aesthetics, capability, and performance. The hull was definitely influenced by the Swan 47, but the rounded midsections were more akin to those of the Skye 51. The razor-blade-like entry, longish fin keel, and large, sweeping rudder would keep the boat moving in a seaway and when the sails were poorly trimmed. The keel foil sections were designed to prevent the boat from stalling. Kaufman was one of the first designers to recognize that performance cruising was fundamentally different from racing, even casual racing.

Cruisers are often undercanvased, overcanvased, or simply out of trim, not because cruisers are poor sailors but because sometimes it just isn't practical to be working the boat as efficiently as possible. If a storm is brewing, cruisers will leave the boat undercanvased even if it means lolling about. Same thing if dinner is cooking below and the chef really needs a flat working surface, or you need the boat flat while the engine or watermaker are running. Sailing with a shorthanded crew, often a husband and wife, a cruiser will sometimes hesitate to make the proper sail adjustment, especially if things are going well enough. And it is not just about being undercanvased. Cruisers can often be slow to reef because they dread the work involved, especially in squally conditions when the sails need to be reefed and unreefed frequently. It is easy to be caught with too much sail up, and the boat has to be able to stand up to these conditions too.

Kaufman wanted a boat that would still make speed and knock off miles even when it was not sailed optimally. That's a true definition of a performance cruiser. Ten years and 90,000 miles later, I can attest that the Kaufman

47 performs superbly through a wide range of conditions without requiring micromanagement by the crew, which is a nice way of saying that sometimes *Quetzal*'s crew does not give a damn about sail trim, like during Captain's Hour. And although this self-management design feature is rarely discussed or written about, it is one of the most important considerations when choosing a serious cruising boat.

Alan Morgan and Kha Shing were delighted with the finished result and insisted on calling the boat the Kaufman 47. Mike, being a humble guy, grudgingly acceded to their wishes. Built in Taiwan, the first three boats were 47 feet long before it was decided to rake the transom aft, adding a couple of feet of waterline. From hull number 4 through 23 (the last one was built in 1987), the design was modified and the boat was called the Kaufman 49, but the only difference was the shape of the stern. The first two boats went to England, and the third hull, *Madrigal/Quetzal*, was the first one imported to the United States. Kha Shing did a wonderful job of executing the engineering plans, Kaufman explained. "I was surprised, but as powerboat builders they really followed the drawings to the tee, and the boat turned out about as nice as you could hope for in the translation from paper to fiberglass."

About half the boats had keel centerboard arrangements, where a centerboard extends from the keel cavity, providing deep draft offshore but shoal 4-foot 10-inch draft when the board is up, a design feature that would have turned me off.

"I like that fixed seven-foot keel underneath me," I told him, "and I hate leeway."

Kaufman laughed. "You won't make much leeway, that's for sure. We had to add a centerboard option for U.S. sailors. There's a lot of shallow water on the East Coast. It was a big selling feature of the Swan 47."

I also asked him about a realistic assessment of the boat's performance. "You will be surprised how fast the boat is. The truth is, I don't really know why it's so fast, but you'll see it lives at 7 knots and above." Attesting to the boat's performance, a twenty-seven year old Kaufman 47/49 won Class 4 of the 2012 Newport to Bermuda race.

I had one more question. "What about the low freeboard? She's really low to the water. Don't get me wrong, I like it. But I mean she's really low."

Kaufman smiled and shook his head. "Well, the boat came in just a bit overweight," he confessed, "and as a result it sat a little lower in the water than we expected. You know, there's a lot of teak in the boat." He chuckled. I told you that designers were honest.

When I think about my passions in sailboat design, I realize how easy it is to become narrow-minded, a victim of your own times and experiences, and find new ideas and newfangled ways suspect—in short, to become an old fogey. I don't dispute that I love the 30- and 40-year-old seagoing designs of Bob Perry, German Frers, Bill Crealock, Sparkman & Stephens, and a handful of other designers of fin and skeg hulls that came of age in the 1970s and 1980s. My admiration is threefold.

First, I like the natural balance that moderate proportions provide. A boat should be fast and seaworthy. The ocean seems biased against extremes in everything, from attitudes to hull design, and today's speed machines are anything but balanced in their proportions. They seem as one-dimensional to me as the lardy Spanish galleons that had one job, to plow before a fair wind and transport as much stolen booty as possible to Europe or China.

Second, I like the aesthetics. Many of the boats of this period blend a respect for the past without detracting from the basic need for utility. A boat needs to turn you on.

Finally, and most importantly, I trust them. Yet this is a slippery slope. Clinging to the past is usually generational blindness, like condemning today's music or lamenting how Facebook is destroying face-to-face communication. One of my favorite nautical writers, L. Francis Herreshoff, was one of the greatest small-boat designers, if not the greatest, ever. He was also a master craftsman with words, and his writings about boats are timeless treasures. But we are all trapped by our experiences and our eras, and in the introduction to his book *Sensible Cruising Designs*, published in 1973, Herreshoff laments the meteoric rise of "plastic boats," which were just starting to turn up on the water. He notes that the cost of the original mold would require many hulls to be built and sold just to recover the initial investment. He foresaw the need for manufacturers to employ salesmen and establish dealer networks to keep the slick machine primed, and he envisioned how manufacturers would eventually cut costs by cutting back on essentials like bow chocks and proper mooring cleats.

Herreshoff saw mass production as the deathblow to affordable family boating, but it turned out to be just the opposite. Sailboat manufacturing exploded in the 1960s, 1970s, and into the 1980s. With increased production, manufacturers were able to offer a variety of designs unimaginable when small local builders turned out one beautiful handcrafted boat at a time. A slew of boats became available as designers and builders pushed the envelope of synthetic materials. This was the golden age of sailing. More than a million sailboats were built during this period, and most of them are still afloat.

Although some may disagree, I suggest what finally squashed the beautiful notion that every person should be able to own a sailboat was not the boat itself or the manufacturing and marketing process but the ancillary costs of ownership and, primarily, the loss of time available to actually sail. Access to the water has become unaffordable as shorefronts worldwide are turned into private residences for the wealthy. Marinas, one of man's finer creations, are becoming scarce and increasingly expensive. And time, the most precious commodity of all, far more valuable than gold, has been devalued as people are forced to squander it in a terribly backward equation—trading it for money. Just how crazy is that? Who, when their allotment of time is all but spent, would not trade every bit of gold for just a fraction more time?

Out of this explosion of production energy emerged a capable, well-rounded breed of boat, coined the "racer/cruiser" or "cruiser/racer," depending on what company was selling it. What made these boats unique is that they were affordable, easily handled, nimble, fast, and, almost amazingly, could be sailed anywhere. A reasonably experienced sailor in 1982 could buy a Passport 40, or a Crealock 37, or a Valiant 40, load his family aboard, and spend the next five years sailing around the world. They could expect the boat to knock off 130–150 miles a day, day in and day out, something early cruisers could only dream of. It would take heavy weather in its stride, without the need to run-off or lie ahull, and still be able to heave-to effectively. And, most impressively, it would be easy to maintain and repair. These boats took a lot of the adventure out of bluewater sailing, and that was a revolution.

A seakindly design, intelligent engineering, and solid construction are hallmarks of all good offshore sailboats. Design, however, trumps the other two. I learned about the importance of design when I sailed *Gigi*, our beloved Contessa 32, around Cape Horn more years ago then I care to recall. Our voyage was just one of many proving grounds for the winsome Contessa. It has been everywhere from Spitsbergen to the Antarctic. While the original

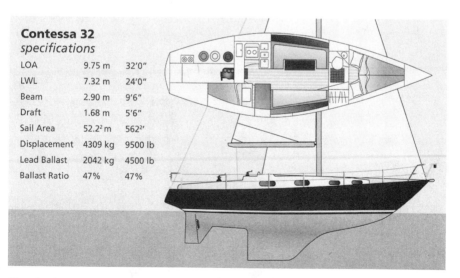

Contessa 32
specifications

LOA	9.75 m	32'0"
LWL	7.32 m	24'0"
Beam	2.90 m	9'6"
Draft	1.68 m	5'6"
Sail Area	52.2² m	562²
Displacement	4309 kg	9500 lb
Lead Ballast	2042 kg	4500 lb
Ballast Ratio	47%	47%

Note the short LWL of the Contessa 32. With a LOA of 32 feet and a LWL of 24 feet, the overhang ratio is 25 percent, which means the boat is beautiful but also means it will heel a lot and will be slower than a boat with a proportionately longer LWL. The Contessa 32 is the most seaworthy small boat ever built. Those flat-bottomed, blunt-nosed boats will be heading for home, pounding viciously no doubt, as the Contessa 32 heads for the horizon.

engineering and construction are certainly above average, it is the design that makes the boat special.

The Contessa 32 is incredibly sure-footed in a blow, almost never pounds, and rarely takes a punch from riled seas. It has a fine entry, a relatively deep forefoot, a longish fin keel, a full skeg-hung rudder, a narrow beam, and low freeboard. The rig is a bit stubby, a result of geographic necessity because most Contessa 32s ply the windy reaches of the English Channel and the North Sea, but it is well balanced and very easy to handle.

This sounds like the perfect boat, but not quite. It has one serious shortcoming—the interior is cramped and uncomfortable. While it works for a non-materialist like me who would rather be at sea than in port, the basic cruising equation works against a small interior. On a typical three-year circumnavigation, for every day spent at sea, ten are spent at anchor or alongside a dock. The boat has to be livable.

Today's boats often tilt the other way, with spacious, dance floor–like accommodations massaged into wide-bodied hulls that are often at war with the sea. While boats like this are great once you arrive at your destination, the passage there can be miserable. Keeping the lesson of L. Francis Herreshoff in mind, I don't really disparage modern boats. Manufacturers are just responding to the way most boats are used, floating condominiums trying to be both a boat and a second home.

Gigi, *a Contessa 32, at the start of her successful mission to break the clipper ship record.*

Sailboats comprise a small percentage of the overall boat market, and bluewater boats are a fraction of a fraction, so why build every boat for the demands of serious sailing? It doesn't make sense, but it does help explain why bluewater boats, even tired old ones, are still in demand. They were built for altruistic reasons, not just economic ones.

Here are some of the design features that I look for in a genuine bluewater boat. Careful readers will notice that many of the features I list are absent in some but not all modern boats. Still, if I have fallen into the same trap that snared L. Francis Herreshoff, at least I am with esteemed company. For the record, I prefer to think that the characteristics that I admire so much are well proven, not just dated. Now don't get me started on Facebook.

Design Features

- A hull shape that does not pound in a seaway or roll unmercifully when running before the wind. A good motion is the most important feature in an offshore boat, period. A soft ride reduces crew fatigue, limits seasickness, and makes life at sea more enjoyable. It also makes the thought of shoving off for a distant island much less daunting.
- A hull shape that tracks well upwind. There is plenty of upwind sailing, even during a so-called trade wind passage. And there's evidence that the world's wind patterns are changing; windward sailing is part of offshore sailing. Close-windedness, or a boat's ability to point, is far less significant than how well it tracks. If a boat can sail 35 degrees off the wind but make 15 to 20 degrees of leeway in typical ocean conditions, what's the point? A few years ago I delivered a modern 46-foot sloop from Connecticut to the Virgin Islands. We had a strong easterly all the way and flew south on what should have been a close reach. I was astonished at the leeway we made—never less than 20 degrees. As a result we were forced to harden up and beat all the way to Tortola. I much prefer a boat that tracks well (doesn't make leeway) to a boat that points high. This is a clear distinction about what makes a boat a bluewater boat.
- The hull and rig need to be well balanced so the boat will react well to self-steering, which, whether by autopilot or wind vane, is critical to the success of any long voyage. If I could choose only one electronic gizmo for my boat, I would forgo GPS, radar, AIS (automatic identification system), sailing instruments, even the VHF radio, and take an autopilot. Steering sucks the life out of a passage, and even on my passages with a full crew, we rely on the autopilot. Some boats, however, especially those with big roachy mainsails and small headsails, don't respond well to self-steering. I talk more about this in Chapter Five when I get into what gear really matters on a cruising boat.

- A keel that can survive a hard grounding and a skeg to protect the rudder. Sooner or later your keel will meet something hard, and you'll snag something you didn't intend to. We hit the skeg hard, slamming a concrete block in Guadeloupe that would have otherwise damaged the rudder. And we collided with an underwater breakwall in Croatia that shook the boat to its core. Poor *Quetzal* takes these assaults in stride, but I have to take a moment to tell you about my friend Benji, and the best grounding story I know.

Benji is a sweetheart of a man, kind and generous, and he desperately wanted to be a sailor. He dreamed of sailing away from the stress of his Toronto computer business, so he purchased a robust Hans Christian 38 cutter. He kept the boat in Florida and hired me to teach him to sail during weekend getaways.

Benji was, unfortunately, not a natural sailor and he struggled to connect the three basic elements of sailing: wind, sails, and rudder. He was a jibing machine, and sailing with him was always an adventure. He also had trouble handling the boat under power because his concentration often waned.

Gradually he made progress and decided that he was ready to take his wife and daughter to the Bahamas. At the last minute he hired me to come along. I knew it would be fun because Benji was always cheerful and had many stories.

The first leg, sailing twenty miles from Fort Lauderdale to Miami, went well enough. We jibed uncontrollably only five or six times. We spent the night at the Miami Beach Marina, just inside the port breakwalls. Benji treated us to a fine dinner and night out on South Beach. Despite the late night, we were up early the next morning to be able to make the fifty-mile crossing to Bimini in the daylight. Benji backed the boat out of the slip and we headed out of the port under power. Just as we passed the breakwalls and started to follow the unmistakable red-and-green channel markers out to sea, Karen, Benji's wife, screamed, "John, there's water coming in here." I dashed below.

"Don't worry, Karen," I reassured her, "I know exactly what the problem is. I'll be right back."

I returned to the cockpit and gave Benji clear instructions. "Benji, we have a little problem below, but I can sort it out. In the meantime, turn around and slowly head back into the port of Miami. Hover off the marina and I'll let you know when everything is okay. Take it easy and pay attention. You can do this."

Benji may not have been a great sailor, but he sure looked like one. He had great clothing, decked out in a billowy white cotton sailor's shirt and sailing shorts with pockets everywhere. He had a Rolex Regatta watch on his wrist, Oakley sunglasses around his neck, and a Leatherman strapped to his waist. He gave me a thumbs-up and then smiled at me confidently as I dropped below.

"These Hans Christians have a terrible flaw," I explained to Karen while hastily removing the floorboards. "They rely on a check valve in the bilge pump discharge line instead of a vented loop. If the valve becomes clogged, sometimes the pump creates a back siphon and actually fills the boat with water. Believe it or not, I have had this problem before."

Sure enough, that was the issue, and pulling the pump inlet out of the water solved the problem immediately. Karen was impressed, and then asked, "Are you sure he's okay up there?"

I nodded. "He's got it under control."

No sooner had the words been spoken then we experienced a terrible, crushing impact. At first I thought a freighter was running us down. Then we listed hard to port and came to a grinding but merciful stop. I staggered into the cockpit. I'll never forget the sight of Benji, standing at the helm with a surprised expression on his face. Somehow, in the span of a quarter mile, he had missed the entrance back into the port of Miami and driven the boat directly onto the beach of Fisher's Island, one of the most exclusive real estate developments in the world. The bowsprit was thirty feet from a $10 million condominium.

Benji actually smiled and said, "Well, you said you're not a sailor until you go aground."

Hopefully your boat won't have to withstand Benji, but it is nice to know that it can. A quick postscript. Benji hired a barge and crane to lift the boat off the beach. Miraculously the hull was structurally intact, a testament to Hans Christian construction.

Design Features, *continued*

- An easy-to-handle sail plan can still be tweaked for better performance. Two secrets of cruising: there's a lot more light air than heavy air, and many cruisers motor more often than they should, or at least admit to it. The solution is not necessarily a lighter boat; it's a proper boat with a generous rig and plenty of sail options.

- A deck layout that keeps you secure when going forward, especially in a blow. No matter how many lines you lead aft, you will still leave the cockpit more often than you think. Bulwarks, tall and well-supported stanchions and lifelines, aggressive nonskid, and well-placed handholds are important.

- A comfortable and seaworthy cockpit. This is where you spend most of your time, at sea and in port. Good sight lines from the helm, easy-to-access sail controls, benches long enough to stretch out on, angled seat backs, and a stout bridge deck are some items to look for. I am always amazed when I watch people pour onto boats at shows. They form a queue on the dock and then, when finally granted access to the boat, they dash below, skipping the deck and cockpit entirely.

- An interior arrangement that works for you. If you sail as a couple, do you really need four double cabins and three heads? Those friends who promise to join you in Bora-Bora rarely show up. Privacy is important but less so than good ventilation, natural light, legitimate sea berths, and a functional galley.

Engineering and Construction Details

While I emphasize the importance of the right design as a priority, a legitimate bluewater boat must be intelligently engineered and solidly constructed. It is easy to be misled by beefy bronze cleats, a solid teak boom crutch, and stainless steel davits hanging off the stern. Is this intelligent engineering? Maybe not, especially when material strength-to-weight measures are considered, and how loading up the ends of a boat hurts performance and seaworthiness.

You can't out-muscle the sea. At best you can try to outsmart it. The late Tom Morris built beautiful world cruisers of moderate proportions that perform well and stand up to storm force conditions. Every detail is engineered properly and then nicely executed during the building process. Excess weight is ruthlessly pared, but seaworthiness is never compromised. That's a construction philosophy that makes sense. Here are some construction features that I think separate bluewater boats from others.

- I am sticking with fiberglass hulls. You know I owned a steel boat for ten years, and I loved her, but metal boats are too time-demanding. I'd rather sail than scrape, but I understand the desire for metal boats and the sense of security they provide. I would go with aluminum before steel, and if I ever buy another steel boat it will be less than ten years old.
- I prefer solid, uncored hulls below the waterline. I appreciate the advantages of cored hulls, especially in the topsides and in the deck, where they reduce weight and offer strength in certain applications. But down south I want solid glass.
- A hull-to-deck joint that does not leak. I prefer a laminated joint to a mechanically fastened one, but they're hard to find, especially in production boats. Most boats have joints that are through-bolted and chemically bonded on inward flanges, and they hold up very well.
- Internal ballast instead of an externally fastened keel held on by bolts. That said, I have logged more than 100,000 miles in boats with an

external keel. However, I like having the ballast integral to the boat as it reflects a different, often more serious construction ethos as well.

- I want the hull to have transverse floors and longitudinal stringers instead of liners and molded pieces.
- I like a deck cored with water-resistant materials like Airex foam. And look for solid laminates in areas below loaded-up fittings. Most boat decks are balsa cored, and for the most part they've held up well. Some old designs, including a few that I really like—the Peterson 44, for example—have plywood-cored decks and are prone to delamination and difficult to repair.
- A boat should have well-engineered sail-control systems with fair leads and intelligent loading. Good-quality hardware often reflects the overall build.

I saw Mike Kaufman off the boat and then sat alone in the cockpit. I surveyed my boat and felt a surge of pride and a tinge of anxiety. I felt like I had a boat that met all my design and construction parameters. Now it was time to see if I was right. It was time to go to sea.

Quetzal's tattered Old Glory. She's seen some miles and is replaced every year. The flag shares the backstay with the man-overboard-pole bracket, which allows the pole to be deployed in seconds.

Ten Old-but-Proven Classics That Can Still Cross Oceans: A List and Some Brief Thoughts

Westsail 32

(Joe Comeau)

WESTSAIL 32. The Helen of sailing, the W32 is the boat that launched a thousand dreams. Of course Helen was the most beautiful woman in Greece, and few would claim the W32 to be the most beautiful boat anywhere. One of the first boats marketed expressly for world cruising, this stout double-ender is based on the full-keel pilot boat designs of Colin Archer and William Atkins. Bill Crealock adapted the Westsail 32 for fiberglass, and the first hull was launched in 1970. Almost nine hundred were built before the company went bankrupt in 1981. Although not a fast boat, the W32 is still plenty capable, and many continue to ply the oceans today.

Price Range: $30,000 to $50,000

CAMPER NICHOLSON 35. This is one of my favorite boats, a proven, handsome classic from the oldest yard in the UK, if not the world. Around two hundred were built, and while most used boats are in the UK, there are usually several for sale on this side of the Atlantic. The Camper Nicholson 35 has a hull shape similar to that of the Contessa 32, the boat that carried me around Cape Horn, with a fine entry, long fin keel, and the rudder tucked behind a full skeg. But there's something else about the Nic 35, as it's called. It's a lovely mixture of style and function, a small yacht with fine finish, capable of sailing anywhere and surprisingly affordable. Not a bad combination.

Price Range: $40,000 to $60,000

Nicholson 35

(Joe Comeau)

TAYANA 37. Designed by Robert Perry, the Tayana 37 is more than just a paean to tradition; it's an incredibly accomplished boat with many circumnavigations on its long CV. Yes, it's a full-keel double-ender with more teak than a Malaysian rain forest, but it is also seaworthy, strong, readily available (six hundred have been built to date), affordable, and, if you're into traditional designs, undeniably handsome. Built by Ta Yang in Taiwan, most are rigged as cutters, although you will find the rare ketch on the market. Many have had their teak decks removed, a definite upgrade, and if they had wooden spars, those too have often been replaced. The majority of boats were built in the 1980s, and I suspect that Tayana 37s will be crossing oceans for decades to come.

Price Range: $60,000 to $100,000

Tayana 37

(Joe Comeau)

SHANNON 38. A classic Walter Schulz-designed cutter or ketch that combines a traditional hull shape with a slightly more voluminous hull form than some of her double-ended competitors. Solidly constructed and with a nice ride in a seaway, even at age thirty-plus, the Shannon 38 is a good choice for a bluewater passage. These boats are out there, in all the cruising outposts, and when you see one lying to anchor you'll admire its beautiful sheerline. The standard interior layout is well suited for a cruising couple, especially with the saloon pilot berth making a perfect sea berth. The cutter rig is versatile when sailing across the wind, but for most trade wind sailing, the high-cut Yankee headsail will be swapped in favor of a big genoa.

Price Range: $75,000 to $120,000

Shannon 38

(Joe Comeau)

(continued next page)

VALIANT 40. If the Westsail 32 put modern-day cruising on the map, the Valiant 40 put the modern in modern day. Considered by just about everybody to be the first so-called "performance cruiser," Bob Perry's design was certainly fresh when it was introduced in 1973. It was quasi-traditional on deck, with the requisite canoe stern demanded by serious cruisers of the time, and the underbody was much more interesting. With a cutaway forefoot, fin keel, and skeg-hung rudder, the Valiant 40 was capable of tracking well upwind and was secure and speedy off the wind. Several early models competed in around-the-world races, and cruisers have been following suit ever since. The bugaboo with Valiant 40s

Valiant 40

(Joe Comeau)

is the blister issue. Between 1976 and 1981, Uniflite, the builder, switched to a fire-retardant resin that caused most hulls to blister badly, below and above the waterline. And while most of these boats are still sailing today, and many have been repaired at great cost, the stigma remains. Valiant moved production to Texas in 1984, and the 40 later became the 42, with a handful of boats built every year. Sadly, all production stopped last year. Ted and Patty, owners of *Little Wing*, the last Valiant 42, have sailed on *Quetzal* several times.

Price Range: For pre-Texas 40s, $70,000 to $120,000, post-Texas 40s, $130,000 to $200,000

BRISTOL 40. This boat could just as easily have been a Hinckley Bermuda 40, a Block Island 40, an Alden Challenger, or a Cape Dory 40. They all feature hulls with pronounced sheers, low freeboard, narrow beam, short waterlines, a cutaway forefoot with a short but "full" keel, and a large attached rudder following the arc of the transom and keel. Most Bristol 40s are centerboarders and some are yawls, neither of which should come as a surprise because the Bristol 40 was designed by Ted Hood. Famous for his sails, Hood also designed many well-respected

Bristol 40

(Joe Comeau)

centerboard racer/cruisers. Bristol Yachts in Rhode Island had a spotty record as a builder, but most 40s were well built, and the boat's sweet shape is at home on the ocean, the key to any bluewater boat. Some boats are now as old as they are long, but I saw a very nice model in English Harbor, Antigua, last year and the couple aboard had been cruising for years and had no intention of swallowing the anchor anytime soon.

   Price Range: $45,000 to $70,000

Mason 43

(Joe Comeau)

MASON 43. A beautiful boat to look at and to sail, the mark of a great design. The Mason 43 helped build Ta Shing's reputation, and the small Taiwan fishing-boat builder eventually became one of the finest sailboat manufacturers in the world. Al Mason's conservative design features a full keel with a cutaway forefoot and a generous cutter rig. The interior is beautifully finished in hand-carved teak, and the overall construction is robust. The 43 has logged countless bluewater miles and circumnavigated several times. Dealing with worn-out teak decks is never fun, and upgrading systems can be expensive, but the Mason 43 is worth putting money into because it is likely to hold its value for years to come. In 1984 the boat was updated and redesigned and became the 44, also a terrific boat but more expensive.

   Price Range: 43s, $80,000 to $125,000; 44s, $150,000 to $200,000

PETERSON 44. Designed by Doug Peterson, known for his performance boats, the Peterson 44 has intrigued cruising sailors from the time it was launched in 1976. Commissioned by California broker Jack Kelly, the 44 includes two features that make it unique. First, it is a cruising boat that is fast; second, it has a center-cockpit layout with the then unthinkable luxury of a private aft cabin with a huge double berth. The first 44s, built by Queen Long, were not finished as well as the early Ta Shing boats, but they were very well suited for serious cruising. More than two hundred 44s were launched before Kelly moved the production to Formosa Yachts, upgraded the boat, and introduced the 46 in 1980. I have seen Peterson 44s and 46s all over the world, and they were on my short list before I bought *Quetzal*. Like many old Taiwan boats of this time, they may need some serious upgrades, from hoses and wiring to removing   *(continued next page)*

Peterson 44

(Joe Comeau)

or replacing teak decks. Of course, you may also find these upgrades completed on many boats on the market.

Price Range: 44s, $85,000 to $120,000; 46s, $120,000 to $180,000

STEVENS 47. The Stevens 47, designed by Sparkman & Stephens, was made for a serious ocean. Fifty-six boats were launched before the boat became the Hylas 47 and later still the Hylas 49. Ruggedly built by Queen Long in Taiwan, the Stevens embodies the hull shape that I talk about throughout this book, with a fine entry, powerful fin keel, skeg-hung rudder, and overall low profile. Most 47s were rigged as cutters, with a tall mast and an ample sail area. The spacious interior features a large aft cabin, a galley in the walk-through, a great saloon, a quarter cabin, and a V-berth. It's livable to be sure, and all the more so because it has one of the softest rides you'll ever experience at sea. Many Stevens 47s have circumnavigated. If

Stevens 47

(Joe Comeau)

you love the Hylas 47 and 49 but can't afford one, take a look at a Stevens 47.

Price Range: $160,000 to $230,000

Gulfstar 50

(Joe Comeau)

GULFSTAR 50. I sailed a Gulfstar 50 ketch from Fort Lauderdale to Japan many years ago and came to appreciate it as a capable and comfortable bluewater boat. Gulfstar, of St. Petersburg, Florida, is all but forgotten these days, and in some ways for good reason. They built some hideous vessels, a series of motorsailers that can only be called fat and ugly. But they also built some handsome world-class boats as well, especially in the 1980s. The 50, designed by Vince Lazarra, has a seakindly hull shape and moderate proportions. The construction wasn't sophisticated, but it was strong, and although many of the hulls have blistered over the years, they have held up well otherwise. Many 50s ended up in Caribbean charter fleets. Most were ketches, although some were sloops. A center-cockpit design, they came with two and three stateroom layouts. Some of these boats are approaching 40 years old and yet there's been a renaissance in the reputation. There are still some bargains out there that will need complete refits, but a nice 50 will cost as much to buy today as it did twenty years ago. It's a lot of bluewater boat for the bang.

Price Range: $80,000 to $140,000

five

Assembling a Crew I First Days Offshore I Three
Keys to Happiness Afloat I Situational Awareness I
Crew Overboard Procedures I Abandoning Ship
Procedures I Distress Broadcasts I Flooding and
Sinking and Not Sinking I Making a Landfall

Departures—
Bermuda Bound

*"In the artificial world of his cities and towns, man often forgets the true
nature of his planet. The sense of all these things comes to him most
clearly in the course of a long ocean voyage, when he watches day after
day the receding rim of the horizon, ridged and furrowed by the waves.
And then, as never on land, he knows the truth, that his world is a
water world."*

—Rachel Carson, *The Sea Around Us*

THE SOUTHWEST WIND FILLED and *Quetzal* sped from the haze that clung to
the Virginia coast like a tenacious bay barnacle. It was our maiden voyage,
and just a few hours beyond the Chesapeake Bay Bridge-Tunnel we were
already shortening sail. We tied a single reef in the main, and then, an hour
later, because the thought crossed my mind, we tied in a second reef. Reefing
is intuitive, or, in the words of Thomas Fleming Day, "It's always time to reef
when you think it is." Although this hackneyed advice is often reprinted on
kitschy brass plaques sold in tacky nautical stores, it's worth remembering.

With the first reef in the main, the 150 percent genoa was furled to
around 100 percent, and then a little more with the second reef. Finally, we
rolled it in completely and replaced it with the hank-on staysail. The rig was
nicely balanced and the ride was relatively flat. The racing mantra "flat is
fast" definitely applies to a performance cruiser like *Quetzal*. Reducing sail
rarely equates to a significant reduction in speed but always improves motion
and control. We were making miles toward the target, Bermuda, a waypoint
that seems to pop up in every chapter and is one of my favorite landfalls.

Mike Kaufman was right—the boat was fast, really fast—and we were charging along at a steady 8 knots.

Bruce, Otto, Lou, and Charlie formed an unlikely but affable crew. None of them had met before, but shortly after throwing their bags aboard we shoved off for an 800-mile nonstop passage from Maryland to Bermuda. There would be plenty of time to get to know one another.

This travel arrangement seems fraught with risk to some folks, especially land people, and I am often asked if I ever got someone on board I just couldn't stand. The answer is no, or, more accurately, almost never. This may sound Pollyannaish, but the evidence is hard to dispute: ten years and more than 90,000 miles later, I've never really had a crewmember I didn't like. I think it's because my trips are self-selective; you have to really want to sail aboard *Quetzal*.

First, you must be persistent in tracking me down because I am not easy to find. I don't advertise my passages, and most people know of me through my magazine articles, books, and lectures. A Google search leads to my website and sailing schedule. You have to be patient. I am famous for not returning e-mails or phone calls promptly because I'm often at sea. But somehow it works out and we eventually communicate, and before long I am welcoming you aboard. My passages appeal to a small group of people, a wonderfully select group who desperately want to experience offshore sailing but who dread signing up for a sailing school course. These folks know what they're getting into, and the only time they complain is when a passage is too smooth, which, given my penchant for getting into trouble, is rare.

No crew is ever typical. Age, health, sailing experience, hopes, and fears vary from trip to trip and person to person. Bruce, a Canadian by nationality and a forester by trade, had sailed with me several times before. He would later be a vital crewmember in our voyage around Newfoundland. He was more of a friend than a customer, but he understood the economics of my life and always insisted on paying the going rate. About my age, he is fit and very funny. Years of traveling through Central America have heightened his senses and filled his joke bag; he knows when to keep things light and when to take them seriously—a very good trait on a boat.

Otto was born in Norway but raised in Michigan. He is self-effacing, with a radiant smile and a knack for anticipating what needs doing, another good trait on a boat. Charlie was a recently retired chemist, and his blurred vision, poor hearing, and limited mobility did not suggest that he would be a natural bluewater sailor, but he would come to surprise and delight me. Lou, a lifelong powerboater, had sailed with me on a couple deliveries and had, almost reluctantly, become intrigued with the possibilities of sailing. "I am not saying I like sailboats more than powerboats," he insisted. "I just really want to travel by boat, and that means a sailboat because powerboats, at least the ones that I can afford, are not capable of going where I want to go." Looking back, he seemed to know there was an urgency to his quest. Sadly he was right.

Expectations and anxieties mark the beginning of every passage. I reminded my four shipmates that pacing is a key component to ocean sailing and urged them to take things slowly. It's natural to begin a voyage with a frenzy of activity. After all, you have only a week or two to knock off everything on your to-do list. However, after a few hours aboard, when you're strangely tired, a little bit queasy, and already missing your family, you realize that a week at sea is infinitely longer than a week ashore.

Every passage begins with a "life aboard *Quetzal*" discussion, complete with my version of the three keys to happiness afloat and an extensive safety briefing.

"Not the potty talk again," Bruce said, laughing.

"Sorry, brother, I have to do it. It's a ritual."

We gather in the cockpit and I begin the only lecture anyone has to suffer through aboard *Quetzal*. I start with the rules, or I should say the rule, because there's only one. Be courteous and tolerant, and respect one another's privacy. On land it would be difficult to take four perfect strangers, sit them in a room, and preach basic common sense like this without sounding like a Disney character. On the boat, on the cusp of a passage, people take it to heart and embrace this utilitarian ideal. John Stuart Mill, the English philosopher and father of Utilitarianism, wrote, "The only freedom which deserves the name is that of pursuing our own good, in our own way, so long as we do not attempt to deprive others of theirs, or impede their efforts to obtain it." This is a slippery slope on a passage. I want each crewmember to find what they're looking for. Their individual quest is vitally important, and yet they must be part of the crew at the same time. I have observed over the years that our accomplishments as a crew tend to be the lasting ones.

Nothing is more dangerous aboard an offshore sailboat than a narcissist. Passagemaking is, in essence, a family activity even if nobody is related. And, as in the case of all families, good communication is essential. Small problems on a boat are like a stalk of ripe bananas; they go bad all at once. You need to confront them before they rot.

It is easy to become irritable on an offshore passage, and it's usually caused by one of three symptoms: lack of sleep, lack of food, or irregularity. It is vital to sleep at sea, and I encourage the crew to nap when possible and to be serious about sleeping at night when off-watch. This is one reason (not the only one!) why I encourage a glass of wine, rum, or beer at Captain's Hour, to help people relax and sleep. A few days without sleep can be debilitating and can not only ruin your enjoyment of the passage but also impair your ability to make sound decisions when conditions deteriorate.

Not eating is usually caused by not feeling well. Let's face it, there is nothing worse than seasickness. Mark Twain, who traveled the world by ship and suffered from mal de mer at the beginning of every passage, wrote, "At first you are so sick that you're afraid you might die, then you are so sick you are afraid you won't." Twain also noted his annoyance when another crewmember feels fine and flaunts it. "If there is one thing that will make a man peculiarly and insufferably self-conceited, it is to have his stomach behave itself, the first day at sea, when nearly all his comrades are seasick."

My crews have tried every remedy imaginable to prevent seasickness, and while some work, many don't, and time seems to be the only ultimate cure. Some natural remedies are hilarious. I had one crewmember bring a small piece of sod. He would sleep on it in a vain attempt to maintain a connection to land and ward off the dreaded curse. It didn't work, and it made a mess in his bunk. He eventually tossed the dirt overboard and resorted to a scopolamine patch. Finding foods that you can keep down, and staying hydrated, are essential to eventually putting seasickness behind you.

Finally, even people who are sleeping and eating can feel miserable if they are not using the head on a regular basis. I am convinced that nobody feels right until they move their bowels, and although this sounds disgusting it is important. I urge people to get regular as soon as possible.

Things turn a bit more serious when the talk turns to safety. The briefing begins with a discussion of personal responsibility, a theme I repeat often in this book. When it comes to safety, it does not matter how much money you spend on fancy equipment because no amount of gear will keep you safe if you don't think about your actions and how they relate to the situation. I have seen plenty of people clip the tethers on their safety harness to a stout jackline and then scoot forward on the lee side of the deck, only to park themselves right below a loaded-up jibsheet, mainsheet, or boom vang. Sure they're clipped in, but if one heavily loaded-up fitting gives way, the resulting impact will knock them overboard or silly before there is time to do anything about it.

I encourage my crews to be aware of their space all the time or, simply put, to pay attention. You don't have to be an experienced sailor to know that you should stay upwind of loaded fittings, keep as much deck space as possible between you and the sea, and take a moment to analyze any problem before reacting. People tend to fall off boats to leeward. The low-side deck edge is the least desirable place to be at all times. Look for a route forward that keeps you on the high side as much as possible. And take your time—even urgent problems usually benefit from a quick reflection instead of a headlong dash to action.

Situational awareness was developed by the military to train soldiers to remain cool when responding to changing conditions in a dangerous environment. On a boat, it's a perfect way to think about merging seamanship and safety. One of the themes I touch on throughout the book is the concept of seamanship. And I do mean concept. Seamanship is a sense, a way of sailing, a way of thinking, a way of living when afloat, a natural weltanshauung that encompasses your boat and your watery world. Seamanship is a noun, and sometimes an adjective, but you should think of it as a verb.

At this point in my talk, everybody takes a deep breath. Who is this hyper-serious John Kretschmer? Isn't it time for a joke or a sea story? They're wondering what they've gotten themselves into. They just wanted to go sailing, and now they have to embrace the notion of seamanship like a religion and promise the skipper they'll try to use the head at every chance. I promise them I will shut up soon, and we take a short break. Nothing sucks the fun out of a passion quicker than a discussion about mundane safety procedures.

Somebody else typically takes a trick at the helm, we trim the sails, make sure we're not on a collision course, and plot our position. Once, in the middle of my safety spiel, we nearly ran down a small fishing boat, averting disaster at the last minute only when we heard frantic screams. We veered

The whisker pole is a vital piece of Quetzal's rigging, deployed whenever the wind is abaft the beam. Here we are flying a reefed main, the staysail, and the poled-out genoa. Note the pole-preventer lines, technically called guys, which run fore and aft. The pole is essentially locked in place, and the genoa sheet, which runs through the pole jaw, is free to be furled. When wind pipes up, the headsail can be furled or reefed and the pole remains in place. As the sail is shortened, the pole is shifted forward. Quetzal has a Forespar combination pole, which means it is an aluminum pole with a carbon inner that is easily extended or retracted by a line-drive system.

off course and narrowly avoided T-boning the small boat, crewed by a bewildered father and his terrified young son.

Falling off the boat is the biggest risk anyone assumes when they make an offshore passage. I tell everybody who sails on *Quetzal* the same thing, "Staying on the boat is your duty, not mine; it's your life and you are responsible for it." I am, however, committed to doing everything possible to make sure everybody who starts the voyage finishes the voyage. The key to retrieving a man overboard is teamwork and decisive action, but I never mince words. The odds of successfully rescuing someone are quite small. To emphasize just how dangerous this situation can be, I tell the story of a person overboard that came within minutes, or even seconds, of being a tragedy.

Back in my yacht delivery days, I was hired to deliver a fast-fading CT 41 ketch from the Virgin Islands to Fort Lauderdale. I had flown to St. Thomas with Mark, a young man who had recently completed a circumnavigation with his parents.

A swoopy Bill Garden knockoff, the CT was laden with ornate teak scrollwork and paeans to traditionalism, with features like a bowsprit, boomkin, boom crutch, belaying pins, and baggywrinkles. Properly maintained it could have been a handsome boat. However, the peeling varnish on the spars reminded me of a once grande dame who had accepted her lot; she was no longer going to be beautiful and had decided to stop wearing makeup. But I delivered the boat because I needed the money—I always needed money in those days—so despite worn sails, a reluctant engine, weak batteries, and more leaks than a cunning politician's press office, I figured we could con the old girl back to Lauderdale without too much trouble. It would be a typical delivery. Just before we were ready to shove off, a young Englishwoman hailed me from the dock. She had recently crossed the Atlantic aboard a big charter boat and was looking for a ride north to the States. I told her that the boat was a bit of wreck, and I wouldn't be able to pay her. Neither condition troubled her, and when she offered to cook, I told her to fetch her bag. She was a sailing hitchhiker, which in the 1980s was a quite common and viable way to travel the world.

A few hours later we were booming along on a lovely reach. The trade winds were in their glory, and we had the baggy genoa poled out and both the main and mizzen booms secured with preventer lines. The old dog of a boat was lumbering along at 6 knots. Kim, our new crewmember, needed to use the toilet, which in this case meant relieving herself over the side because the head was out of order. Mark and I naturally averted our eyes as she made her way to the stern. For more privacy she locked her legs around the wooden rail, held onto the mizzen sheet, and leaned outboard. I heard a quiet, "Oh shit," then a splash.

That was it. She was overboard.

"Man overboard!" I screamed as I launched the sun-rotted horseshoe buoy. After a moment's panic, we snapped to life and began to execute a classic quick turn man-overboard maneuver. Every small-boat sailor learns this technique of steering onto a beam reach as quickly as possible, and holding the course for a count of twenty before coming about. After a wide tack the boat is put on a broad reach momentarily before the sheets are hardened and you are able to point up toward the person in the water.

Mark and I frantically began freeing the sails. He raced forward to drop the whisker pole, and I went after the preventers. This took a lot longer than twenty seconds, and by the time we were ready to tack we had sped well past where Kim had fallen overboard. The ensuing tack was a disaster as the headsail sheets hung up on oversized brass Dorade vents and teak belaying pins.

Finally I realized that what we were doing, trying to effect a rescue under sail, was idiotic, and I started the engine, giving thanks when it sputtered to life. Powering through the tack, I told Mark to roll in the headsail and tighten up the main- and mizzen sheets. It was several minutes, probably more than five, before I turned the boat 180 degrees onto the reciprocal course.

Suddenly plunging and punching into what had seemed like moderate seas when were we reaching, the clumsy boat kicked up sheets of spray as we searched the horizon looking for our shipmate. She was nowhere in sight. Resisting the urge to speed up, I motored slowly and carefully, fighting the wheel to stay on course. I staved off another pang of panic, knowing that it would not do Kim, or me, any good. Several minutes passed with no sight or sign of her. Had I gone too far? I had no reference point, nothing other than a compass heading, my watch, my instincts, and Mark's sharp eyes. This was pre-GPS; I was still using my sextant to navigate. I hollered for Mark to hold on and, convinced that we must have missed her, turned abruptly back to the original course. The situation was getting desperate.

Motoring with the wind and seas behind us, we sped up dramatically. What was I thinking? Clearly we had not gone far enough on the previous tack. I resisted the urge to turn the boat again and continued on for another minute or two before bringing the boat back through the wind. I was confused and had no idea where to steer. I was zigzagging all over the ocean.

Finally, miraculously, Mark spotted her. She had drifted significantly to leeward, and I chastised myself for not factoring this into my search pattern, as if I had an actual search pattern. I steamed toward the tiny human head at full speed. Seeing her bob in the water put the rolling six- to eight-foot seas into graphic perspective; they dwarfed her, and even at close range she disappeared in each wave trough.

Mark threw a life jacket, but at 100 feet we were too far away and it was well off target. Then he pitched a seat cushion and a fender, and although they both came within twenty feet of her, she was too exhausted to reach them.

It was dangerous for us to maneuver close to her, so I positioned the boat upwind of her and we floated a line and life jacket toward her. It passed less than ten feet from her, but she could not muster the energy to grab it or even swim toward it. She was just holding on, barely treading water, her strength ebbing with every wave that washed over her.

Mark wanted to go into the water to save her, but I overruled him. "Then we'll have two people overboard. No, we have to get the boat to a position where she'll drift down to us."

I pushed the throttle ahead and steered directly downwind, then turned 90 degrees. The boat rocked violently from side to side. Mark cut the life-lines and I jockeyed the boat backward and forward, trying to make sure that we would intercept her drift. Like a piece of jetsam, she was carried by the waves right toward us. When it was certain we'd have a chance to reach her, I dashed forward. Draped over the side as far as we dared, we each clutched an arm and hauled her aboard.

Every time I tell this tale, I relive the horrible experience. The memory is vivid and has not dulled with time. Although I lost contact with Kim within days of reaching the States, she has, through her ordeal, accompanied me on every passage I have made since. She also lives on in the minds of Amy, one of my frequent crewmembers. Amy has heard Kim's story at the beginning of so many voyages that she has written a short story about Kim, a woman she's never met but feels she knows. And in the story Kim relives her whole life while she awaits rescue.

I certainly learned from Kim's near disaster, and I assure the crew that we are not going to repeat the same mistakes should we have a similar emergency. From that day on I have always discussed a potential man-overboard emergency with the crew and, more importantly, formulated a plan. Our biggest mistake was to lose contact with Kim almost immediately. By worrying about the boat, we took our eyes off the prize. To bring my point home, I usually throw a piece of fruit—a grapefruit or small melon is perfect because it's about the size and shape of a human head—into the water and yell "man overboard." Then we follow it trailing astern in the waves. By putting a finger on it, a pointer, you can extend visual contact dramatically. Your finger gives your eyes a return reference point as the target disappears in a wave trough; you know where to look when it reappears on a crest. Whoever sees the person go overboard becomes the "point person" of the rescue. They immediately alert the crew and put their finger on the person. And they never take their eyes off them.

The first person in the cockpit punches the MOB key (man overboard function) on the chartplotter and notes the course heading. We also have a VHF in the cockpit equipped with DSC, digital select calling that has a one-button emergency feature, and this is punched too. It may be of limited use offshore, but every option must be deployed. Then we start the engine. There is no reason to attempt a sailing rescue. Period. As sailors we learn man overboard techniques from the perspective of a small boat. But we're not dinghy sailing on the ocean, and sails distract from the main task of finding and retrieving the person in the water as efficiently as possible.

The next job, and it should happen within seconds of starting the engine, is to launch all the emergency flotation devices. On *Quetzal* we carry a man overboard pole, an inflatable man overboard module, and a horseshoe buoy with a strobe light, all in quick-release brackets. We also tie the fenders to the stern rail; these can quickly be ditched and probably offer the best flotation.

The problem with all this emergency apparatus is that it rarely reaches the person in the water. Once dispatched into the sea, it blows rapidly to leeward—even the ballasted man overboard pole—and the distance between the person and the equipment usually increases as time goes on. But it does leave a trail of debris, floating bread crumbs if you will, that can be useful in guiding you to the person in the water.

Finally, roll in the headsails, sheet in the main, and bring the boat through the wind 180 degrees to the reciprocal course. With a full crew, this entire process, from the first shouting of man overboard to a controlled return approach, should take less than two minutes. This is the time when situational awareness saves lives. Think and react. Remember, the person in the water will not be at the MOB position; it is just another data point. Don't steer in wild gyrations trying to return to the precise MOB coordinates. Stay on the reciprocal course, which should correspond to the general heading on the plotter. Use common sense. A boat sailing at 6 knots will travel approximately a quarter mile in two minutes. It does not take long to retrace a quarter mile. Above all, follow the pointer person. Hopefully the pointer kept watching the person as the boat came through the wind and moved forward if necessary to have an unobstructed view. Also watch the gear in the water. Is it blowing hard to leeward? Adjust your course and keep just upwind of the windward-most floating object.

The person in the water must fight off panic and remain calm. It's always best to float face down, in a "navy float," with your knees pulled into your chest. Sometimes this is called a dead man's or prone float. By keeping your face down, you are forced to keep your mouth closed and to breathe out, not in. Then lift your head, look forward to make sure a wave is not about to swamp you, and take a deep breath. Floating on your back leaves you vulnerable to swallowing seawater. Once that process begins, your chances of survival decrease rapidly. Conserve energy by moving as little as possible. Frantic waving at the boat is not helpful. If you have flotation, you can survive a long time in warm water. Even in cold water, if you conserve energy you can stay alive long enough to be rescued.

COLD WATER SURVIVAL TABLE

Water Temperature		Exhaustion or Unconsciousness	Expected Survival Time
°F	°C		
32	0	<15 minutes	<15–45 minutes
32–40	0–4	15–30 minutes	30–90 minutes
40–50	4–10	30–60 minutes	1–3 hours
50–60	10–16	1–2 hours	1–6 hours
60–70	16–21	2–7 hours	2–40 hours
70–80	21–27	3–12 hours	3 hours–indefinitely
>80	>27	indefinitely	indefinitely

The will to live is a powerful force. If you don't have flotation, you'll have to make a critical decision. If you feel that you can make it to something jettisoned by the crew, give it a try. If you don't think you can swim to it, then save your energy. This is a tough call because flotation makes a huge life-saving difference. There is a powerful incentive to wear an inflatable PFD all the time. If you do manage to reach a fender, horseshoe buoy, or anything floating, lift as much of your body out of the water as possible to ward off hypothermia for as long as possible. Your job is simple: be alive when the crew returns to pick you up.

The process of retrieving the person will depend on the conditions. A throw line and a Lifesling-style towable buoy are essential. It is vital to make physical contact with the person in the water as soon as possible, but take painstaking care to not run them over or tow them under once you have a line to them. Drop the swim ladder and, if conditions permit, put the dinghy in the water and rig a long painter. Dinghies can be easier to board, and they also give the crew a platform from which to help the person in the water while maintaining contact with the mother ship. I always tell the crew that once we have the boat in close range, we are not going to lose the person. We are going to do whatever it takes to get them back aboard. But I am not sure if I believe myself.

No matter what, though, even if the person in the water is unconscious or disabled, rule one is to stay aboard the mother ship.

The next uplifting topic on the safety agenda: when and how do we abandon ship?

There's usually a collective groan and a snide comment when I begin, but I press on, knowing that if an emergency were to arise, having talked about it beforehand, and having a plan, may very well save our lives.

"You want to step up into a life raft." As hackneyed sounding as it is, it has merit. Never leave a floating vessel. Unless sinking, fire, or explosion is imminent, even the mostly reluctantly afloat hulk is almost always a better platform for survival than a life raft. There are many documented cases of crews abandoning ship, never to be heard from again while their boat is found still floating or washed up on a beach. Being in a life raft is as close to hell as you can come while still being alive. It is a vessel of last resort. Boarding a life raft is extremely dangerous, and if you do make it aboard the damn thing, you will be cold, soaked to the bone, and instantly seasick. On the other hand, as miserable as bobbing in a life raft may be, it very well may save your life one day.

We have a clear-cut exit strategy for leaving *Quetzal.* Just like the man-overboard procedure, teamwork and clear thinking are essential when it's time to abandon ship. The first task is critical: everyone must be wearing a personal flotation device. Then I assign everyone a specific job.

On this passage, Bruce was the life raft person. It was his job to free the raft from the rail, make sure the painter (line) was attached to something strong, and be ready for me to give him the go-ahead to launch it. By this I meant throwing the raft overboard, preferably on the lee side of the cockpit, and then inflating it by pulling the painter. I explained that the entire valise went overboard; there was nothing to unpack. It was Bruce's job to then pull the raft alongside the boat.

We talked briefly about how to board the raft. In rough conditions it is usually best to step on top of the canopy or hood and work your way around to the opening. Many new rafts, including the top-of-the-line Switlik SAR-6 (search and rescue) that we use in the offshore passagemaking workshops I conduct, have a canopy that folds up and down to allow easier boarding. In survival conditions the only way into the raft is from the water, with the strongest crew boarding first, then helping the others in by pulling them aboard on their backs. It was also Bruce's responsibility to always carry a knife to cut the painter free of *Quetzal.*

Charlie's job was to dash below and grab the abandon-ship bag mounted with Velcro on the aft bulkhead. This bright yellow float bag weighs around 20 pounds and contains an EPIRB, flares, signaling devices, a handheld radio, a sat phone, a GPS, fishing gear, first-aid supplies, a manual desalination device, emergency rations, and other survival items. It was Charlie's job to make sure that the abandon-ship bag made it into the raft. Once the bag was in the cockpit, he and Bruce would stand by as the deck team, ready to make a sail change or maneuver if I requested. If no maneuvers were imminent, Charlie was also responsible for dashing below and rounding up bottles of drinking water. One advantage of gallon plastic water bottles is that they have a handle that allows them to be tied together. Even if they don't make it into the raft initially, they will float and hopefully can be rounded up later.

Lou had a deep, clear speaking voice, and this qualified him to be our radio officer. It was his job to man the VHF and SSB radios, both mounted in the aft cabin nav station. I told him to write down our position in simple latitude and longitude notations, dropping the cardinal directions and rounding to the nearest minute by eliminating all numbers to the right of the decimal point. In other words, if our GPS position was 35 degrees 42.16 minutes north latitude and 72 degrees 15.83 minutes west longitude, I wanted him to say simply, "Our position is 35 42 and 72 16." Anyone within range on VHF Channel 16 or SSB frequency 2182 KHz would know that we were north of the equator and west of Greenwich, and if they didn't know that, they probably would not be much help in rescuing us anyway.

There are three levels of distress broadcasts: Sécurité (pronounced "say-kyur-ee-tay"), Pan-Pan, and Mayday. Sécurité implies that there is not yet an immediate risk to life, but a problem exists. Pan-Pan is more serious and implies that a life-threatening risk may develop soon. Mayday leaves no room for doubt; urgent assistance is required to prevent immediate loss of life. For that reason a Mayday should never be issued casually. First responders are preparing to risk their lives to save yours—never lose sight of that fact.

I told Lou that our most likely first broadcast would be a Pan-Pan. The procedure is to say "Pan-Pan" three times, slowly and clearly. Then follow up with the vessel's name and position, again spoken slowly and repeated three times. This is followed by a brief description of the emergency and a request for all vessels to respond and stand by. Once contact is made, the standby vessels are appraised as the situation develops.

A Pan-Pan scenario might go something like this: "Pan Pan Pan, this is the sailboat *Quetzal, Quetzal, Quetzal*. Our position is 38 24, 65 41; 38 24, 65 41; 38 24, 65 41. We are taking on water and assessing the situation. Any and all vessels, please acknowledge and then stand by. This is the sailboat *Quetzal*. Out."

Otto's job was to accompany me and help me do everything possible to prevent *Quetzal* from sinking. Even then, on *Quetzal*'s first voyage, I knew the boat intimately, having combed every inch of the bilge while familiarizing myself with her. Otto is one of those talented people who can build a boat from a set of plans and finish it to perfection. He was at home with any tool, and I knew he was the right man to have next to me should we need to make an emergency repair. Everyone on board had a vital role in our ultimate survival. That's what a passage on *Quetzal* is all about. That's what any bluewater passage is all about. Taking responsibility for your own actions.

I had been talking a long time, and fortunately it was Captain's Hour. This is a wonderful tradition on any boat I am skippering, a break before dinner and night watches when the crew assembles in the cockpit and shares a drink, alcoholic or not, a nice snack, and lively discussion. Bruce took orders and returned with drinks for all of us. We toasted *Quetzal*, our voyage, and one another. I explained that I had one more story to tell them and then mercifully the safety briefing would be over. "It takes a lot of water to sink a boat," I began, "and a few years ago I almost found out just how much."

I was delivering a brand-new Hylas 49 from Fort Lauderdale to the Virgin Islands. The same steady easterly trade winds that make sailing in the Caribbean such a delight once you're there conspire to almost guarantee headwinds and sloppy going for the 1,000-mile passage trying to get there. In one of those geographic anomalies that can be hard to visualize, the route from Florida to the eastern Caribbean is primarily an east-to-west affair, not a north-to-south run. For every degree of latitude sailed, you need to knock off two degrees of longitude. It's a deceptively challenging passage.

My crew was the new owners, John and Sue, and two prospective Hylas buyers, Jim and Bill, who had signed on for a serious sea trial. Motoring down the New River, which slices through downtown Fort Lauderdale before heading offshore, I dutifully went over the watch schedule, man overboard drill, and abandon ship procedures, as I had just done with Bruce, Otto, Lou, and Charlie—and as I always do.

We cleared Port Everglades and were soon met by a lumpy Gulf Stream. I was eager to take advantage of the fair northwest winds, but I knew the Stream would be rough. The boat was being delivered to a Caribbean charter fleet and was minimally equipped. It was fitted with a bimini sunshade but not a spray dodger, and soon everybody aboard was wet and cold. And everybody but Jim and me was seasick.

Halfway across the Stream, the new owners and Bill, with buckets in hand, retreated to their cabins. The boat didn't have an autopilot, and I told Jim I would stay at the helm until we were past Great Isaac Light, and then he could spell me. Beyond the light we'd be clear of the Gulf Stream and in the lee of Grand Bahama Island, where the motion was sure to improve.

Two hours later, and still about ten miles from the light, Jim poked his head out of the companionway. "We have a lot of water in the bilge, and the pumps don't seem to be working."

"I'm not surprised," I said. "Damn new boats. Can you pump it out manually? When I come below, I'll check the pumps."

Jim slammed the companionway hatch closed just as another wave crashed into the cockpit. Twenty minutes later, Jim emerged again. "I can't keep ahead of the water. It's above the floorboards." He was dressed in his foul-weather gear and ready to take the helm. "You need to look at this now."

As soon as I dropped below, I realized Jim was right. The water was well above the floorboards and sloshing from side to side as the boat rolled miserably in the Gulf Stream swell. The electric pumps were useless, and the manual wasn't much better. The pumps were clogged with wood shavings and other bits of construction debris, a common new boat problem. As fast as I cleared the strainers, they clogged again.

Suddenly the water began to rise noticeably. Quickly it was over my ankles.

Trying to remain calm, I roused the crew. I told them to put on their foul-weather gear and a PFD and stand by in the cockpit. The tone of my voice made it clear that there was no time to tarry. It was just getting dark as I began to tear the boat apart looking for the leak. Leaks often turn up in the engine room, but the stuffing box and stern tube seemed to be intact. I had already checked every through-hull fitting below the waterline. Where was the water coming from? Was it time to put out a Mayday? I had plenty of questions but few answers.

Everybody had gone to their positions. Jim, still steering, was also ready with the life raft. Bill had grabbed the abandon-ship bag on his way to the cockpit. Sue was assembling spare water jugs and lashing them together. I was impressed; they had listened carefully during the safety briefing. I told John to carefully write down our coordinates and to use the handheld VHF radio to broadcast a Mayday. I was confident that the powerful U.S. Coast Guard radio receivers would pick up our transmission, or that somebody on the nearby island of Bimini would.

"Jim, start the engine, and motor at full throttle right toward Great Isaac Light. It's on a rocky little island but at least it's an island. If we're going to sink, I'd rather sink in twenty feet of water where the boat can be salvaged and we can swim ashore."

Shortly, a commercial fishing boat that was anchored in the lee of the lighthouse answered our Mayday. The captain said he would stand by and was ready to come to our rescue. This was incredibly reassuring news. Meanwhile the water below was rising steadily. Within minutes the engine, completely submerged, sputtered to a stop. Then, with the batteries also underwater, the lights failed. Jim and Bill trimmed the sails, but the sodden boat barely moved. At least we were in the lee of Great Isaac and the seas had calmed. The fishing boat, with its deck lit, was raising anchor and getting ready to come alongside.

Still below, I wondered at what point the boat would start to sink, and would I be trapped inside when it started to go down? The water was above the counters in the galley. The cabin had become a slurry of cushions, pots and pans, and clothes. Anything not tied down floated about. In some spots the water was chest high. I was scared and furious. I couldn't accept the fact that I was about to sink a beautiful, brand-new boat. Flashlight in hand, I made one last search for the leak. Wading forward, I pushed my way into the quarter cabin. The mattress was floating, the board beneath it was floating, and the drawers below the bunk had been washed out of place.

And then I saw it, a stream of water. There seemed to be a hole in the hull. I plunged underwater to take a look. There it was: a two-inch hole that was supposed to house a spare depth-sounder transducer. It had been mounted at the extreme turn of the bilge, where it was impossible to make it flush to the hull. Somewhere in the Gulf Stream the transducer had been jarred free. While the transducer was nowhere in sight, thankfully a wooden plug had been strapped to the shoddy fitting. I grabbed it and shoved it down into the cavity. We were not going to sink after all.

Back aboard on our maiden voyage, *Queztal* was flying toward Bermuda and was on pace for a record passage, at least a record for me. Four days out of the Solomons, we were just sixty miles from the tiny fairyland island of Bermuda.

Unfortunately the ugly dawn that greeted us on day five had no intention of letting us slip quietly into the harbor at Saint George's. There would be no records set on this passage, and the Dark and Stormies waiting for us at Tavern by the Sea on Somers Wharf would have to wait a bit longer. The wind backed abruptly, first to the south, then to the east, and decided to treat us to a gale. Our progress slowed dramatically.

Tough slogging within a day's sail of landfall is a much different affair from tough slogging offshore. When you know that your misery will end soon, there isn't the despair that accompanies the knowledge that you are in for a long, hard fight with no respite in sight. We all laughed when a nasty wave slapped aboard, submerging Charlie and setting off the inflatable PFD on his harness. Charlie had endured the passage much better than I had suspected. He was smart, a good helmsman, and understood his limitations. His dream of buying a cruising boat and sailing the Caribbean seemed much less absurd than it had four days earlier. And in fact he would do just that. He bought a Tayana 42, and he and his wife cruised along the East Coast and in the Caribbean.

Otto had thoroughly enjoyed the ride and was melancholy that it was coming to an end. Bruce, always a good shipmate, had never failed to scramble on deck to help tie in a reef or do his share of the cooking duties. We did give him grief over his cheap Canadian Tire rain suit. He had taken pleasure in chiding the crew about their costly foul-weather gear, bragging that he had spent $30 on his perfectly adequate gear. Slowly but steadily the red vinyl suit dissolved during the passage. His jacket turned into a vest as the arms wore away, and his bibs into shorts when the pants disintegrated in a hard rain. He looked ridiculous, but to his credit he wore it to the end.

Lou was thrilled to be nearing Bermuda. He loved the idea of landfall, a validation of his first true offshore passage, and the raison d'être of his conversion from powerboater to sailor. He had loved every minute of the passage and was prepared to leave his mark in Bermuda.

We reached the Saint George's approach channel just before dark. The wind had increased all day and was now steady at 40 knots. We accidently jibed as we entered the harbor and shredded the mainsail, a learning experience for the crew and an expensive mistake for me. After a frantic docking procedure at the customs wharf, we were told to clear out because a full gale was forecast later that night. We ended up seeking shelter in a tiny cove behind Smith's Island. It was too windy to row ashore, and I didn't want to leave the boat. We celebrated with a warm beer, and collapsed into our bunks. So much for bringing Bermuda to its knees.

Lou was greeted by his wife, Julia, and they spent a week aboard in Bermuda. He was working hard, selling her on the sailing life. Julia said she was willing to give it a try. They had a great week on the boat, and in the fall they joined me for another week of sailing around Newport, Rhode Island. Lou was on a fast track and becoming a good sailor. Later that year he took the plunge and bought a sailboat, a Pearson 36. He told me that he knew it wasn't an ideal bluewater boat but it was a good boat for coastal cruising and improving his skills. I agreed heartily.

Sadly, Lou didn't sail his new boat much. He was diagnosed with pancreatic cancer not long after purchasing the boat and died a few months later. Julia wrote that she was grateful that Lou had been able to follow his passion to become a sailor. She said that while in the hospital he spoke often of his days at sea and their profound impact on his life. Right up to the end he hoped to recover and sail away with her. Nothing makes us more aware of life, and of living, than death. Lou's cruising dreams may have been unfulfilled, but that does not diminish their power.

Thoughts about EPIRBs—and Other Tips to Ensure Rescue

Every sailboat heading offshore should carry an EPIRB. *Emergency position-indicating radio beacons* have saved thousands of lives over the years, and the latest models, 406 GPS EPIRBs, sometimes called GPIRBs, are the most effective large-scale search-and-rescue (SAR) devices ever made.

While these ruggedly built, compact beacons are game changers for offshore sailors, they can also instill a false sense of security. Sailing across oceans can be dangerous, and nothing will eliminate all risks associated with passagemaking. Circumnavigator Beth Leonard wrote an informative piece in the November 2011 issue of *Cruising World* about the realities of EPRIBs and offshore search-and-rescue operations, and I share many of her opinions. www.cruisingworld.com

How do EPIRBs work? You can either switch them on manually or rest assured they will automatically deploy when submerged. It's essential to remember that they should be activated only in the case of life-threatening emergencies. Think about this: when you set off your EPIRB, you are asking other people to risk their lives to save you, and that's a serious step and should never be taken lightly. As recreational sailors it is not our right to be rescued; it's a privilege that we must never abuse. *(continued next page)*

EPIRBs transmit on a frequency of 406 MHz and send an encoded SOS signal that is picked up by polar-orbiting satellites. The Cospas-Sarsat system is an international humanitarian search-and-rescue (SAR) organization. In the United States it is overseen by NOAA. This 406 MHz signal, which is yours alone and registered in a national database, is then sent to an unmanned fully automatic ground-based station called a LUT, or local user terminal, for verification. Once it is confirmed that the distress call is from you, and that you're on a passage—information obtained by calling the contacts you provided when registering the beacon—the LUT forwards the information to Mission Control Center (MCC). This vetting process has dramatically reduced false alerts that previously slowed Coast Guard reaction times. MCC, which is located in Maryland, then initiates a search-and-rescue operation through the nearest RCC (rescue coordination center). The United States operates two air force RCCs, but the eleven Coast Guard RCCs undertake almost all the maritime SAR missions. The enormous advantage of GPS EPIRBs is that they can pinpoint the location of the beacon to a couple hundred feet. Most EPIRBs have lithium batteries that allow for 48 hours of continuous transmission.

In theory, potential tragedies can be averted with this brilliantly conceived system. However, the reality of SAR is very different. It's almost never a smooth process. First, the Coast Guard and air force both prefer to use helicopters for rescue operations because they're more maneuverable and efficient. Once on

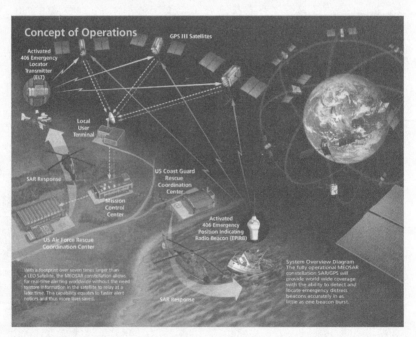

Once activated, an EPIRB sets off a chain of responses that hopefully leads to a marine rescue, provided you have registered your device and have met a host of other conditions. Don't take getting rescued for granted. (NOAA)

the scene they can put swimmers in the water and complete the rescue mission on the spot, or they can drop supplies and pumps.

But these helicopters have a limited range, and offshore sailors are often well beyond the reach of these aircraft. A Coast Guard HH-65 helicopter has a range of about 90 miles, while the HH-60 has an effective range of about 150 miles from a coastal base. Even fixed-wing SAR planes have a limited range, and the Coast Guard admits that mounting a rescue operation that's more than 500 miles from a base is not feasible. The United States is responsible for SAR operations up to 600 miles from the coast, although they occasionally exceed this limit. This means offshore sailors will most likely need to be rescued by a diverted merchant vessel.

AMVER, automated mutual assist vessel emergency response, is a database managed by the Coast Guard to monitor participating ships that check in regularly and agree to undertake emergency operations when called on. Vessels carrying the U.S. flag must participate in the system, and although it's voluntary for foreign-flag ships, most participate in the spirit of cooperation that has long existed among mariners. Ships almost always agree to divert for a rescue operation when contacted by SARSAT (Search and Rescue Satellite Aided Tracking), refusing only when the conditions create safety concerns. However, in remote locations they can be days away from a stricken vessel.

My good friend Etienne Giorre was rescued by a containership when his trimaran capsized during the 2010 Rhoute de Rhum singlehanded transatlantic race. The race committee was tracking Giorre, and even before his EPIRB was activated they knew he was in trouble. A seasoned sailor, former class winner of the OSTAR transatlantic race, and successful manufacturer of the ATN brand of innovative sailing products, Giorre reacted to his misfortune calmly. Once he realized he had actually capsized, he swam back into the boat and fetched his emergency ditch bag that contained the EPIRB, satellite phone, and VHF radio. He then inflated his life raft and stayed with his overturned but still floating boat. He made contact with the race director and 10 hours later was picked up by a Portuguese ship.

EPIRBs do save lives, but if you are not part of a carefully monitored race or rally, the story can be very different.

The Coast Guard admits that there can be problems when SAR operations fall between jurisdictions. Some countries are more dedicated to mounting rescue operations than others. Some just don't have the resources even if they have the will. Another problem is that the emergency signal that is received is frustratingly vague and contains no details of the situation. While responders know the location of the beacon, they don't know whether the crew has already been rescued, if they've perished, or if it is a real emergency. For this reason it is a very good idea to carry two EPIRBs, even if the second one is a smaller, more affordable PLB (personal locater beacon). By activating two distress signals, you can be confident that emergency responders know you   (continued next page) need help. And contrary to what you might hear from safety-equipment manufacturers, you still must be prepared to wait for several days or longer before being rescued and will need a well-stocked ditch bag to ensure your survival. Also, you should be prepared to take an active role in your survival.

Here are several things you should do:

1. In addition to carrying one ship station 406 GPS EPIRB, you should also have aboard at least one PLB and possibly more PLBs, which are also 406 EPIRBs. Make sure that all the beacons are properly registered. If they're not, they're not very helpful. Make sure the batteries are up to date. Multiple distress signals from the same location help validate the need to commit assets, in Coast Guard lingo, to a rescue operation.

2. Carry a GPS tracking device like SPOT (satellite personal tracker) that sends updated position reports to your contact list via text or e-mail and also has "help" and "911" functions. SPOT operates on the low-orbit Globalstar satellite network. The range of SPOT products and features continues to expand. SPOT Connect allows for short personalized messages in lieu of a standard "all's well" type of message that accompanies your GPS position. Tracking allows your contacts to follow the boat's progress throughout a passage. SPOT position updates can also be posted on Facebook and Twitter. Make sure the people on your 911 list know what to do if they were to receive an emergency text or e-mail. Make sure they also understand that sometimes messages don't get through and not to panic. I once dropped my SPOT overboard, and folks back home were quite stressed until we checked in via satellite phone.

3. Be sure to have a fully charged satellite phone with preprogrammed numbers of people who you can trust to react to your situation. Store the phone in a waterproof container in your ditch bag. Also preprogram the RCC numbers for the areas where you will be sailing. See the websites listed below. Also have a fully charged handheld DSC VHF radio. Digital select calling allows for a preprogrammed emergency call to be broadcast by pushing one button. New handheld VHF radios also incorporate GPS and include position with the broadcast.

4. Buy a high-quality life raft. This is no place to skimp because when you need it, you really need it. Of course with this said, don't leave the boat until you have to. Even a partially submerged boat is much more visible than a life raft. The life raft is a vessel of last resort.

www.beaconregistration.noaa.gov (forms for registering EPRIBS)

www.sarsat.noaa.gov/rcc.html (RCC locations—enter these phone numbers in your sat phone)

six

Choosing a Route I Pilot Charts I West to East
Crossings I Mediterranean Summer I Losing a
Staysail I East to West Crossings I Knockdown
on the Eve of a Landfall

Atlantic Crossings—
The Atlantic Circle

*"It had been a miserable passage. In midocean, a fierce wave had
exploded against the old ship's topsides, straining a structural tim-
ber until it had cracked like a chicken bone. The* Mayflower's *master,
Christopher Jones, had considered turning back to England. But Jones
had to give his passengers their due. They knew next to nothing about
the savage coast for which they were bound, but their resolve was
unshakable."*

—Nathaniel Philbrick, *Mayflower*

QUETZAL WAS 700 MILES from anyplace with human inhabitants. Trace an
arc from Bermuda across the North Atlantic through Halifax and Cape Race
in Newfoundland to Flores, the westernmost island in the Azores chain. We
were just a tick above the 40th parallel and a pinch west of the 45th meridian—to some, a no man's sea; to me, one of my favorite addresses on Earth.

This is the heart of the Atlantic, where the west and southwest winds are
interrupted only by an occasional easterly gale or a wayward tropical storm.
Depressions sweep by to the north, leaving cool and cloudy conditions below,
which are preferable to the sun and sweat of tropical passages. It's the haunt
of curious fulmars and flittering storm petrels that skim just above heaving
gray seas. The Gulf Stream has slowed a bit at this point, but it's still a magic
carpet and generously gives sailors 20 to 30 miles a day just for showing up.

We were two weeks out of Fort Lauderdale, Florida, bound from Fort
Lauderdale to Portugal, with a week still to go to Horta—our Azores landfall. The crew was holding up well, although small signs of stress were becoming evident. Jim, who at age sixty-eight was older than most people who sail
with me, was tired and spending a lot of time in his cabin. John, who had

made several passages with me before this crossing, was a bit homesick and using the SAT phone to talk to his dog. Pat was reverting to a more primitive state and becoming obsessed with catching tuna and mahimahi. But Ed, whom I was worried about the most before shoving off, had found his stride and was relishing the passage.

Ed's younger brother Bryan and I had been best friends in school, and although I knew Ed, he was six years older than we were, a generational leap when you're a kid. After college Bryan went to law school and I went to sea and we drifted apart. I didn't know that Ed had become interested in sailing until he turned up as part of the crew of a boat I was delivering from Tortola to Fort Lauderdale.

We were shocked to see each other when we met at the bar before the passage. I learned that he owned a Catalina 400 that he sailed on Lake Michigan and had made a lot of money with a home oxygen-supply business. He was surprised to hear that although I had just flown in that afternoon, I was planning to leave right after dinner. In fact he was incredulous. "But it will be dark by then." I shrugged my shoulders and told him he'd better get used to it because we were not going to stop at all on the passage. "You mean we're going to sail for a week, day and night?" He found this notion astounding.

We were delivering a beautiful Hylas 49 owned by Ed's friend Frank, an experienced scow racer who was longing to make ocean passages. In those days Fort Lauderdale was still the best place on the U.S. East Coast to sell a boat, and Frank, the owner, had decided to unload his Hylas and have a custom cruiser built in New Zealand.

We slithered out of the crowded Moorings Marina in Road Town, on Tortola, just before midnight and soon were bombing along on a perfect reach. Ed was the cook, and despite battling his stomach every time he went below, he served one excellent meal after another. We were watch mates and happily chatted the three hours away, remembering our childhood days in Michigan and anticipating future voyages together.

His naiveté amused me. He told me how he had hit a rock in Green Bay, Wisconsin, because his GPS displayed only latitude and he was never sure of his position. That seemed unlikely to me, and he was incredibly relieved when I told him that he probably just needed to scroll to another page on the device.

Ed's sense of the moment is priceless. A true romantic, he can be moved to tears by a brilliant sunset, a heartrending song, a pod of dolphins, or the memory of an old girlfriend. He isn't troubled by the technical details that so many sailors obsess over. He sails like an artist; he would rather draw pictures with his course line than steer blindly toward a waypoint. His never-ceasing sense of awe was at times hard to believe but always inspiring.

Ed crewed on many deliveries with me over the next few years, including one that took us into the vortex of Hurricane Mitch, which I discuss in detail in Chapter Eight, but suffice it to say that it was challenging. Ed eventually had his boat trucked from Michigan to Florida, and I used it for a few training passages and he always tagged along. He was developing into a competent offshore sailor and made several passages on his own between Fort Myers and Key West, Florida. Once I purchased *Quetzal*, Ed was the first person to sign up for the transatlantic passage.

Despite his progress as a sailor, I wondered whether he would be able to sustain a romantic vision of the Atlantic all the way across, and I didn't want to be the one to snuff out his idealism. He was also still terribly prone to seasickness, and I was afraid it might become debilitating on a long passage. At 3,000 miles, give or take, this was a long passage by anyone's standards. I told the crew to expect to spend at least twenty days at sea and be prepared for more. All totaled, we were hoping to make it to Portugal in a month.

Ed, who once again assumed the cooking duties, made some dietary changes that helped with his seasickness. He stopped drinking coffee and stayed away from rich and greasy foods, although that didn't stop him from baking cakes and his famous quiches for the rest of us. But it was more than

Celestial navigation may seem quaint in the age of GPS, but it is alive and well on Quetzal. *We take sights, reduce them, and plot position. One negative about an enclosed cockpit is that it makes taking sights difficult. We often have to work from the foredeck, usually adjusting the heading to ensure that we have a clear view of the sun and the horizon. Yes, of course we use GPS, but there's something most rewarding about finding your position from natural satellites, not man-made ones.*

diet that helped him conquer his ever-present queasiness. He discovered that he loved being at sea. He was going through a difficult time ashore with a struggling new business and a messy personal life. But as serious as both issues were, they faded further from his consciousness with every mile we put under the keel.

The ocean environment is selfish; it demands your full attention, and worries from the mere 30 percent of our planet covered by land have a hard time finding you in the vastness of the other 70 percent. For the first time in his adult life he felt free, at least free from the day-to-day responsibilities that ruled his world and caused him so much angst. Ed, by nature, assumes the problems of those he loves, and this usually ends up being a frustrating and thankless agenda that leaves him racked with guilt. At sea his duties were simple: cook, sail, stand watch, and never miss Captain's Hour.

This passage, in 2004, was my sixteenth transatlantic. Since then I have made four more crossings, so I do have some experience here. When it comes to east to west passages, I had by 2004 concluded that skipping Bermuda was

The starboard-side pilot berth, with webbing to hold the crewmembers in place, and temporary hooks to hang clothes and jackets. Quetzal's mission is to go to sea and make passages, and with five or six aboard, space is always a bit tight. Normally gear is stowed in hanging lockers and drawers, but when the weather is cold and/ or wet, you need quick access to your foulies. The gear here hangs after a passage across the Atlantic. We also have hooks in the shower compartments in both heads for foul-weather gear. When considering a boat for bluewater sailing, make sure it has plenty of room for stowage.

a more efficient way to cross the pond if you wanted to actually sail and not spend a disproportionate amount of time under power.

Unfortunately, I don't always follow my own advice. Don't misunderstand me, I love Bermuda and have dropped the hook in St. George's Harbor seventeen times that I can remember. However, in May and June, the best time to cross the Atlantic, Bermuda lies in an area of high pressure with light and inconsistent winds.

Of course it is all just a matter of perspective because some mariners see these mild conditions as a passagemaking plus. A growing faction of sailors is fully prepared to power across the Atlantic by remaining smack in the middle of the light-air "horse latitudes." A lot of sailors now simply motor in the light-air horse latitudes, carrying enough fuel to make the 1,800-mile passage from Bermuda to the Azores, or the entire 3,000-mile passage to Europe.

Quetzal is a terrific sailboat and a poor, inefficient motorboat, and that suits me just fine. I must confess, however, over the years I have done plenty of motoring in the Atlantic, especially on yacht deliveries when time was money. However, I much prefer sailing. I like contending with ever-changing conditions and the often demanding physical work of making the boat perform under sail. And I love the navigational challenges of safely and efficiently finding my way to the other side of the world. Navigating—even in this GPS epoch that has sucked most of the uncertainty and a lot of the satisfaction out of the art—is still one of my favorite aspects of offshore sailing, especially route planning. I can happily while away hours poring over pilot charts and my dog-eared copy of Jimmy Cornell's masterpiece, *World Cruising Routes*.

I have found that following the Gulf Stream, a route blazed by Columbus on his way back from the New World, and maybe his most impressive discovery, is still the most reliable way to get from, yes, west to east. A close examination of the pilot chart shows that when departing from Florida, following the great circle route to the Azores actually tracks close by Bermuda. You may recall that the shortest distance between any point on the Earth's surface is along the arc of a great circle. That's why planes flying from the United States to Europe pass north over Iceland; it's the shortest distance.

But winds and currents sometimes make a passage to Bermuda more of a detour that you will pay for later as you try to work back up to the prevailing westerlies. Staying west of Bermuda while working your way north in or near the Stream until at least latitude 40 offers the best chance for favorable winds and fast passages under sail.

We had chosen this route and it had paid off. We'd made about 150 miles a day, a 6 knot average, and had done very little motoring. But the Atlantic never lets you slide all the way across without a test, and on day fifteen the winds veered to the east and kicked up. The seas built quickly as the current and wind went to war with each other. Fortunately, short bursts of hard rain temporarily flattened the seas. This odd phenomenon, noted by sailors as far

Reaching along off Newfoundland. I have had three genoas during the ten years I've sailed Quetzal, a Kaufman 47. Peter Grimm of Doyle Sailmakers in Fort Lauderdale, Florida, has built them all. Each time I opt for a smaller headsail, having gone from a 150 percent to a 135 percent to my current headsail shown here, a 125 percent. I like the smaller headsail for two primary reasons. It furls (reefs) better to around 100 percent, and it's cut a bit higher, allowing me to sail more efficiently with the staysail. Quetzal's headsail is made of 8.8 ounce high-mass fiber weave. It's a cruising sail, not a racing sail, but its performance is good and its durability is excellent. I opt for the heavy-duty upgrade that includes reinforced corners. A sail lasts me typically around 20,000 to 25,000 miles.

back as Jason and his band of Argonauts, is caused by both the weight of the freshwater and by the raindrops disturbing the sea surface and causing a slight disruption in the wave pattern. As soon as the rain passed, the seas turned nasty again and our progress slowed.

We shortened sails all through the day. *Quetzal* was fitted with a 150 percent genoa, which is a terrible sail for bluewater sailing, but it had been almost new when I bought the boat and I couldn't justify buying the sail I really wanted, and have now, a 125 percent super-strong, high-cut genoa that allows me to sail more readily as a cutter. A large genoa furls (reefs) inefficiently, to say the least, and when reduced beyond 20 to 30 percent it loses shape and also sharply raises the center of effort as more sail is slopped around the headstay, raising the foot of the sail in the process. A big sail also puts up a lot of resistance when you furl it in a strong wind. It's easy to make a hash of things.

With the winds steady at 25 knots and gusting higher, I decided to shorten the genoa even further, from approximately 100 percent to maybe 80 percent.

We should have simply rolled the sail up and set the staysail, forgoing a bit of horsepower for a smoother, easier ride. But I was greedy for speed, and I felt that taking a few bites out of the headsail would be sufficient to ease the ride a bit but keep our speed up.

Luffing the genoa, we cranked in on the furling line, which was loaded on the secondary winch. But the furling line wouldn't budge. "Don't force it," I said to Pat, who was manning the winch. "Let's see what's wrong first." Jim steered off the wind to stop the sail from flogging, and I dashed forward. The problem was obvious: the furling line had slipped off the drum and wrapped itself around the turnbuckle below. It was a mess, and also a worry, because we had no way to shorten sail.

"We'll have to go up there and deal with it," I said, masking my disgust for letting this happen, an obvious case of sloppy seamanship. "I'm going to need a hand." Ed was harnessed up and ready for action and I nodded at him. "I'll help," he said. I could tell he was proud to be the one called on. "What tools are we going to need?"

"I'm not sure," I said, "but grab the Leatherman, a big screwdriver, and a pair of needle-nose pliers, and meet me on the bow. And be sure to clip on to the jackline before leaving the cockpit."

Although we had fallen off the wind, the bow was still plunging in confused seas. Sprawled on our bellies, we tried to free the line, but it was slow going. We realized that we would have to let the sail all the way out, drop it, rewind the furling line around the drum, and then hoist the sail again—a big job in a strong wind.

The sail flogged madly as it came out in a rush. John, who was the most experienced member of the crew and would later join a boat for a Cape Horn passage, quickly let the halyard go. Pat eased the sheet, and Ed and I hauled the sail down on deck. Occasional waves washed the bow, thoroughly soaking us. Ed was focused and animated. This is why you cross the Atlantic, for moments like this when your actions really matter and impact your existence.

By the time we raised the genoa, the wind was gusting to gale force, so we hastily furled it and hanked on the staysail instead, the very thing we should have done before the trouble began.

Back in the cockpit we were all quite satisfied with the afternoon's work. Despite losing a couple of hours to the project, the knowledge that the boat was back on course, under control and fully operational, was most reassuring. Ed served up a hearty Captain's Hour snack and broke out our special bottle of Oban single-malt Scotch for the occasion.

Ironically the crew seemed to be relieved to be sailing on the wind after weeks of broad reaching. Most of us learn to sail by pounding away upwind, tacking from one close-hauled heading to another. Easing out the sails to crack off onto a reach seems anticlimactic and a bit boring. I told them they were crazy, and 24 hours later they were yearning for those halcyon reaching days when the world was not angled 20 degrees or more, when a hatch could be left open for ventilation, and when the waves stayed mostly in the ocean and not on deck.

The easterly eventually tracked north of us as we began steering southeast toward Horta. Fair southwesterly winds returned and landfall became imminent. What is it about landfalls? On the one hand they validate a passage, the reward for doing your job. Joseph Conrad put it like this: "In all the devious tracings the course of a sailing ship leaves upon the white paper of a chart, she is always aiming for that one little spot—maybe a small island in the ocean, a single headland upon the long coast of a continent, a lighthouse on a bluff, or simply the peaked form of a mountain like an ant-heap afloat upon the waters. But if you have sighted it on the expected bearing, then the landfall is good."

But there is something more to a landfall than satisfaction, even in the GPS age when landfalls have gone from being eventful to inevitable, as you watch the digital distance to the waypoint decrease every few seconds. There are few events filled with as much promise as the prospect of stepping ashore after a long passage. It is almost as though your time at sea has cleansed you, and you have hopes that somehow you'll be a better person now that you've returned to earth. The forced isolation of the passage gave you time for reflection, and the experiences of the passage, even a mundane one, have had a profound effect on your psyche. Sadly, it's been my experience that the euphoria fades fast as the hustle and bustle of the so-called real world hits hard, throwing you off stride. The people you left behind are not always that interested in your self-awakening, and actually may be a bit resentful of the fact that you managed to carve some time away from the madness of modern life. "Okay," they seem to be saying with glaring eyes, "you had your fun. Now start pushing the rock back up the hill, Sisyphus."

And they don't always empathize with the hardships you've just endured, alas.

When it comes to landfalls, the Azores taunt you, especially if you're bound for Horta, on the island of Faial, the most popular harbor in the archipelago and a truly charming place. Invariably the first land you spot is the improbable island of Pico. Lying just a few miles to the east of Faial but towering over it, well-named Pico explodes out of the ocean like an island version of the Tower of Babel. It looks like the way a child draws an island, tall and pointy. Of course grown-ups, especially men who have been at sea for a couple of weeks, see the shapely island with a small knob at the summit in a different way. No matter what image it conjures, at nearly 8,000 feet high it is visible a long way off—sometimes, depending on the light, from more than fifty miles away. It can make for a long day of anticipation as you make the approach, especially because the wind often dies as you near the islands.

We arrived after midnight and eased alongside the customs wharf. Café Sport, the best bar in the Atlantic, and a legendary watering hole for sailors, was just closing for the night. However, seeing the desperation in our eyes as we stumbled up the hill from the port, Jose, the owner, decided to stay open long enough for us to have a celebratory beer. Ed's friend, and soon to be wife, Linda, was there to meet him, a wonderful romantic surprise for a romantic man. However, the demands of business and family tracked Ed down quickly, even in Horta, and by the next day he decided that he would have to forgo the

Approaching the Azores, with the amazing island of Pico in the background.

Café Sport, the best and most famous bar in the Atlantic. I have been here many times, and always look forward to returning.

last leg to Portugal and return to Chicago. His Atlantic interlude, a blissful existence of being frequently cold and wet but immensely satisfied, was over.

John, Pat, Jim, and I stayed in Horta a couple days, just long enough to catch up on our sleep, have some terrific meals, provision, and top our tanks. The passage from Horta toward the Mediterranean is usually more of a beam reach than a deep reach as the prevailing winds shift to the north. These winds, dubbed the Portuguese trades, curve clockwise around the Azores' high-pressure system and are moderately strong and fairly consistent. They turned up right on schedule and hurried *Quetzal* toward the continent. We cut Cape St. Vincent, the ruddy Portuguese headland that is Europe's extreme southwest tip, quite close and admired the view. We sailed into Vilamoura, Portugal, a massive resort marina along the Algarve coast, thirty days outbound from Fort Lauderdale.

We hastily went our separate ways. These quick departures are always a bit bizarre after the forced intimacy of a long passage, but everybody had a flight to catch and a life to return to.

But then Nari and Nikki, then ages eleven and nine, joined me, and the three of us sailed along the bottom of the Iberian Peninsula and into the Mediterranean. We had a memorable summer visiting Cadiz, Gibraltar, Morocco, and many Spanish ports along the Costa del Sol. At times I felt vulnerable sailing with just my two young children. There was one wild approach into a marina near the Portugal–Spain border, with Nari steering through a narrow channel as I scrambled on deck to drop the main. And there was the night Nikki found out that her favorite team, the Miami Heat, had traded her favorite player, Brian Grant, to the Lakers for some nobody named Shaquille O'Neal. She cried inconsolably despite my attempts to sooth her with gelato.

In all, though, it was a great experience for us, and we still often reminisce about that summer. Nari stood her first solo night watch, Nikki learned to plot on the chart, and the three of us became rather adept at executing Med moorings.

In late July we were holed up near Almeria, the easternmost corner of Andalucia and close to the point where the coast of Spain begins to bend a bit to the north, when my new girlfriend, Tadji, came to visit us. The girls knew Tadji well. She was Ms. Rodriguez to them, a teacher at their elementary school in Fort Lauderdale, and teachers outranked everybody else in their minds. I met Tadji because she was Nikki's after-school reading tutor. And being a writer, and someone devoted to reading, I made it a point to pick Nikki up every day I was home that spring. Tadji, who is half Iranian and half Colombian, a wonderfully exotic mix of DNA, had never been sailing but was passionate about traveling. When we met, the girls and I were living on the boat, and she found it fascinating that I was going to take the boat to Europe. She spent a wonderful week aboard in Spain and became enchanted with the possibilities that cruising offered.

I spent the fall sailing across the western Mediterranean to Rome and back through the Balearic Islands and Sardinia. These were working trips, and I was joined by new and mostly former crewmembers as my trips were becoming less about training and more about shared adventures. By early November *Quetzal* was back in Spain, not far from Gibraltar, preparing for the passage back across the Atlantic. Another friend, Steve Maseda, joined me and the two of us sailed through the Pillars of Hercules and out to Santa Cruz de Tenerife in the Canary Islands, off the northwest coast of Africa, where the next transatlantic crew was awaiting our arrival.

The Atlantic is well suited to a clockwise circumnavigation, and the term Atlantic Circle has become part of the cruising lexicon. The passage I described from the southeastern United States to Portugal is one of several options for eastbound Atlantic sailors. As I mentioned earlier, plenty of boats continue to call at Bermuda, and there are advantages. A Bermuda landfall breaks the passage into three legs and substantially shortens the distance to the Azores, making it a two-week passage instead of three. Also, many European sailors returning home from the Caribbean and North America turn northeast at the Azores and head toward the English Channel. A prevailing southwest wind typically makes this a good run, although I've had some tough slogs up to the United Kingdom over the years. Another route, one I would like to take in the next few years, is crossing well north of 40 degrees. Voyagers typically call at Nova Scotia and Newfoundland before heading east to Ireland or Scotland, tracking above the 50th parallel. This is the shortest way to Europe—the distance from St. John's, Newfoundland, to Galway, on Ireland's west coast, is less than 1,800 miles. It's also much more challenging, with increased chances of encountering fog and icebergs. The likelihood of gales is also higher.

The trade wind route, which we were about to embark upon, is surely the most pleasant way to cross the Atlantic, and really the best option for westbound passages. Coined "the lady's trades," the steady northeast and east winds that wash the Atlantic from the Canary Islands to the coast of Central America provide ideal sailing conditions. Other than during the late summer hurricane months, when this route should be avoided like the plague, the weather is consistently fine, and gales are almost unheard of. I have made this crossing seven times, and without fail it's been a joyride.

Ken, then the associate publisher of *Sailing* magazine, and three friends met Steve and me at Marina Atlántico, in Santa Cruz de Tenerife. Rick, Angie, and Beth all raced aboard Ken's old Tartan Ten one-design on Lake Michigan, and they were avid competitive sailors. Steve, also an accomplished racer and the one-time Melges 24 class president, rolled his eyes as Ken told me how seriously they were taking our upcoming passage. Steve, who is also a cruiser and has logged thousands of miles with me on many deliveries, understands the inherent differences between passagemaking and racing.

"This is not going to be some cruise in the park, Kretschmer. We're going to sail this boat hard," Ken explained.

I nodded. "I don't have a problem with that, Ken, really. Sounds good to me too. We'll keep the old girl moving."

We shoved off as soon as we loaded the last of the provisions. The Canary Islands form an impressive archipelago of seven large islands running mostly east-west and just sixty miles off the coast of Morocco and the disputed territory of Western Sahara. They're an underappreciated cruising ground, and most of the thousand or so boats that call in the Canaries every year are there for one reason—passages to the Caribbean.

I always tell myself that I am not going to rush out of the Canaries, and one time I actually tarried. I was delivering my mom's old Jeanneau Gin Fizz back to Florida from Spain, and we arrived in the Canaries in early September. We spent nearly three months exploring Tenerife, La Palma, Hierro, and La Gomera, the island that Columbus departed from on his first voyage.

La Gomera almost changed the course of history. Columbus anchored his small fleet in San Sebastian, La Gomera's well-protected harbor, to make final preparations for his epic voyage. He was distracted, however, by the island's lovely widowed governor, Beatriz de Bobadilla. The *admiralante* found one reason after another to delay his departure, and, as the legend goes, he pulled himself away from Beatriz only on direct orders from the other woman in his life, the one with the money, Queen Isabella.

The major tactical decision a vessel faces upon leaving the Canaries is how far south to sail before turning west. Santa Cruz de Tenerife is just north of the 28th parallel, and the trade winds are not always firmly established until you drop below latitude 20. That's 500 miles, which is a large chunk of a 3,000-mile passage. It is tempting to shave some distance to the Caribbean by sailing a more direct route, but it's almost always a mistake. Sailing south-southwest until you pick up the trade winds is a well-proven strategy. Some navigators sail to the latitude of their destination before heading west, but that's a bit extreme. Others carry on south to the Cape Verde Islands, off the coast of Senegal, which not only breaks the crossing and shortens the distance to the Caribbean but almost always ensures steady trade winds for the main passage west. Antigua, our destination, straddles the 17th parallel, so we traced a course that began arcing west-southwest once we dipped below 20 degrees. Once we reached latitude 17, we'd aim right at the mark.

Ken and crew were determined to beat my best crossing time, which up to that point was sixteen days. When I average all seven trade wind passages I've made, it's eighteen days, showing just how consistent the winds are on this passage, maybe the best ocean crossing on Earth. It's interesting to look at how surprisingly little time difference there is with the types of boats I've sailed.

The first time I crossed was in *Gigi*, the Contessa 32, and we sailed from the westernmost Canary Island of La Palma and arrived in Montserrat, near Antigua, in nineteen days. In *Buddug*, a 33-foot motorsailer, we lumbered into St. Martin twenty-two days out of Tenerife. In *Epoch*, the Gin Fizz, we also arrived in St. Martin twenty days out of La Gomera. In *Kinsale*, a Beneteau First 38, we arrived in Barbados out of Las Palmas, Gran Canary, in sixteen days.

In three crossings *Quetzal* has made passages of sixteen, seventeen, and eighteen days. Ironically, these times are not dramatically different from those achieved by the much maligned Admiral of the Ocean Sea. Twice Columbus crossed from the Canaries to the West Indies in twenty-one days.

We were lucky as northeast winds whisked us away from the marina in Tenerife and didn't let up until we tied up in English Harbor, Antigua. It was a great passage, although my crack racing crew seemed to lose focus early. It didn't take long for Captain's Hour to take precedence over sail changes. Hand steering gave way to pushing the buttons on the autopilot. It was almost as if *Quetzal* knew the way and we were along for the ride. William Snaith wrote in *On the Wind's Way*, one of my favorite sailing books, "The bow plunges steadily on, as if it, and not we, knows where we are going."

While we flew the spinnaker occasionally, my new 125 percent genoa did most of the work. Boomed out with a whisker pole, it carried us along a deep reach, or even dead downwind, at anywhere from 6 to 10 knots. The main was given the passage off as we ripped off one 160- to 170-mile day after another. We could have sailed a bit faster, sure, but *Quetzal* was happy. The rig wasn't stressed, the rudder wasn't overloaded, the autopilot was coping easily, and life was pleasant. It was amazing to watch the racers turn into cruisers. Still, we raised Antigua on day sixteen, equaling *Quetzal*'s best passage.

We made our way south to Trinidad and north to the Virgin Islands as we lingered in the Caribbean for most of the winter and spring. In April *Quetzal* returned to Fort Lauderdale, completing an eleven-month, 12,000-mile Atlantic Circle.

My sailing business was quite busy, and I spent the next few years conducting passages that took us as far south as Panama and as far north as Newfoundland. By the spring of 2007, I was ready to head back across the Atlantic. I had a great crew signed on, *Quetzal* was in good shape, and I anticipated another nice ride east across the pond.

I was in for a surprise.

I know as well as anybody that sailing across the Atlantic should never be underestimated. It's a long way from one side to the other, and, as I stated earlier, the Atlantic rarely lets you slide across her protean surface without testing you. This is especially true on the west-to-east passages. Naturally some crossings are more challenging than others, but every now and then the Atlantic turns downright mean-spirited, and you're reminded that chance still rules the waves. These are the crossings that make you contemplate a career change to farming, and fill you with an intense desire to burn the pilot charts. Of course these are the passages that also provide the best lessons, and this crossing would prove very instructive.

The route was a well-worn one, Fort Lauderdale to Spain, and I assured the crew that we'd fetch up in Puerto Santa Maria in a month's time. The only difference from the previous passage was that this time we planned a brief Bermuda landfall.

I'd like to blame the crew, but I made the call to make Bermuda our first waypoint. My reasoning was sound, or so I thought. Because we were sailing with a bigger crew than in our last crossing, our supplies of food, water, and fuel would need to be stretched further, and I liked the idea of topping up in Bermuda instead of cramming every corner of the boat with provisions.

We shoved off on May 13 and figured that the big decision would be how long to ride the Gulf Stream before angling east toward Bermuda. We were hoping for a couple of big current-assisted days to start the passage, but it didn't work out that way. The morning of the second day, we encountered a rare northeast gale, which of course was a direct headwind and had not been predicted. Any wind out of the northern quadrant raises steep, unruly seas in the Gulf Stream. We had no option but to beat east out of the current and then tack toward Bermuda. We logged a whopping 88 miles on day two, and that would not even be the worst day of the trip. However, our tactics during this modest gale, to drastically reduce sail but keep moving by forereaching, would later prove invaluable.

I was joined by Doug, Chris, Ron, Warren, and my good friend Rick. Everybody had sailed with me before, and I loved knowing that I had three engineers aboard to effect repairs when gear failed. We raised Bermuda on the eighth day and tied up to a rickety dock along the St. George's town quay. Bermuda had not fully recovered from the battering it took during Hurricane Florence the previous fall.

The only real inconvenience of leg one was that the engine stopped producing hot water for showers. We traced the problem to a faulty heat exchanger, and my friend Bob Pingel, *Quetzal*'s patron saint, tracked down a new one and had it on a plane to Bermuda ASAP. The engineering staff aboard had it installed in no time, and just 72 hours after our first rum swizzle and last Dark and Stormy, we were heading back to sea.

The second day proved troublesome, and we ran into another northeast gale. The Bermuda weather service had forecast strong winds, but the Force 8 conditions caught many boats, including us, by surprise. The wind built all afternoon, leaving us few good tactical choices. We could either tack more or less due north, maybe even a little west of north, taking us well away from our desired northeast heading. Or we could continue clawing our way east for a better velocity made good (VMG) toward the waypoint. But this option took us below the rhumb line, more into the variable horse latitudes. The rhumb line is the straight line penciled onto the chart, and unlike a great circle route it is not usually the shortest distance between two points. But it is the line that you sail, the line that you study, and the line that you curse when you can't steer it.

I chose the latter course, to work east, and it proved to be a mistake. The decision was partly based on Herb Hilgenberg's advice. The weather guru for Atlantic sailors, Herb has been selflessly broadcasting detailed weather reports and providing free routing advice for yachts since 1987. He's a remarkable man and much loved by cruisers. Like every other boat crossing the Atlantic that summer, we eagerly awaited his afternoon forecasts. Herb felt that two deep low-pressure systems, one northeast of Bermuda and one south, made the east-southeast schlep the best short-term option. He made no bones that it was only the better of two bad choices. In my gut I suspected that we should have been heading north, to reach the westerlies, even if it added miles to the passage. We needed to get to at least 40 north, about 500 miles north of Bermuda, but instead we were plodding in the wrong direction.

The gale blew itself out, and we were left becalmed, bobbing on stirred-up seas with the sails slatting. This might be my least favorite condition, and after a brief attempt to sail, we decided to fire up the diesel. In those days *Quetzal* had a Westerbeke, and it was always a bit temperamental. We had motored for only a few hours when the engine overheated. The new heat exchanger worked so well that the old engine didn't know how to cope with it, and it blew out a freeze plug in the block, causing us to lose coolant repeatedly. I didn't have any spare freeze plugs aboard. Who does? The engineers were able to fix the problem with a Canadian Loonie—a one dollar coin that I found rolling around the nav station—and some epoxy. It seemed to work, but we were wary and decided to use the engine as little as possible, primarily just to charge the batteries.

We sailed across the Atlantic the old-fashioned way, battling light, fluky winds and imprisoned in the horse latitudes. It is interesting how weather reports lose their significance when you can't do much about them. According to Herb there was wind north of us, naturally, and another gale south of us, which we would have preferred to annoying calms. Our spirits hadn't plummeted to the depths of Tartarus, to be sure, but I knew that the frustrations of calm weather threatened to mar the crew's experience.

I remembered my first Atlantic crossing aboard *Gigi* many years before. I was a young, immature captain, and although my sailing partner and *Gigi's* owner, Ty, had almost no sailing experience, he was wise enough to know that he had to keep my spirits buoyed. Our passage had bogged down as one gale after another kept us from leaving the English Channel, but Ty kept me laughing and pushing on and we eventually made our way to Antigua. Although the conditions between these two trips were polar opposites, the results were the same—a sense of despair that the passage was coming undone.

Our situation aboard *Quetzal* was anything but dire, but several crewmembers were keenly disappointed when they started to realize that they might have to jump ship in the Azores because they simply didn't have enough time off to finish the passage. I did my best to keep the mood light by telling sea stories. Rick kept us shaking our heads with a never-ending stream of puns. Warren, the senior member of the group, told quirky stories but had to avoid laughing, even at his own jokes. Early in the passage he fell in the companionway and bruised his ribs. He was in pain most of the crossing, but you'd never have known it.

Finally, on day nine the westerlies turned up. The wind shook the lethargy out of us and sailing was fun again. We ripped off three good days in a row topped by a 180-mile run, our best 24 hours of the passage. On June 1 we were twelve days out of Bermuda and still 300 miles from Horta. I had predicted a twelve-day passage, alas, but at least we were hopeful that with two more good sailing days we'd be in Horta for happy hour at Café Sport.

But it seems the Atlantic had other plans for us.

That night the barometer dropped to 1,008 millibars, a slight drop but not alarming. A spectacular carmine sky greeted us at dawn, and we all did our best not to think about the old saw of red sky by morning . . . but change was coming, and by midmorning the wind had backed through the south to the east and finally parked in the east-northeast, which of course was just where we needed to head. Soon the winds were steady at 30 knots. We had a reef in the main and the staysail and, although it was tough slogging, we were making decent progress. Sailing very close to the wind, we managed to keep the boat moving at 5 knots punching right through the waves.

Suddenly there was a loud *Ka Bang*! I was below. I was sure the mast had buckled. Not the case. I flew back up to the cockpit in time to hear Doug shout, "We've lost the staysail." The staysail and the stay were whipping in the wind. Loaded up with the drum, mounting hardware, and aluminum extensions, the staysail was a lethal battering ram. One second it was lifting in the breeze, the next it was crashing into the boat like a wrecking ball. We tried to furl the sail, but there was no purchase on the line. There was no way to lower the stay without going up the mast. There was only one thing to do.

Despite the assault that *Quetzal* was under, we took a few minutes to suit up and make a plan. It was pretty simple. We had to corral the stay as soon as possible or it would shatter a hatch, or we could even lose the rig. Ron, Chris, and I crawled forward. Doug took the boat off autopilot and took the helm. Rick and Warren manned the sheets.

"Bring us up," I screamed back to Doug, and he carefully eased the boat into the wind. The wayward stay swung inboard and I lunged at it and held it for all I was worth. But the sail started to pull away, with me holding it, so Chris grabbed me. Ron held Chris. It would have been funny if it hadn't been so dangerous. Rick and Warren frantically tried to furl in the sail, but the extrusions were bent like pretzels.

Chris and I managed to get a line around the furling drum and lash it to the windlass. The sail was flogging wildly, threatening to knock us off the foredeck. "Fall off, Doug, fall off," I screamed. "But pay attention. What-ever you do, don't jibe." There was no irony in my tone. Running off with just the main meant that a jibe would take the mast with it.

"I'll try," Doug shouted back hoarsely.

The three of us tried in vain to lower the sail. Chris and I pulled like mani-acs, but the sail wouldn't budge. I had told Ron to let go the halyard, but in the confusion I had pointed to the wrong halyard.

"Are you sure it's this one?" Ron said, suspecting that I was wrong.

"Of course I'm sure. It's just jammed."

Ron, a fine sailor and a fine man, finally said, "Well I'm just going to try to ease this other one and see what happens." With the staysail halyard free, instead of the pole topping lift, the sail came down easily despite the mangled extrusions.

Doug carefully brought the boat upwind as we staggered back to the cockpit. We eased out a bit of headsail, which thankfully was undamaged, and put *Quetzal* on course. The engineers were dying to know what had caused the problem, and the answer infuriated us. It was a faulty toggle, and a brand-new one at that, installed just before the crossing as part of a new furling system. Sold as stainless steel, it clearly wasn't, and Doug, the dean of engineering at the University of Tennessee, concluded that it looked like pot metal. A bad part, and a bad day. And it was about to get worse.

That night a full gale developed as the low to the north of us intensified and swooped south. Without the staysail we were reduced to using a tiny amount of headsail and a deeply reefed main. Fortunately, the new Harken furling system we'd installed before the passage was up to the job as we shortened the headsail all night long.

A reluctant dawn crept above the horizon, almost as if the new day had no desire to see what the ocean had wrought. Northeast winds were sustained at 45 knots, Force 9 on the Beaufort scale, and we later learned from the weather service in Horta that nearby ships recorded gusts above 60 knots. We decided on around-the-clock watches and shortened them from three hours to two, with two men in the cockpit at all times.

Staring at the chart at the sodden nav station below, I realized we had two and a half options. We could run-off, which would immediately ease the motion but would take us from the Azores and require diligent helmsmanship running before what had become huge seas. The second full option was to press on, forereaching into the teeth of the storm, as we were doing. The half option was to heave-to. I say half option because without the staysail, which doubled as a storm jib, we would have to rely on the deeply furled headsail, and that worried me. I decided to keep that option in my pocket. I chose pressing on. *Quetzal* seemed to be handling the conditions, and it kept moving us closer to our landfall. Also, by sailing close-hauled on a starboard tack, we had to be moving away from the low.

That night the storm reached its peak, Force 10. Doug and Chris had the 2200 to midnight watch. It was, in a perverse way, beautiful. Witnessing the raw energy of the wind and waves in a full storm at sea, especially from the perspective of a small boat, is something you don't forget. The autopilot was doing a decent job of steering, but Chris was positioned behind the helm to grab the wheel if need be. Doug was trying to keep his balance on the high side of the cockpit, tucked beneath the spray dodger. We had the full cockpit enclosures zipped in place, but it was still wet in the cockpit.

Lying below, I felt the boat lurch. Then I heard Doug shout, "Hold on, Chris." A marauding wave crashed aboard just aft of the bow and swamped the cockpit. *Quetzal* was laid over hard to starboard, knocked down, but then she quickly righted herself.

The cockpit had been swamped, but the scuppers were draining the water quickly. Other than a blown-out panel in the enclosure, we were okay. Doug and Chris assured me that they were okay, and they insisted on finishing their watch. They were both fine sailors, and I was damn lucky to have them aboard. "I might have to charge you more for the knockdown," I joked as I dropped back below.

But one hour later the wave that leveled *Quetzal* was anything but a laughing matter.

From below it sounded as though a freight train was running right over us. The roar of the wave breaking was deafening, and again *Quetzal* was laid on her beam ends. This time I wasn't sure if she was coming back up. I was pinned to the side of the berth in the aft cabin. Gravity had me in a headlock. I couldn't move. "Come on, *Quetzal*," I pleaded. "Please, please, come up."

And finally she did. I pulled myself out of the bunk and screamed to Rick, Ron, and Warren. "Are you guys okay?" They were stunned but not hurt. The cabin was a shambles, but I didn't care. I had to get to the cockpit.

Ripping back the companionway hatch, I shouted, "Are you guys here? Tell me you're here! Are you here, goddammit?" All I could think was that the wave had carried them with it.

Doug answered. "We're here. I think we're okay. Wow, what a wave."

Chris was piled into a corner behind the wheel. "Yeah, I'm here, and yeah, Doug, what a wave."

The cockpit looked as blighted as a Florida neighborhood after a hurricane. It was naked and exposed. Bare stainless steel frames were all that was left of the spray dodger and bimini. The enclosure was in tatters. Amazingly, though, *Quetzal* was still sailing, pounding her way to weather. We had been knocked down a second time but had bounced right back up again.

Ron joined us in the cockpit, and he and Chris wrestled the dodger frame and what was left of the canvas below. Doug and I inspected the rig, and it seemed fully intact. Same with the sails. Rick and Warren started making some sense of the cabin, but it was a thankless task. The midships head door had flown off, exposing the head to a barrage of flying spices. Cumin and curry were everywhere.

I suited up and sent the crew below. I was relatively well rested and determined to con *Quetzal* into the light of day and then into Horta. It was time for landfall. We were only 60 miles away. I also didn't want to expose the crew to the ravages of another misguided wave.

An ugly dawn greeted us again, but we had clawed our way to within 40 miles of Faial and were making decent progress. The winds fought us every inch of the way. Those were some of the toughest 40 miles I have ever sailed.

Beating, tacking, pounding, punching, kicking up sheets of spray, we pushed *Quetzal* toward the finish line. Ron and Rick relieved me, and I took a needed break. By noon we were just 8 miles away. At 1500 we were still 4 miles out. Hurricane force katabatic blasts cascading down the steep hillsides pushed us back every time we inched close to land. Doug managed to start the engine and, more impressively, kept it running as we finally motorsailed into the harbor just before dark. We were 16 days out of Bermuda.

The scene in the harbor was chaotic. The terrible weather had prevented boats from leaving, and there were no slips available at the marina. Yachts were anchored everywhere, and boats were dragging their anchors all over the harbor. It took us three tries to get our big Bruce anchor to set. When it finally took hold, I felt myself relax for the first time in days. Once we were certain it was holding, we hitched a ride ashore.

Café Sport was packed, and the sea stories were flowing faster than the beer, and in many languages. An Irish sailor insisted on buying us a round. He couldn't believe we had just arrived. "You're mad to have come in through this, mad."

A New Look at an Essential Route-Planning Tool: Pilot Charts

I first discovered pilot charts in the cartography department of the library at Michigan State University, and I have been addicted to them ever since. They were much more interesting than whatever class I was skipping. I was drawn to their confident wind and current arrows showing the trade winds, the variables, and higher latitude westerlies, and I loved the small-scale projection that made large swaths of ocean comprehendible. Pilot charts were made for dreaming about voyages—and that's all I did in those faraway days. The charts allow even a casual observer to notice the prevailing winds, currents, tracks of tropical storms, temperatures, and even the range of pack ice and icebergs. In essence they are long-term climate records published in chart form and depicted by the month. They were better than the sports pages!

Of course I eventually made a few voyages and came to realize that pilot charts were not just for dreaming but essential tools for route planning. I collected pilot charts for every ocean and loved the fact that they never went out of date. Every time I unrolled a pilot chart, I felt connected to the brave mariners who sailed before me. Pilot charts were created by Matthew Fontaine Maury, who joined the navy as a midshipman in 1825 and went on to become one of America's preeminent navigators and oceanographers. In 1847 he published his first wind-and-current chart of the North Atlantic. Maury relied on ship captains and navigators from all over the world to supply him with observations from their voyages. This was still the great Age of Sail, and clipper ship captains and owners were desperate for information to give them a competitive advantage. They faithfully supplied Maury with information from their logbooks. Maury's pilot charts were a huge navigational breakthrough. For the first time, skippers had hard data for route-planning decisions. This wonderful cooperation from mariners has continued, and Maury's original pilot charts have been periodically updated during the ensuing 150 years and continue to be published by the NGA (officially, NGIA National Geospatial-Intelligence Agency) and are also available as downloads.

As timeless as pilot charts are, I must confess that they do have shortcomings. First, the areas with the most accurate and detailed information are the shipping lanes—those most frequently plied by commercial vessels—and these are regions that sailboats often avoid. Along this line, sailors today are reaching into distant corners of the watery world, areas that don't have a statistical baseline for accurate observations. Additionally, large ships, even sailing ships, tend to underestimate wind strength, especially as it applies to small sailboats. Fifteen knots to a large fully rigged ship is barely enough wind to fill the sails, but to a modern sailboat it's an ideal Force 4 breeze. Finally, and most importantly, the world's climate has been changing, and bluewater sailors are on the front lines of observing this gradual shift in oceanic weather patterns. Will pilot charts go out of date? And because they're based on years of reporting, how can one update them?

Enter Jimmy Cornell, the guru of bluewater sailing information. Cornell, the author of *World Cruising Routes*, the bible for cruising sailors, and his son Ivan have created new pilot charts based on data gleaned from the geospatial and remote-buoy data gathered from meteorological satellites. This data, collected from 1987 to the present, is printed in pilot chart format by the Cornells in their privately published *Ocean Atlas: Pilot Charts for All Oceans of the World*.

One of the specific geographic areas that the Cornells highlight is an area where their charts differ from traditional pilot charts. It is in the Pacific, just beyond the Bay of Panama, on the route to the Galapagos. I sailed that route twice last year on expeditions to the Galapagos, and I discovered firsthand that Jimmy and Ivan are on to something. And believe me, I say this with a heavy heart because my instinct is to trust hundreds of years of history more than twenty-five years of science. But as we bucked a surprisingly strong south equatorial current and pesky north winds beating our way back to Panama, both changes picked up by the Cornells' pilot chart, I had to admit that satellites are hard to argue with.

Overall the Cornells' atlas is beautifully presented, with sixty oceanic charts and sixty-nine detailed charts of specific routes for cruising sailors. The authors also do a great job of graphically presenting the position of the intertropical convergence zone, better known as the equatorial *(continued next page)* doldrums. They also show how the dominant high-pressure zones of each hemisphere shift from month to month. Knowing the position of the Azores High is one of the keys to a successful Atlantic crossing.

I suspect that the Cornells' *Ocean Atlas* will gradually supplant traditional pilot charts, at least for bluewater sailors, and that's a change that I am going to have to accept. Maybe it's time to realize that Jimmy Cornell, with his tireless work to present the best routes for skippers, is sailing's very own Matthew Fontaine Maury.

They're kindred spirits.

seven

Heaving-to I Chafe in Heavy Weather I
Forereaching I Lying Ahull I Myths Debunked I
Sail Trim in Heavy Weather I Preparing for Heavy
Weather I To Drogue or Not to Drogue

Storm Strategies

"The barometer at sea is not a very reliable guide. It must be the sky which commands the most attention."

—Adlard Coles, *Heavy Weather Sailing*

"The ocean waits
to measure or to slay me
the ocean waits
and I will sail."

—Webb Chiles, from his website

THE SIX OF US were squeezed around a finely varnished table in Taberna de Pim, a snug restaurant that overlooks the black sands of Porto Pim just beyond Horta. Frequented by locals, Taberna is known for its *moda dos acores*, or octopus stew, and we had a heaping family-style portion before us.

We'd been in the Azores a couple of days and the wind was still howling. Our delay in making landfall meant that most of the crew, actually all the crew except Doug, would have to abandon ship in Horta. Fortunately my friend Steve Sullivan had flown in to help crew, but this was our farewell dinner, and as the carafes of Portuguese wine flowed, our conversation turned to the subject that was still on everyone's mind: heavy weather. Ron and Chris wanted to know where the havoc a few days before (see Chapter Six) ranked in the pantheon of my storm experiences.

They were certain it had to be in the top five, maybe even the top three. They were lobbying hard for a high ranking, and I was in no mood to disappoint them. I assured them it was top five material, and we toasted our ordeal, proud that we had survived and incredibly relieved that it was now relegated to sea story status.

A week later I was on watch alone, sharing the cockpit with my thoughts. It was a cool, breezy night, and *Quetzal* was charging toward Cape St. Vincent, Portugal, as another Atlantic crossing was almost in the books. The Azores approach storm, as it was now dubbed, seemed a world away, but I couldn't help thinking about Ron and Chris's question again. I began scribbling in my journal, trying to recall the mightiest storms that have rocked my world. I started a list, and then, remembering another storm from long ago, crossed out the previous entry and added another. Soon the page was overflowing, and each new entry triggered a flood of memories.

Two things occurred to me as I worked on the list: first, that I'd been in far too many storms, and second, the Azores approach storm of 2007 was hard-pressed to make the top ten.

Ranking storm experiences is risky, as memories tend to be more emotional than analytical. Also, two key factors must be considered, the boat's seaworthiness and the crew's capability, because they can define the experience just as accurately as can wind strength and wave heights. Our first offshore passage aboard *Epoch*, our Jeanneau Gin Fizz sloop, is a good example. At the time, this storm was a monumental event in my nascent sailing career. My crew consisted of my girlfriend Molly and my mother. Our combined sailing experience amounted to almost nothing, a couple of overnight passages on calm seas and cover-to-cover reading of *Heavy Weather Sailing*. Worse, I hadn't yet learned to trust the boat, and that's never a good mindset for offshore sailing. What seemed like terrifying winds and seas, and what convinced me to heave-to for a couple of days, would certainly not have the same impact on me today, especially aboard *Quetzal*. Does that diminish the experience? No, but it does put it in perspective.

With the experience I have today, I would have adopted different tactics, been more confident and aggressive, and likely have a completely different memory of a gale that was, at its height, generating occasional wind gusts of Force 9 on the Beaufort scale. It was a serious situation, just not a particularly dangerous one. And I am almost sure now that we would have carried on toward Bermuda.

The top ten list that I finally came up with on watch that night has been modified again, as a couple more storms have made the grade since 2007. Ron and Chris will be happy to know that their storm is still ranked, but just barely. They are both signed on for another Atlantic crossing in 2014.

I hope that won't give them an opportunity to move up a few notches on the list.

Top Ten Storms (full descriptions are in Chapter Eight)

1. Force 13: a midwinter Atlantic crossing aboard *Isobell*, an Ocean 71 ketch
2. Cape Horn Snorter: 60 knot winds and massive seas after rounding the Horn aboard *Gigi*, a Contessa 32

3. Hurricane Mitch: 70 knot winds on a delivery of a Hylas 46 to the Caribbean
4. North Sea Gale: Force 11 conditions east of England on *Isobell*
5. Capsize: a tropical storm south of Bermuda on *Gigi*
6. Hurricane Bob: 80 knot winds on a training passage aboard a Hylas 44 offshore of the Bahamas
7. Gulf Stream Storm: wild, breaking seas on a training passage aboard *Quetzal*, a Kaufman 47
8. Bay of Biscay Gale: sustained Force 10 conditions aboard *Gigi*
9. Azores Approach: the storm of Chapter Six
10. Cape Hatteras Storm: 50 knots, huge seas rounding the infamous cape in a Swan 41.

Just typing the list kindles vivid memories, or I should say nightmares, of bleak skies and angry seas. While the beautiful days at sea blur in my mind's eye, I remember the storms with amazing clarity. There's something about the ocean's fury that is hard to forget. And there is much to be learned from reliving these tempests, from storm tactics to boat tendencies to the psychology of keeping the crew engaged.

One nasty wave doesn't ruin the majesty of fast sailing on the ocean.

The boats range from 32 feet to 71 feet, and crew experience also varies widely. Before I launch into the specific storm stories, we need to discuss storm-sailing strategies. The list is here just to tease you, or to keep you reading. In Chapter Eight I write about the above-mentioned storms, some in more detail than others.

There are four basic tactics to consider when contending with heavy weather: two passive measures—heaving-to and lying ahull—and two active measures—forereaching and running-off. While many factors influence storm tactics, including sea room, boat type, crew experience, and weather forecasts, in general I am a proponent of heaving-to as a first option and forereaching when the weather becomes truly severe. Running-off is viable, especially in the right boat, but avoid lying ahull until every other card has been played. Let's look carefully at when and how each tactic should be executed, and what decision points force a change of strategy.

Heaving-to

Heaving-to is a time-honored way to take the sting out of a blow by buying time and easing the motion aboard. I have hove-to many times, and almost without fail it's been effective—up to a point and in the right boat. Heaving-to is not just a storm strategy; it's also a vital seamanship skill. Small-boat sailors know how to heave-to, to back the sails and counteract their force with the rudder and bob peacefully until the next race starts. Big-boat sailors also occasionally heave-to to take a break, to simply turn off the wind and forget that they're stranded on a sailboat, if just for a while.

The process is relatively simple. First, bring the boat up hard on the wind, and then come about without releasing the headsail sheet. Once the headsail is backed, effectively putting the boat in irons, put the helm down so the boat tries to come back into the wind. The backed jib is trying to pull the boat off the wind while the mainsail and rudder attempt to drive the boat back into the wind, effectively parking the boat. Naturally you will have to trim the main and adjust the rudder position to find the right balance that keeps the boat in a position anywhere from 45 to 60 degrees off the wind. I have hove-to to cook a decent meal, to effect an important repair, to get much-needed rest, and most frequently to time an imminent landfall for first light. Heaving-to in a gale is another matter altogether.

There are plenty of nuances to heaving-to in heavy weather. But no matter how cunning the skipper, the sad truth is that some modern boats simply won't heave-to at all, or at best will lie abeam of the wave pattern, leaving the boat vulnerable to getting clobbered by breaking waves. A boat with excessive freeboard, a wide beam, a flat forefoot, and a narrow-cord fin keel will tend to rotate around the keel each time a wave strikes. Instead of tracking

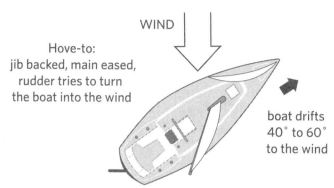

WIND

Hove-to:
jib backed, main eased,
rudder tries to turn
the boat into the wind

boat drifts
40° to 60°
to the wind

Heaving-to is the best strategy in most heavy-weather situations. It is important to find the right balance between the sails and the rudder. Some boats with longer keels will heave-to under just a storm jib or a staysail, reducing wear and tear on the mainsail. Others will need the mainsail deeply reefed. Although bluewater sailors can be skeptical of mast-furling and boom-furling mains, the ability to fly any size main is a big advantage in seeking the right balance. Also, if you intend to fly a trysail or a storm mainsail to heave-to, make sure you determine tack and control points on the mast and deck. (Joe Comeau)

into the wind and taking oncoming waves on the chin, modern boats are often blown off the wind and take waves on the beam, or sometimes even on the quarter, which then precipitates a vicious pivot back into the wind. In a deep gale, these gyrations can be incredibly dangerous.

It is not just the hull and keel shape that make modern boats resist heaving-to; it's the rig as well. The trend is toward fractional rigs featuring large mainsails and small headsails. And while this combination can be easy to handle in fine weather, it can also limit your choices in heavy weather. Fractional rigs are often difficult to balance because the main, even when reefed, overpowers the jib. While a large main can help push the center of effort aft—a good thing when hove-to—finding the right balance when hove-to is challenging. Some modern rigs heave-to better with just a deeply reefed main or just a storm jib and a hefty amount of applied rudder. Practice heaving-to in moderate conditions to discover your boat's tendencies.

And speaking of rudders, many modern hull designs put a tremendous load on the rudder when hove-to. Without much of a keel and semblance of a forefoot to provide lateral resistance, more of the directional responsibility falls to the rudder. As a general rule, the more rudder that has to be applied to keep the boat into the wind, or properly hove-to, the harder it is on the rudder. It's just like when you're underway—when the sails are well trimmed, you need less rudder action. Modern hulls sit higher in the water than older designs, and while modern hulls may be more buoyant, they also tend to pitch and pound when hove-to. This up and down motion puts a tremendous strain on the rudder, the rudderpost, and the rudder bearings. You simply cannot risk losing steering in heavy weather, so you can't allow the rudder to be damaged or become inoperable. If you lose the ability to steer, you are completely at the mercy of the sea.

So, you say, Kretschmer just pays lip service to heaving-to as a storm strategy. He doesn't really like it; in fact, it sounds like he hates it. That's not the case, really. Please remember that I prefaced my comments about heaving-to by saying "in the right boat." And that's the key to almost any storm strategy. Know your boat, and its strengths and limitations. Modern boats are better suited to running-off and forereaching in heavy weather. On the other hand, heaving-to in a relatively low-slung boat that tracks

The most important thing to do when you spot squalls is to prepare for an immediate sail change. It is hard to know if a squall will pack wind or rain, or both. I typically put the second reef in the main, or, if running or reaching, I drop the main. I stand by with the headsail, knowing that with my top-quality furling gear I can furl or reef the sail very quickly. Squalls typically—but not always—move perpendicular to the angle of the wind. Take this into consideration when choosing a course of action. Many times you can run-off before a squall, especially if the main is under control and you are not worried about jibing.

Squalls with moderate to heavy rain usually make good radar targets, and this can give you an idea of their size and movement.

true and has a well-supported rudder is another matter—it's a great way to ride out a gale.

If it has a split rig, that's even better. We hove-to in the so-called "storm of the century" off Belize in my old steel ketch *Fortuna* with a reefed staysail and reefed mizzen. It was such a non-event that it didn't even make my top ten storm list. (Although the subsequent grounding at Lighthouse Reef atoll was a horror story.) I have ridden out several gales hove-to in *Quetzal* without worry, and it's a safe and viable strategy up to 50 knots.

There are definite techniques and parameters that make heaving-to more effective. First, try to get the boat to lie as close to the wind as possible but without stalling or actually coming through the wind; 45 degrees is about ideal. Naturally, continue shortening sail as the wind increases, and try to keep the sails balanced. The more forward speed you can eliminate, the better. Split rigs—ketches, yawls, and schooners—are ideal for heaving-to because the mizzen places the load aft, taking pressure off the rudder. In a sloop or a cutter, you will need either a third reef in the mainsail or, better yet, a storm trysail.

A Mediterranean squall off the coast of Malta.

As a little aside, don't practice setting the trysail for the first time in a gale; it won't go well. We talk about storm sails later in this chapter, but it is not uncommon to buy a trysail for peace of mind but to have no idea how to actually fly it until you need it in heavy weather. Why do I know this? Because I'm guilty as charged.

Whatever sails you're flying when hove-to, be alert for chafe. Headsail sheets are terribly prone to chafing when hove-to because they often lie across the shrouds. If possible, heave-to under a staysail or a storm jib set on the staysail stay. An offshore boat should be fitted with a staysail stay and a heavy-duty staysail for serious bluewater work. Staysail sheets are typically led inboard the shrouds and are less prone to chafe when the sail is backed. I sometimes rig a block and barber haul to create a fair lead for the staysail sheet when hove-to.

Chafing occurs dramatically faster in heavy weather. I learned about chafe aboard *Gigi*, our Contessa 32, during my Cape Horn passage. Several times the headsail-furling line chafed through in critical situations. The culprit was a small, sharp edge on the furling drum, and although it seemed minor, it cut through the line in minutes when the sail was furled and the line was under load, exactly when I didn't need a problem. It isn't much fun to go from a deeply furled headsail to a full genoa in a gale. Eventually, after replacing the line twice, I filed the edge smooth and solved the problem for good.

When hove-to, the boat will drift slowly to leeward, roughly in a direction that falls somewhere between the compass heading and the reciprocal of the wind direction, depending on how much forward speed the boat maintains. While it is best to have as little forward motion as possible, in reality most boats, especially modern hulls, maintain a knot or two of speed, and a small bit of forward speed actually counteracts leeward drift to some degree. Take the time to heave-to on the most logical heading—that is, a heading that keeps you close to the pre-storm rhumb line, or the one that takes you away from a dangerous lee shore. Don't underestimate how much you will drift to leeward while hove-to. It can easily be as much as 2 knots, which translates into nearly 50 miles in 24 hours. Fifty miles seems like a lot of sea room until you're in a gale.

This drift does have one very positive effect. By crabbing to leeward, the boat creates a slick to windward. This tends to keep waves from breaking aboard, and that's a huge advantage of heaving-to. In his book *Sea Quest*, Charles Borden writes that legendary singlehanded sailors Jean Gau and Alan Gerbault both chose to heave-to in survival storms. They also rigged oil drip dispensers from the windward side of their boats to make the natural windward slick even larger, drop-by-drop. This sounds messy to me, and the Coast Guard might not look kindly on the idea these days, but they both later wrote about riding out monster storms quite happily hove-to in their stout Tahiti ketches.

A sea anchor may prevent much of the drift to leeward when hove-to, and can also steady the motion. Lin and Larry Pardey, two of the most experienced small-boat sailors of all time, recommend rigging a parachute-style sea anchor from the bow when hove-to. They suggest using a bridle to shift the relative position of the sea anchor to prevent the boat from coming head to wind or, worse, turning beam-to the seas. It is vital to pay out plenty of rode to reduce what can be jarring loads transferred back to the boat. The Pardeys have ridden out severe storms with this technique.

While I have great respect for Lin and Larry, I am hesitant to recommend this technique unless you have the right boat for it. Their Lyle Hess-designed *Talisman* is a modern-day Bristol Channel cutter, an incredibly seaworthy design built with heaving-to (as they waited for ships approaching Bristol Channel roads) in mind. More modern boats just don't heave-to as well, and it will be challenging to maintain a relative position to the sea anchor. Also, my two experiences with sea anchors in severe gales have convinced me that I don't want the web of lines required to control them anywhere near the keel, prop, and rudder. I am a bit paranoid about keeping the rudder safe. An undeniable advantage of heaving-to with a sea anchor deployed is that it can slow leeway significantly, and if you're hove-to off a lee shore, that may be a life and death advantage. Sometimes buying time is the most important tactic of all. We talk more about sea anchors later in this chapter.

Ultimately there comes a time when heaving-to stops being effective. How do you know? The boat tells you. When the slick no longer keeps the waves from breaking or the bow from being forced off the wind, it becomes clear that a different strategy is needed. When you can no longer keep the bow consistently into the wind, you have to try something else. My next move aboard *Quetzal* is to forereach, but before we discuss this controversial tactic, let's talk about running-off because, like heaving-to, it is often a first approach to managing heavy weather.

Running-off

Running-off may be the best short-term tactic, especially if a short-term gale is forecast and the seas are not predicted to build to dangerous heights. I have used this tactic in severe weather several times, as you'll read about later. Running-off is different from "following a squall," when you run-off as the wind shifts dramatically at the onset of a squall and you ride it out by steering off the wind until the local system passes. It does this relatively quickly, and you regain your original course, having lost a bit of time and progress toward the destination but otherwise being no worse for the ride. Running for hours, and sometimes days, before a deep ocean storm is significantly more challenging.

The old idea of running before a storm was to slow the boat and take more of a passive approach by maintaining just enough speed to keep control. And to also try to prevent the boat from surfing down the face of waves where it might broach or, worse, pitchpole bow over stern. Sailors would tow warps, heavy trailing lines that dampened the waves to some degree and acted like a drogue. Joshua Slocum was the first yachtsman to write about towing warps to keep control of *Spray* as she was blown back toward Cape Horn during a furious storm on his epic circumnavigation. Wrote Slocum, "Anyhow, for my present safety the only course lay in keeping her before the wind. She was running now with a reefed forestaysail, the sheets flat amidships. I paid out two long ropes to steady her course and to break combing seas astern and lashed the helm amidships. In this trim she ran before it, shipping never a sea."

While it's never a good idea to doubt the wisdom of Joshua Slocum, the *padrino* of all small-boat sailors, the notion of running-off and towing warps is a bit outdated. But there's no reason not to have every weapon available in your heavy-weather arsenal, and being prepared to slow the boat when running by carrying a drogue makes perfect sense. I have one stowed away in *Quetzal*'s lazarette, but I have never deployed it. I talk in more detail about drogues later in the chapter. Today, most sailors feel that slowing the boat is more dangerous that running with the sea. One of the first sailors to see the light was Bernard Moitessier.

Sixty-five years after Slocum's voyage, Moitessier and his wife, Francoise, were struggling to keep *Joshua*, their 39-foot ketch, from broaching in the huge following seas of the Southern Ocean. They had left Tahiti bound for Cape Horn, the so-called "logical route" back to Europe, and Moitessier realized it would be a long, tedious, and dangerous voyage if they kept slowing the boat by towing warps. In a fit of inspiration, he cut his warps away and, in so doing, freed *Joshua* to sail down the waves. He realized that by taking the waves between the quarter and the stern, the boat would respond naturally to the rudder. The tenor of the passage changed from that moment on, and *Joshua* rode the waves around Cape Horn and into the annals of sailing lore.

Modern boats are better suited to running-off before a storm than they are to heaving-to. Light, flat hulls with freestanding rudders positioned as far aft as possible can, in many instances, surf down waves safely and swiftly while maintaining good steering control. This technique requires intense concentration and, as the storm builds, increasingly skilled helmsmanship. Watch YouTube videos of Open 70 class boats charging down huge Southern Ocean waves in the Volvo Ocean Race to get an appreciation of the demands of downwind helming. It is difficult to stay alert and focused for more than an hour at a time, so crew size and experience are vital. Running-off also puts a lot of demands on the steering system, which must be able to respond rapidly and forcefully as the boat skids down the face of a wave. Of course by maintaining speed, the relative force of the wind and waves is reduced, and waves that do slop aboard are not usually troubling.

The three main problems with running-off:

1. It is exhausting and usually requires manning the helm in lieu of using the autopilot or wind vane, and there's a limit to human endurance, especially for cruisers sailing with a shorthanded crew.
2. By running at speed, you are prolonging your exposure to the storm by staying more or less directly in its path of travel. If a deep low is the source of the storm, depending on where you're positioned, running may actually take you right into the heart of the system.
3. Modern boats are often forced to carry the main when running, and the possibility of jibing in big seas is not only dangerous to the crew but carries the disturbing possibility of losing the mast and rig.

Knowing when to abandon running-off can be a difficult decision to make and a dangerous maneuver to execute. If you listen, your boat talks to you, and then it's up to you to act. As conditions deteriorate you are always on the verge of something bad happening, and that bad thing is likely to be a broach or, worse, a capsize. The same design factors that make some hulls prone to surfing make them deadly in a broach. While many factors impact stability, and ratios like the capsize screening index need to be taken in context, it is safe to say that hull forms with excessive beam and lots of freeboard—that is, those with a high center of gravity—may have excellent initial stability, but they also have dangerously low ultimate stability.

A bluewater boat must be able to recover from a knockdown to at least 130 degrees, and many modern boats are not close to that number when you look carefully at their stability curves. To be sure, stability, especially in a dynamic sense, is a complex equation. But calculating the angle of vanishing stability is not a mystery, and stability curves should be included in every off-shore boat's specs. Further, once the boat is knocked down and begins to roll, the rudder that has been placed well aft for better steering control becomes useless as the bow digs into the wave, followed by the boat's forward shoulder. The rudder is barely in the water and offers no help in trying to steer out of the crisis. If you think back to the rogue-ish wave that crushed *Quetzal* in Chapter Two, I believe that a different boat would have continued the roll and that you would be reading another book right now. *Quetzal*'s angle of vanishing stability is around 132 degrees, and her capsize factor is 1.76, both solid numbers for an oceangoing boat. When the seas begin to break and you feel the loss of steering control while rushing down the waves, then you must abandon running-off. Some sailors think this is the time to slow the boat down by trailing warps or a drogue in order to try to regain steering. I think a better course of action is to begin forereaching.

Forereaching

Forereaching is my preferred tactic for coping with severe weather. In some ways forereaching is similar to heaving-to except that the boat is moving forward, its natural motion, and not crabbing to leeward. By forereaching you trade the slick caused by heaving-to for the stability caused by having some forward motion. Forereaching requires strong stormsails, robust rigging, and a hull and deck that can take a pounding. In survival conditions expect your boat to be knocked down, but that's a better alternative than broaching before a breaking sea or being thrown on to your beam ends while hove-to.

Forereaching calls for reducing sail proportionately as the weather deteriorates. It is important to keep a balanced rig to maintain steering and enough speed to prevent developing lee helm. Usually you try to take waves 45 to 60 degrees off the bow and essentially jog along at 2 to 3 knots.

One of the great advantages of forereaching is that most autopilots and wind vanes are effective on this point of sail because the load on the rudder is less than with other storm tactics. If you are hand steering, you have the advantage of bringing the boat up into the worst waves, taking them just off the bow. This is the strongest part of the boat and the one offering the least resistance to an onrushing sea. Big-boat racing sailors are often forced to beat their way through storms because they're not set up for alternative storm tactics. Think of forereaching as a less violent, more sustainable version of this approach.

Wind and waves rarely line up in a gale. Wave direction can be distorted by many factors, even a long way from land, and there's almost always a preferred tack. In moderate gale conditions the preferred tack might be where the wave pattern is away from the direction of the wind, allowing the boat to sail free between waves but still head up when necessary. In a severe deep-ocean storm with breaking seas, the preferred tack is usually the one closest to the wind, allowing the boat to take the seas as near to the bow as possible. One danger is that a breaking wave can bring the boat about, backing the sails. And if the waves are steep, there's a tendency to stall in the troughs and lose momentum before encountering the next wave. This is less of a risk in a deep-ocean storm where the wavelength extends significantly in proportion to the wave height, creating less of a steep-sided canyon and more of a long valley in the troughs.

Some experienced mariners recommend running the engine to control boat speed when stalled in the troughs between towering waves. I don't. A better solution is to steer off the wind just a bit, filling the sails to power up the boat. Engines don't like to be heeled excessively and can lose lubricating oil pressure if angled beyond 25 to 30 degrees—a bad thing. Also, with the boat bucking around madly, it is not uncommon to stir up the fuel

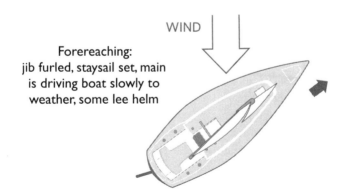

WIND

Forereaching:
jib furled, staysail set, main
is driving boat slowly to
weather, some lee helm

Forereaching also requires a bit of trial and error to find both the right sail combination (or, more accurately, how deeply to reef) and the proper angle for taking the seas. This is not necessarily beating, but rather close-reaching under much-reduced canvas to find the right slot in the wave and swell pattern to inflict the least damage to the boat. Forereaching is a boat's most natural motion and is easy on the rudder. (Joe Comeau) tanks, resulting in clogged filters and the engine cutting out when you need it most. Finally, fouling the prop is a very real possibility in heavy weather when a wave washes a sheet or a furling line overboard and you don't notice it until it's too late. Once the prop is wrapped, the engine becomes useless and unavailable when it might provide that last desperate measure of safety. Engines should be used only as a last resort in most storm conditions.

Arguably the best reason to forereach in a deep gale is that you can steer a course that will take you away from the storm. The most direct way out of a low-pressure system in the Northern Hemisphere is to sail to the right of the storm's path, which means keeping the winds close aboard to starboard. You may be sailing at only 2 to 3 knots, but you are making miles away from the storm—taking an active role and moving away from the worst conditions—which has a very real positive effect on morale.

Managing the mind-set of the crew is one of the skipper's most important jobs in a storm. Fear leads to inaction and then finally to panic, and that's a deadly course to follow. The majority of sailing disasters result from boats and crews taking passive approaches to storm conditions. Staying engaged with the boat and the situation is the single most important heavy-weather tactic. You made the decision to go to sea and you own your decision. It's your storm and you have to deal with it. You can't just push the reset button.

Lying Ahull

Lying ahull might also be called The Last Resort. Lying ahull calls for dropping all sail, lashing the rudder amidships, securing everything on deck and below, and hoping for the best. Some boats will drift better than others, but every boat is vulnerable when left to the mercy of breaking seas. If things go well, your boat will drift more or less downwind, but don't count on it. Most modern monohulls tend to lie beam-on in gales, which is actually the meaning of the phrase *lying ahull*: when the force of the wind overcomes the force of the water as it acts on the hull.

If you are forced to lie ahull, it is worth experimenting with the helm. Sometimes lashing the helm to leeward helps to keep the boat from rounding up. Also, streaming a warp astern can increase directional stability. Running under bare poles is a more active form of lying ahull and can definitely be more effective than leaving the boat to fend for itself. This was Slocum's strategy during his Cape Horn gale. If your boat is not as well behaved as *Spray*, a steady hand on the wheel can keep the boat before the wind, reducing the chance of the boat turning broadside to the waves.

We often lie ahull on *Quetzal*, but not as a storm tactic. I love to swim at sea, and whenever we do we take all sail down and let the boat drift with the wind. I trail lines with big fenders, primarily for swimming safety, but I have also noticed that they tend to keep the boat pointing downwind. But the rocking, rolling, and slamming about, even in calms seas, is horrible. If you want a taste of lying ahull, try it on a relatively calm day. It will convince you that it's the last thing you want to do in a storm.

Heavy-Weather Myths Debunked

Before getting into fitting-out for heavy weather and preparing for storms before they arrive, let's debunk a few common myths. First, the notion that with today's excellent satellite-weather forecasting, you can essentially avoid heavy weather. This sanguine notion is the voice of inexperience. If you plan to sail across oceans and cruise the world, you will encounter heavy weather. Think about how accurate local forecasts are in your hometown. Now add the vagaries of the ocean environment and the uncertainties of changing climate to the mix and you can pretty well count on encountering some unexpected storms in your travels. The Azores approach storm of 2007 was not forecast and caught much of the Atlantic crossing fleet by surprise.

The second myth is that you can outrun heavy weather if your boat is fast enough. While there is some truth to the notion that you can limit your exposure to storms by taking aggressive steps to sail out of harm's way, particularly if you know the path of the storm, generally this is not viable for most cruising boats traveling at 6 to 7 knots. Time is better spent preparing for the ensuing blow. I do have to admit, though, that I have never understood why boats lying in the predicted track of a tropical storm don't move out of the storm's way rather than assuming the bunker mentality and hunkering down for the blow. If you are at anchor in Antigua, in the Leeward Islands of the Caribbean, and a hurricane is a couple of days away and tracking west, why not make all haste south to Grenada or, better yet, Trinidad? It's only 300 to 400 miles due south, and in two days you can be completely out of the storm's swath of destruction. Today's tropical storm track models are very accurate, at least in the big picture, so the choice of where to sail is usually very clear. I think this is a better strategy than doubling and tripling your mooring lines and offering prayers and bribes to every available deity in hopes that the storm will change course.

The 2012 tragic loss of the replica tall ship *Bounty* in Hurricane Sandy points to flaws in both strategies mentioned above. If there ever was a time for hunkering down, this was it, as Sandy spread terror across the Atlantic like a malignant tumor. While I understand the skipper's angst about having the storm surge damage his ship in port, the potential for losing the ship and the crew by taking what in reality was a movie prop to sea in hurricane conditions was a terrible combination of arrogance and negligence. Captain Robin Walbridge and crewmember Claudine Christian paid for this mistake with their lives, and only heroic actions from the Coast Guard prevented more loss of life.

There was no way the *Bounty* was in a position to outmaneuver Sandy, but what's difficult to understand is why she didn't at least try. With the storm tracking northwest toward the New Jersey shore, the *Bounty* cleared out of New London, Connecticut, and, after rounding Montauk Point on the east end of Long Island, laid a course right toward the approaching storm. No attempt was made to outflank the storm by sailing east. Nobody knows for sure why Walbridge sailed back toward the coast and ultimately collided with the storm off Cape Hatteras.

Boat Design and Heavy Weather

Early and often in this book I have mentioned that the boat matters, and nowhere is this more true than when you are caught in heavy weather. Good boats exist because of bad weather. While the majority of cruising takes place in light to moderate conditions, you need your boat to be able to stand up when things turn ugly. You need to trust your boat. The boat has to be able to take a prolonged pounding, respond to heavy steering demands, and provide a safe haven below. These are serious demands.

Bright, wide-open interiors, which are certainly the trend in interior yacht design, are undeniably more livable than dark, narrow cabins divided into small spaces. According to my wife, Tadji, that makes sense. She reminds me often of the 10:1 cruising ratio: for every day at sea, ten are spent in port during a typical circumnavigation. Unfortunately, the days are weighted differently, and days spent at sea in a storm have disproportionate value. When you drop below in *Quetzal*, you are in a cramped three-foot-wide hallway. If the boat lurches, you can't lurch with it, or at least not for long, as you're quickly brought up against a bulkhead. There are handholds every few feet as you make your way forward, but handholds are a bit overrated. Having a bulkhead or furniture facing to support your weight is much safer. Think of standing on the train. Holding the overhead support bar is better than trying to balance without a handhold, but leaning against something solid feels much more secure. Next time you look at a boat with an eye on serious cruising, stand in the companionway and picture yourself making your way forward in a storm. If you feel like you're stepping onto a dance floor, you might want to look at another boat. A good cruising boat needs to offer sanctuary below, not room to practice the salsa.

The boat also needs to be able to take a pounding. What do I mean by this? To survive Force 9 storm conditions, which are 41 to 47 knots, the boat has to be able to take waves breaking across the deck and filling the cockpit without structural compromise or swamping. The weight of seawater is roughly 64 pounds per cubic foot. Even a moderate wave breaking on deck weighs more than a ton, and it impacts with the force of the wave speed—in short, it packs a powerful punch. A huge, breaking storm wave lands on deck with literally "tons of pressure." The boat has to withstand this crushing load, and sometimes repeatedly. The rig has to be able to survive a knockdown, which means the boat is heeled to a point where the mast spreaders are in the water.

When you think about preparing the boat for bluewater, try to picture it knocked down, usually not a pretty picture. One of the reasons why sailboats are so expensive is that their gear has to endure intense and often shifting loads. Blocks, shackles, clutches, and other sail controls made of inferior materials, or not built strongly enough, are exposed as frauds in heavy weather.

The truth is that most boats are built to these high, exacting standards. Sailboat manufacturers are, in the main, remarkably responsible and keenly aware of the hostile environments their creations work and play in. As wood was replaced by fiberglass, structural failure has become extremely rare as the cause of loss in storm conditions.

What has changed with the coming of synthetic materials is the shape of boats. In the desire to become more commodious, they've become wider, flatter, and higher sided and in many ways less seaworthy. Because today's boats are not as well suited to passive storm strategies, they need to be micromanaged in heavy weather, and this gets back to the idea that rugged and responsive steering systems are essential in a modern cruising boat. It is the single most important system aboard, and this leads back to my philosophy of protecting the rudder at all costs.

Heavy-Weather Sails

Every boat planning to make an ocean passage, from a rugged double-ended Westsail 32 to a nimble, light-displacement J44, needs to be equipped with stormsails and a strategy for flying them.

Mainsail

Let's start with the mainsail. It should be heavier than a typical main; *Quetzal*'s main is 9 ounce cloth, for example. The main should have reinforced corners. It must have three reefs, with two being permanently rigged with outhauls, and the facility to add a third reef outhaul easily. The traditional method of reducing the mainsail is with slab or jiffy reefing. This system of lowering the halyard, securing the reef cringle either manually or with a downhaul to the reef hook, and tensioning the reefing outhaul is time-tested and almost bulletproof. It is not difficult to lead all control lines aft, making it possible to reef the main from the cockpit, the system I have on *Quetzal*.

Many boats today have furling mainsails, either in-mast or in-boom systems. Can these mainsails, designed primarily for ease of handling, survive storm conditions? Are they able to be reefed down enough to cope with heavy weather? The answer to both questions is yes, with a qualifier. The furling systems and the sail itself have to be top quality. In many ways, the ability to reef a sail to the size of a hand towel from the security of the cockpit is an advantage, especially because the sail can be reefed off the wind.

As you will read in the next chapter, we rode out the remnants of Hurricane Mitch in a Hylas 46 fitted with an in-mast furling mainsail. The Hylas 49 I sailed from New York to the Caribbean and back for many years was fitted with a carbon fiber mast and electric in-mast furling, giving us push-button control from the cockpit. How well did it work? We rode out several Atlantic gales without trouble. Although I have sailed with plenty of boats fitted with boom-furling systems, I have not been caught out in a gale in one.

While the idea of lowering the center of effort by furling the main into the boom makes a lot more sense than moving the loads forward by rolling the main into the mast, the boom systems have one basic disadvantage: you have to be dead upwind to reef, and in a gale that can be challenging. However, more and more boats are opting for in-boom systems, and I suspect that in the near future they will be as ubiquitous aboard cruising boats as headsail furlers are today. More about reefing techniques in Chapter Eight.

Trysails

Now what about storm trysails—better described as storm mainsails? Are they still necessary, and should bluewater sailors carry them? First, a confession: I don't have one on *Quetzal*. That being said, I put trysails in the same category as drogues and sea anchors. There is no reason not to have every option available to you when dealing with storms. A trysail is usually a better sail for heaving-to than a deeply reefed mainsail because without a boom, the overall center of effort is lowered, and it can also be rigged to avoid any chafe. A deeply reefed main is a better sail for forereaching as it is much more efficient. Neither mainsail nor trysail are in play when running off or lying ahull, so it comes down to heaving-to.

Most sailmakers recommend fitting a separate track on the aft edge of the mast specifically for the trysail. The track should go nearly down to the deck so that the sail can be fitted and ready to hoist without having to feed the slugs onto the track in gale conditions. *Gigi* was fitted with a trysail, and we hove-to with it while waiting for a favorable tide in the Le Maire Strait near Cape Horn. We had all sorts of problems with it, primarily caused by the halyard flagging against the mast and trying to find a way to secure the tack.

We discovered that the track was mounted too far to the side of the mast, and the halyard chafed at the masthead because the lead to the trysail head was not fair. This is important because if the main halyard chafes through, your options for storm management are greatly reduced. Also, although we had practiced raising the trysail in New York City before the voyage began, actually controlling the tack in a gale was much more difficult than we realized. We ran the sheet to the jib car first, then to a jury-rigged block on deck, and then finally to the end of the boom, which we had to raise back in position after we had lowered it to the deck. Another point to consider with a trysail: it must be well supported by the mast—even a sail of 100 square feet can set up mast pumping. Running backstays may be necessary. The point here is not to dismiss the importance, or the effectiveness, of a trysail but to look at the realities of actually using it in heavy weather. Like a lot of safety gear, just buying it makes you feel better, but unless you have a thorough plan for using it, it just takes up space.

Storm Jibs and Storm Staysails

Storm jibs are another matter—they're essential for an offshore boat. Too many times while delivering boats I have been forced to rely on a deeply furled genoa for a stormsail, and it is always a bad compromise. Furled headsails offer great versatility and ease of handling. I wouldn't go to sea without one. But in storm conditions, they're a liability. I firmly believe that a staysail stay, or an inner forestay, whether permanently rigged or temporary, is vital for the deployment of a storm jib or a storm staysail. The typical process aboard *Quetzal* goes something like this. As the wind builds, we reef the main and the furling 120 percent headsail, trying to maintain balance. Once the headsail is furled beyond 80 percent, we roll it in all together and set the heavy hank-on staysail. The effect is immediate as the center of effort is lowered and shifted aft, and I always ask myself why I didn't do that sooner. With the staysail and two reefs in the main, *Quetzal* can maintain control on all points of sail in gale conditions. If conditions continue to deteriorate, we take a third reef in the main and replace the staysail with the storm jib, also set on the staysail stay. With this configuration I feel very secure, whether hove-to or forereaching.

One rule of thumb for a storm jib is that it should be roughly 3 percent of the I measurement squared. I am not sure where this comes from, but it is conservative and very accurate for serious ocean sailing. On *Quetzal*, the I is 56 feet, so that squared is 3,136 feet, and 3 percent of that is 94 feet. My storm jib is 100 square feet. The staysail, on the other hand, which is more of a heavy-weather sail than a pure working sail, is 200 square feet. It's a huge difference, but I love the sail and rarely used the storm jib. They are both hoisted on the staysail stay, sometimes called the inner forestay.

Heavy-Weather Boat Trim/Securing the Boat for a Blow

A couple of points need to be made about trim in heavy weather, and here we can learn a lot from racing sailors. I am talking about boat trim, not sail trim, and it's vitally important. Weight aloft and weight concentrated in the ends of the boat dramatically alter a boat's stability and performance. A genoa furled around the headstay adds significant windage. If you know a storm is coming your way, dropping the sail and stowing makes sense. Remove items lashed on deck and stow them below. Reducing windage should be a priority in preparing for heavy weather.

New trends in cruising boats seem to point to loading up the ends with things such as stainless steel cockpit arches with solar panels and antennas, massive bow rollers set up with two heavy anchors, and tons, literally, of ground tackle. All this weight is concentrated in the exact wrong place. Weight should be low and centered to maximize a boat's stability and performance. Keep this in mind before adding dinghy davits. Do you really need to put another 500 pounds on the stern?

When a storm is coming, be proactive in preparing for the worst. This sounds obvious, and maybe even a bit patronizing, but I have seen sailors shut down when they know they're in for a blow, and deny the facts written in the clouds or on the weather fax. Priorities can easily be confused. You don't need to spend precious time trying to get more weather information or communicating with folks ashore or other boats. Get your boat squared away.

There is no specific order of events, but there should be urgency preparing for a blow at sea. Secure the deck and don't be lazy. Don't lash that bucket, fishing pole, or boathook when it is just as easy to store it. If possible, muscle the anchors into a secure position in the chain locker. If that's not possible, lash them securely. Having an anchor jump out of the roller during a storm is a nightmare. A clean, uncluttered deck is a safe deck. Problems in heavy weather are often the result of that lashed dinghy suddenly shifting and crashing into the lifelines, or the sailboard coming adrift, or the panels connecting the dodger to the bimini ripping apart. Suddenly you're on deck dealing with something that should have been stowed but is now exposed to the weather and you're not concentrating on handling the boat.

Make sure your stormsails are pulled out of the bottom of the lockers and are ready to be deployed. Check the sheets. Are they ready to run? Dig out the drogue and the sea anchor if you think you'll need them. Sorting out this gear during a storm is never easy, and it exposes the lockers to spray and swamping. Make a thorough survey of the deck. You'll always find something to address.

Take time to eat and prepare food for the next day or two. Try to get some sleep. If I know the weather is going to change for the worse, I'll nap during the day in anticipation of a long night. I think of sleep like gas in the tank. I know I'll be better at dealing with the conditions if I am not exhausted. I need to run on a full tank. Sometimes the crew is surprised that I can sleep before a storm, but this is a lesson I've learned the hard way. Study the chart and try to lock it away in your brain. Know which way you can run with plenty of sea room. Know the direction of the nearest lee shore. Know what course will most likely take you away from the storm.

Finally, take time to discuss the situation with the crew and describe your plan of action in detail. Exude confidence because your mood directly influences the mood of the crew. Do everything you can to avoid a sense of doom; don't brood, and resist at all costs the bunker mentality. Keep everybody engaged and informed. I have learned that the psychology of maintaining crew morale is just as important as knowing the ins and outs of heaving-to or forereaching. The boat will talk to you, and you will know what to do. It's just a matter of finding the resolve to do it. Your crew, on the other hand, may not talk to you or, worse, they may be terrified and try to shake your resolve. Fear does terrible things to people. Your biggest challenge as a skipper is to help your crew deal with their fears so that they can be productive when you really need them.

Sea Anchors and Drogues

Let's end this chapter by taking a look at the controversial subject of sea anchors and drogues. While I have a lot of experience heaving-to, forereaching, and running-off in storms, my experience with sea anchors and drogues is limited. I have used a parachute sea anchor on a Hylas 49 in a moderate North Atlantic gale, not because we felt we needed it but because we were curious how the boat would respond. And I have used a Jordan drogue in a Gulfstar 50 on a Pacific crossing while running before huge seas with a disabled steering system.

The parachute-style sea anchor is very effective in slowing a boat's drift to leeward. This is reason enough to carry one, especially because it doesn't take up a lot of room and is easy to stow. Parachute-style sea anchors were originally just that, parachutes. Commercial fishermen began using them after the war to keep working during storms.

Sea anchors are set off the bow, usually to windward, and typically open quickly. Rode is then played out as the boat drifts aft. Sometimes the sea anchor can fill with air while on deck, making it difficult to set. Most commercial sea anchors deploy in bags, eliminating that potential problem. The result is that the boat lies head to the wind and waves, held more or less in place by the sea anchor with just a marginal leeward drift.

Out in the Atlantic I was surprised how heavy the loads were on the boat. The Hylas 49 has robust forward cleats, but I was genuinely worried they might be ripped right off the deck when the sea anchor rode pulled tight and the bow jerked 30 degrees one way and then the other. Eventually we managed to position the sea anchor so that it was riding the same wave pattern we were, albeit two wavelengths away.

The problems occurred when the sea anchor was on the crest of the wave and we were in the troughs. Retrieving the sea anchor turned into a struggle when the trip line tangled and then fouled. The only option was to motor ahead, pulling in the rode frantically to make sure that it didn't foul the prop or rudder. Before we finally wrestled the sea anchor aboard, it was dangling below the bow for a few anxious minutes. A proper trip line would have made this task a bit less harrowing, but I just don't like the idea of having lines in the water and the possibility of snagging the prop, keel, or rudder. I view a sea anchor for what it is, an anchor, a method of stopping or slowing the boat, and not necessarily a device for heavy-weather storm management. But always remember, this is just one sailor's opinion.

Drogues are designed to be set off the stern. Their primary purpose is to slow the boat down while running-off before big waves. Drogues are the modern version of what Moitessier called warps, and they work far better. There are two basic types of drogues, those that slow your speed to manageable levels but still allow for the boat to make headway, and those that essentially stop the boat. The best known of the latter type is the Jordan drogue. We used a more traditional drogue in the Pacific and it worked very well.

The steering system failed all at once on the Gulfstar 50 that I was delivering to Japan. I spent hours jury-rigging a new steering chain, not an easy repair. But when we went to bring the boat back on course, I realized that I had mounted the steering cables backwards. When you turned the wheel right, the boat went left. It was maddening, and I was frustrated, to put it mildly. We had been hove-to while I completed the repairs, and I regretted not being able to take advantage of the strong trade winds and large following seas that wanted to push us directly toward our waypoint—Hilo, Hawaii. I needed a break and was not ready to repair the system. Instead we lashed the emergency tiller amidships with the boat pointed downwind, and launched a drogue. It was an inexpensive conical canvas webbing, but it did a great job of keeping the bow off the wind, and we managed to drift toward Hilo through the night. The next morning I swapped the cables and we got back underway.

I carry a Para-Tech drogue aboard *Quetzal* but have never deployed it. I am firmly in the Moitessier camp and feel that the boat responds best without being shackled by a drogue. When running-off becomes untenable, I switch to forereaching instead of rolling the dice by running before breaking seas. I carry the drogue because of how well it worked on that trip across the Pacific on the Gulfstar 50. I like the option of slowing the boat to time my arrival on a downwind approach, or when I need a rest but don't want to lose ground by stopping forward progress by heaving-to.

eight

Heavy-Weather Sailing 2.0 | Equipment Failure |
Force 13—Atlantic Crossing Gale | Cape Horn
Snorter | Hurricane Mitch | North Sea Force 10 |
Capsize in Force 10 | Unexpected Hurricane Bob |
Cape Hatteras Storm | Bay of Biscay Force 10 |
Other Notable Heavy-Weather Experiences

Storm Stories

"Being hove-to in a long gale is the most boring way of being terrified I know."
—Donald Hamilton, *Cruises with Kathleen*

"I hate storms, but calms undermine my spirits."
—Bernard Moitessier, *The Long Way*

"When the wind is from the west
All the waves that cannot rest
To the east must thunder on
Where the bright tree of the sun
Is rooted in ocean's brest."
—Rumann son of Colman, translated from Eighth Century Gaelic by Frank O'Connor

ONE OF MY FAVORITE BOOKS is Adlard Coles's *Heavy Weather Sailing*. It was first published in 1967, and I read it a few years later when I was still a kid. I was fascinated by storms even then, and the black-and-white pictures of towering waves, battered boats, and synoptic charts with tightly packed millibars and wind bars loaded with arrows sent chills down my spine. I had never been sailing on the ocean, and had actually sailed only once, on a Sunfish on a small Michigan lake, yet I desperately wanted to test myself at sea.

The other book that commanded a cherished spot next to my bed was Sir Francis Chichester's *Gypsy Moth Circles the Globe*. I can still picture *Gypy Moth IV*, with just a miniscule spitfire jib sheeted flat, rounding the Horn in a ferocious storm. *Yachting Monthly* magazine called it "one of the most unforgettable pictures in the history of small-boat passage making." That picture changed my life. Come hell or high water, I was going to sail around Cape Horn one day.

Francis Chichester supplied the motivation for my dreams, but Adlard Coles offered up details on how I might survive the storms I felt destined to encounter. Even today I can't break my addiction to this classic, and I reread *Heavy Weather Sailing* every few years. The latest edition was published in 2008, edited by Peter Bruce after Coles died in 1985. Bruce has maintained the understated, analytical approach to describing how sailors cope with storm conditions and updated the book with more recent storm stories.

This chapter is, with all humility aside, my small, personal version of *Heavy Weather Sailing*. It details my experiences in some of the storms that made my top ten list from Chapter Seven that are not described elsewhere in the book. What makes my experiences unique is that I have dealt with storms in a variety of boats and with very different crews. There are certainly lessons to be gleaned from my encounters, and more likely than not they've been lessons learned the hard way, or even the wrong way. I seem to learn only from my mistakes, and I hope the storm stories that follow will help you avoid some of the same pitfalls.

Force 13—Atlantic Crossing Gale

Date: January/February 1991
Location: 300 miles east of Newport, Rhode Island
Boat: Isobell, Ocean 71 ketch
Crew: 3

This is the storm that I mention, almost flippantly, in Chapter One, with me listening to the shortwave radio and hearing about Charles Taylor staging a coup d'état in Liberia. Shortly after that broadcast, the situation became dramatically worse.

According to the radio officer on the nearby Dutch tanker *Tania Jacob*, the wind was steady at Force 11 and consistently gusting to hurricane Force 12, or more than 63 knots. "We're even seeing some Force 13," he told me in a casual tone that belied the savage conditions. "And your weather service says the seas are 30 feet to 50 feet and the air temperature is –2 degrees C (28 degrees Fahrenheit)."

I knew the situation was serious, but Force 13? "The Beaufort scale doesn't go to 13, does it?" I asked.

He sensed the fear in my voice on the other end of the VHF radio. Chuckling, he said, "Then call it Force 'unlucky,' skipper. We will be standing by on Channel 16 if you need assistance. Good luck."

It was January 31 and we were 300 miles off the U.S. East Coast. We were bound for Sweden. Yes, Sweden. The logical question is: why would anybody sail across the Atlantic in the middle of the winter? The answers were economic, personal, and illogical. I was a delivery skipper, and the new owners wanted the boat in Sweden as soon as possible. That was simple. A midwinter crossing wasn't cheap, and nothing can make a sailor overlook a few double-digit gale percentages on the pilot chart faster than the prospect of a nice payday. And finally, I was compelled by the challenge of a winter crossing. That's another one of those things you either understand in your soul or you don't.

Even I wouldn't test the wintry North Atlantic in just any boat. *Isobell* was a twenty-year-old Ocean 71 ketch, designed by Van de Stadt and built by Southern Ocean Shipyard in the UK. Ruggedly constructed and designed for heavy weather, *Isobell* was able to withstand the six weeks of near constant gale force conditions that defined this passage. The Ocean 71 was, in many ways, a fiberglass version of the legendary offshore racer *Stormvogel*. Launched in 1961, *Stormvogel* was famous for winning the Fastnet Race, the Bermuda Race, the Cape Town to Rio Race, and a host of others. William F. Buckley chronicled his voyages in *Sealestial*, a chartered sister ship to *Isobell*, in the books *Atlantic High* and *Racing Through Paradise*. But that's getting ahead of the story because one of the longest nights of my life loomed just ahead. With a long fin keel, a deep forefoot, relatively low freeboard, and a powerful skeg-hung rudder, *Isobell* was made for handling heavy weather.

I knew I needed an excellent crew for the passage, but most of my usual shipmates thought I was crazy for wanting to sail across the Atlantic in the winter and took a pass on my invitation to join the fun. Poor Molly reluctantly signed on, at least for the first leg from Newport to the Azores. Fortunately, my dear friend Joe Murton from London also agreed to make the passage. Joe had just built a steel boat and was looking for some heavy-weather experience. I didn't disappoint him on that score. After shaking fresh ice out of the rigging, the three of us shoved off from Newport on January 26, 1991.

Our plan was to sail near or just below the 40th parallel to the Azores, a route that I hoped would keep us south of stray icebergs and in a tolerable climate zone. By staying in or near the Gulf Stream, we were looking at expected mean temperatures in the 40s (degrees F). Breaking the trip in the Azores added extra miles because we then had to sail back north to the English Channel. But it seemed like a sensible plan, especially with a small crew, an ever-present threat of ice, and extreme winter gales farther north. The weather forecast was promising, and the first two days of the passage were actually relatively warm and pleasant, allowing us to hurry past Georges Bank and the worrisome shallows that extend well off the East Coast of the United States. We were hoping that a large cold front would stay north of us.

That didn't happen. A series of nasty line squalls heralded the arrival of the front, and soon the wind backed to the southwest and piped up to gale force. A secondary low-pressure system had moved up from the Carolinas and merged with the cold front. Extreme weather was coming our way. We reduced sail steadily during the daylight hours. The main was reefed, then dropped, as we flew along on a reach with the mizzen, staysail, and small jib. Then we furled the jib. Finally, as darkness swallowed us we doused the mizzen and continued on a deep reach under staysail alone, at times hitting 14 knots with the wind gusting to hurricane force.

The wind had clocked back to the west and the seas were massive, but steering was still manageable, with the autopilot coping just fine. I never considered towing warps or reducing sail further to slow down the boat. We were actually snug beneath a makeshift canvas pilothouse that Joe had fashioned back in Newport.

Molly had the first watch. At 2100 she screamed, "We've lost the staysail." Joe and I struggled into our foul-weather gear and dashed on deck. I was amazed at the frenzied ocean around us. It looked like an old black-and-white negative, with the foam of breaking waves the only light source. In another boat these would have been pure survival conditions, but the Ocean 71 is the most seaworthy boat I have ever sailed. Without the staysail we were running under bare poles but still hitting double-digit speeds, and occasionally surfing down what had become massive seas. The wind felt as if it would lift me off the deck as I made my way forward, and I remember thinking that I had to stay low to not be carried away.

I quickly discovered why we had lost the staysail. The halyard had chafed through, and when the sail lost luff tension, all the bronze piston hanks ripped apart like plastic. The sail plunged over the side and was connected to the boat only by the tack and the sheets. We wrestled it aboard and stuffed it into the forward sail locker. Then we hauled the storm jib on deck, only to find that the luff had been cut to fit the furling gear foils on the forestay. This was an oversight of the skipper, namely me. I should have inspected the sail before shoving off. Taking the furled jib off the forestay in Force 13 conditions would have shredded it into hankies. And raising the storm jib in its place, feeding it into the headstay foils, would have been almost impossible.

We decided to raise the storm jib by tacking it to the staysail tack point and hoisting it loose luffed, meaning that only the head and tack of the sail were attached to the boat. It would soon prove to be a poor decision. It was a struggle, with the sail whipping wickedly, but Joe and I managed to raise it, and Molly trimmed the sheet. The motion was immediately better, and Molly was able to engage the autopilot.

A powerful wave crushed *Isobell* on the starboard beam and washed the decks just as Joe and I went below to warm up. The boat skidded off course and the storm jib backed violently. Then the tack shackle, which carried all the load of the sail, exploded. Without any hanks to keep it along the stay, it flew upward and turned into a marauding wrecking ball. It wiped the masthead clean of instruments, lights, and antennas and then plummeted into the water. Together with the sheet, which had ripped the staysail block right off the deck, the storm jib wound around the prop shaft with a death grip. The moaning of the shaft was terrifying. If the shaft was torn from the boat, we'd sink in the frigid waters of the winter Atlantic.

I grabbed my knife and was back on deck in a flash. Frantically I tried to cut the halyard end, which had jammed in the mast, thinking that it might free the sail if it could run through the mast and out through the masthead. But it was no use. Then, stretching over the side as far as I dared, I tried to cut the sheet, but it was just beyond my reach. I nearly sliced the knuckle off my thumb instead, and it hung by a mere strand of flesh.

But there was no time to think about it because Joe was screaming, "Now, now, John." He had pulled the sheet closer to the boat. I finally managed to cut it, and we watched the freed sail and sheet disappear into the blackness astern.

Once again we were running under bare poles. Molly, flailing the wheel one way and then the other, was doing a great job of steering, keeping the stern to the seas. Joe and I lay panting on the deck, knowing that we should hurry back to the cockpit. But we were completely spent. Freakishly the spreader lights popped on—for no reason, it seemed, other than to reveal a bloodstained deck. It looked gruesome, and I realized I had to deal with my thumb. Before I could, a jarring crash sent us dashing below.

The problem was in the engine room. The generator had sheered its mounts and toppled onto the Perkins diesel, threatening to destroy our main engine. Joe hurried to get a line as I wedged myself between the engine and the generator, a human fender, and a stupidly vulnerable position to place myself in. Using my legs I managed to prop up the generator, and Joe lashed it in place like a cowboy wrestling a steer.

Returning to the cockpit, my thumb wrapped in a towel, I was utterly exhausted when Molly informed me, "It's your watch. You're the one who wanted to sail across the Atlantic in the middle of the winter."

The storm force winds continued through the night and into the next day. We had no choice but to continue to run under bare poles. Luckily the wind was pushing us right where we wanted to go. Even a 75,000-pound boat rolled from gunwale to gunwale without a steadying sail. It was vital to keep the stern directly before the waves, and we steered in one-hour increments. Concentration was paramount, and we were lucky to have three capable crew for steering duty. The winds moderated by the following evening, and we cautiously unrolled a tiny bit of headsail. We had survived a Force 13 storm.

The two primary lessons that I took away from the storm were, first, how quickly things can deteriorate when one piece of equipment fails, and, second, in the right boat, running-off, even under bare poles, is a viable storm strategy. Within minutes we'd gone from flying along under staysail to near chaos with deadly whipping sails, sheets, and blocks flying around the boat.

This sounds eerily like the situation on deck during the lead-up to the Azores storm mentioned in Chapter Six.

As for tactics, we were content to run because we were essentially sailing directly on course throughout the storm. The Ocean 71, with its near 9-foot draft, low freeboard, and powerful underbody, tracked true running under bare poles, although it was still terrifying anytime we flashed our beam toward the seas. I doubt a smaller boat would have been able to employ the same point of sail. Additionally, although we had both a storm jib and a heavy staysail, both were rendered useless in a matter of minutes, a frightening reminder of the force of the wind in a deep ocean storm.

Rob at the helm, dressed for northern sailing. Although we use the autopilot, we also do plenty of hand steering on our passages. The oversize wheel makes it difficult to climb back to the helm station, but it sure is nice when "driving."

Cape Horn Snorter

Date: February 9, 1984
Location: 360 miles north of Cape Horn, 100 miles off the coast of Chile
Boat: Gigi, Contessa 32
Crew: 2

> *"The Horn lived up to its reputation again. In twelve hours its malign influences had transformed an innocuous summer low coming in out of the Southern Ocean into the most dangerous of storms, what old time square rigger sailors used to call a Cape Horn Snorter."*
>
> —Derek Lundy, The Way of a Ship

Technically, our Southern Ocean storm was not a Cape Horn Snorter. But *snorter* is a great word, and having rounded the Horn just a few days earlier, I think it is fair to use the phrase here. This memorable storm occurred on my long-ago voyage from New York to San Francisco by way of Cape Horn. The passage has been chronicled in many articles over the years and in my book *Cape Horn to Starboard*. We were sailing *Gigi*, a Contessa 32, and had planned a three-legged journey retracing the 16,000-mile route of America's Gold Rush clipper ships.

This storm occurred on leg two from Rio de Janeiro, Brazil, to Valparaiso, Chile, the Cape Horn run. *Gigi*'s owner, Ty Techera, was my crew. *Gigi* may have been the smallest boat to ever double Cape Horn to weather, which means to sail nonstop from the 50th parallel in the Atlantic, south around the Horn, and then north to the 50th parallel in the Pacific. The old sailing ship shanty described the passage: "*From 50 south to 50 south you won't grow fat and lazy, for the winds that blow off Cape Horn will surely drive you crazy.*"

We also may have been the first American yachtsmen, or at least small-boat sailors, to complete this difficult passage. But our voyage was never meant to be about records, and sailing in the shadow of Cape Horn you quickly realized that being the "first this" or the "smallest that" was meaningless. We had rounded Cape Horn a few days before and were nearly a month out of Rio de Janeiro when we encountered the worst storm of the entire passage.

In the Southern Ocean, where incessant westerly winds and huge seas sweep across vast reaches of ocean, the latitude belts have tough-sounding names to remind sailors what they're up against. While the "Furious Fifties" had been quite manageable, the "Roaring Forties" seemed determined to live up to their dirty reputation. No sooner than we had crossed the 50th parallel in the Pacific when a southwest gale developed. The winds quickly raised a fierce chop, and we beat into it, shortening sail all day long. Although we had sufficient sea room, 100 miles, the southern coast of Chile may be the most notorious lee shore on the planet, and I didn't want to get anywhere near it. I also didn't want to tack west, or even southwest, and lose hard-fought ground, so we sailed as close to the wind as possible on a port tack and clawed our way north.

The winds were steady at Force 8 (34 to 40 knots) and gusting higher. We had two reefs in the main and a small amount of furled headsail deployed, fighting for every inch of both sea room and forward progress. A different boat would have struggled to make progress, but the Contessa is made for hard windward sailing, with its fine entry, ridiculously low freeboard, deep draft, and moderately high-aspect rig (at least for its day). But a furled headsail produces lousy sheeting angles and a high center of effort. I knew that we'd have been better off with the staysail, but I was reluctant to trade course for speed. Or at least that's what I told myself. A note in my journal is revealing: "I just don't feel like climbing out there and getting soaked. We seem ok."

The northwest winds persisted. Four days of gale or near gale headwinds is very tough going in any boat, but it is particularly miserable in a small boat. We were wet all the time and able to pound out just a hundred miles or less each day. The winds finally moderated on February 9, but it was only the proverbial calm before the real storm. There's an old saying that isn't always true, but in this case it was: "The waves are the wind's messenger." It sounds more like Shakespeare than NOAA, but even the bard would have realized that the distinct swell rolling in from the south meant trouble ahead. Within twelve hours the wind was steady at 45 knots and routinely pegging our wind speed meter at 54 knots. We would later learn that the Chilean Coast Guard came to the aid of several vessels and classified the storm as Force 11, with 30-foot seas. What makes the Southern Ocean unique is how quickly depressions form and how rapidly they intensify.

We were lucky that the wind was blowing from the south and we were headed north. Because the majority of the 16,000-mile passage was against the prevailing winds, any downwind sailing was seen as a luxury. The seas were truly mountainous. Trust me, my memory has not turned this faraway tempest into something it wasn't. I just watched the old, grainy video I have of this storm, and I am still amazed by the massive seas and how the wind whips the tops of the waves like a child blowing out birthday candles. I am also rather amazed at how cavalier Ty and I appear. At that point in the voyage, thirty-three days at sea and most of it spent sailing upwind in the Southern Ocean, we were hardened and completely at home in our rugged environment. We didn't sense how vulnerable we were. Riding on nature's raw edge is where and when you are most profoundly alive.

We shortened sail in degrees, rolling in the headsail regularly, then taking the main off completely. The ride was exhilarating as *Gigi* would surf on the long crests, skidding and squirming at breakneck speeds until the wave outpaced her. I have a vivid memory of being picked up by a wave, sinking down into it like an artillery shell into a howitzer, and then firing forward as the wave top overcame the base and started to break. It was madness. I can also recall seeing fish in the wave curls that were higher than we were.

The euphoria faded as the storm raged into the night. Although we had just a foot or two of headsail set, I knew we had to set the storm jib on the staysail stay to lower the center of effort and push it aft. Inching forward on my fanny, I started to hank on the staysail just as a wave crashed aboard. *Gigi* was swamped by the cascading wave, and rushing water swept me into the netting along the lifelines. I came up laughing, and yelled back at Ty, "Hey, watch what you're doing." Then I noticed that the lanyard on my safety harness was not clipped to anything. I felt a chill sweep over me. I suddenly knew just how vulnerable we were.

With the storm jib set, the ride slowed and improved, but it was dicey all through the night. Twice we nearly broached. I told Ty that we had to change tactics and start to forereach, but he talked me out of it. "It's more dangerous to try to change course than to just keep running with it." He was right, and fortunately by the next morning the winds began to moderate.

Once again I had ridden out a severe storm by running downwind. Again, I never considered towing a drogue to slow down, although I am not sure why. If you look at the Ocean 71 and the Contessa 32 in profile (see the Contessa 32 on page 89), they have very similar hull shapes. They're from the same era and have the same design ethos that puts seaworthiness ahead of all else. They're two of the three most capable boats I've ever sailed. The third is the Hylas 49, which has a similar shape as well (see page 46).

Another factor that puts our Cape Horn Snorter in perspective is the crew. Although there were just two of us aboard, Ty and I were completely in concert with the boat. I had sailed *Gigi* from New York to the bottom of the world by that time, and I knew her every move, her every shudder. Sitting in the companionway I could predict her movements intuitively. Thoroughly knowing your boat is a critical advantage in heavy weather.

Hurricane Mitch

Date: November 1998
Location: 150 miles northeast of Eleuthera Island, Bahamas
Boat: Hylas 46
Crew: 4

Determining when to shove off on an offshore passage, and when not to, is a fundamental decision for skippers. Weather information is better today than ever before, and the ability to receive weather updates while underway has also dramatically improved, but the fact remains: you never really know you made the right decision until you get out there. This storm story discusses my encounter with the remnants of Hurricane Mitch, the deadliest Atlantic storm on record at the time. In hindsight, I could have avoided the storm altogether had I been a bit more patient, but delivery skippers don't get paid for being patient. Although we encountered winds gusting to hurricane force, we coped with the rapidly changing conditions very well by forereaching and heaving-to as the storm escalated. This storm is very instructive because another boat, the 42-foot cutter *Kampeska*, was just fifty miles north of us. Their crew chose to lie ahull, and a huge wave sent *Kampeska* in a 360-degree roll, totally debilitating her.

I was delivering a Hylas 46 from Fort Lauderdale to the Virgin Islands, a route I knew well and had sailed more than thirty times over the years. We were waiting for a decent weather window and keeping a close eye on Hurricane Mitch. The storm had cut a murderous swath along the coasts of Central America with winds that reached 155 knots and corresponding storm surges. Read Jim Carrier's riveting *The Ship and the Storm* to fully appreciate the wrath of Mitch.

Lumbering north toward the Yucatan Channel, Mitch began to fall apart. As the muddled mass of low pressure reached the Gulf of Mexico, it was forecast to lose steam as it ran into a high-pressure system to the north. It seemed like the perfect time to leave.

We cleared Fort Lauderdale on November 3, 1998, and hurried across a gentle Gulf Stream toward the Bahamas. The Hylas was brand new and, like most boats heading into charter service, not well equipped. My crew consisted of the new owners, husband and wife, and my dear friend Ed, whom you read about in Chapter Six. Ed had wanted to make the passage despite having been in a recent car accident that shattered his leg and forced him to limp around the boat with a cane. For two days we had perfect weather and sped east of the Bahamas.

The passage from Florida to the Caribbean is much more challenging than some realize. It is easy to assume that you head south to the islands, but that's not really the case. It is mostly an east-to-west affair, not north to south. Fort Lauderdale is at 26° N latitude and St. Thomas is at 18.5° N—a difference of 7.5 degrees. Longitudinally, Fort Lauderdale lies at 80° W and St. Thomas at 65° W—a difference of 15 degrees. So as I mentioned earlier, for every degree of latitude made good, you must sail two degrees of longitude. Adding to the fun is that the prevailing winds are from the east and become stronger and steadier as you punch farther south. My well-honed strategy was to push east to clear the Bahamas, then sail as close to the rhumb line as possible, knowing that we might have to lie in a long tack at the end of the passage.

On day three our luck ran out. Instead of dissipating, Mitch regrouped and headed east toward the Florida Keys. The storm that 24 hours earlier had been downgraded to a tropical depression suddenly had 45 knot winds with gusts to 60 knots in a newly reorganized tropical storm. Mitch crossed the Keys and then followed the coast north to Miami. Fowey Rocks Light Station off Biscayne Bay recorded a 63 knot peak gust. Instead of tracking north, Mitch continued to confound forecasters by turning east-northeast toward the Bahamas and gaining even more strength in warm Gulf Stream waters.

Once again the waves were the wind's messengers, a phenomenon of hurricanes, and soon a pronounced swell rolled in from the south-southeast. By noon the winds were up to 25 to 30 knots from the south, and the trusty barometer on my Casio watch was falling fast. Things were getting interesting. We were flying east under a deeply furled main and headsail. The ride was becoming progressively worse as the seas were transformed into powerful ocean rollers. I tuned my shortwave receiver to the NOAA broadcast, and in a scene right out of a cheap movie, just as the computerized voice of Perfect Paul announced "Tropical Storm Mitch has re-formed and is—" a wave washed aboard and silenced the radio for good. We knew Mitch was coming our way but had no details. We later learned that the eye of the re-formed storm passed 50 miles north of us. We were on the right-hand side of the storm, the worst place to be in a tropical storm in the Northern Hemisphere.

By 1600 we had steady Force 9 conditions and stronger gusts, a feature of tropical storms. We could hear the storm winding up and preparing to deliver big blows. The Hylas 46 was fitted with an internal roller-furling mainsail on the mast. We were still sailing on course with tiny sails. We wanted to take advantage of the wind direction, to make miles toward the waypoint, and at the same time move away from the storm. We were heading southeast, and the low-pressure system, which was rapidly becoming extratropical, was charging toward the northeast. Late-season hurricanes typically become extratropical when they move into more northerly latitudes over cold water. At this point they no longer suck their energy from warm tropical waters but instead from the horizontal temperature contrasts from frontal air masses. Their forward speed increases dramatically and is tacked on to the wind speed of the cyclone.

The wind was just forward of the beam and the seas were becoming extremely dangerous. I prayed that the roller-furling mainsail system would hold together. The boat was not fitted with an autopilot, and I steered for hours on end. The owner was able to take a turn at the wheel, but his wife was not. After a nasty fall she retired to her cabin and didn't emerge until we reached St. Thomas. Ed tried to steer, but with his shattered leg he couldn't support himself in the cockpit. True to form, though, he kept sending up cookies, granola bars, and sandwiches, anything to keep us going.

Storms always seem to save their worst mayhem for the dark hours. That night the winds frequently pinned our wind speed indicator at 63 knots. The seas continued to build, ultimately to 30 feet, as we learned later. The winds had backed from the south to southeast. We were essentially forereaching at this point, and the boat was handling incredibly well, easing along on course at 3 knots. At times I was underwater at the helm as waves washed over the boat. There was no spray dodger, and I had lashed the bimini, so there was no protection in the cockpit. My biggest concern was chafe, primarily on both furling lines. Having either the main or headsail furling line chafe through and suddenly unveil a full sail would have been disastrous. Every hour we adjusted the furling line positions, just by inches, to prevent chafe by transferring the load to different point on the lines.

I am certain we could have continued to forereach through the storm, and hastened our exit from the system, but the owner and I were too exhausted to steer all night. I decided to heave-to. Timing our tack into the wind between crests, we backed the sliver of jib. I experimented with the helm and eventually found the right balance, and the boat came to rest around 50 degrees off the wind. Our crabbing to leeward created windward turbulence, the so-called slick, and the ride was more than tolerable. I was even able to make spaghetti for supper.

The winds peaked around 2200. We learned afterward that several ships and yachts reported gusts over 70 knots. I will never forget sitting in the cockpit watching the wild sea surrounding us. The boat would ride up the face of a wave and slide harmlessly to leeward as the waves pressed under the keel. Mitch was moving fast, at 40 knots, which contributed to much of the wind speed. By midnight the worst was behind us. By 0200 the winds had backed all the way to the northeast and we were underway again, on course and making 7 knots slaloming through, around, and over confused seas.

Unfortunately, Mitch timed its assault on the North Atlantic to intercept a fleet of boats taking part in the Caribbean 1500 rally. Fifty-two boats, ranging from 30 feet to 60 feet, had departed Norfolk, Virginia, bound for the British Virgin Islands. As the storm track became obvious, many boats sought shelter in Bermuda. Some hove-to north of Mitch's track while a few others carried on, trying to get south and ahead of the brunt of the storm. But Mitch was moving too fast, and soon they were enduring the same storm conditions we were. The crew of the *Kampeska* was lucky to survive.

According to a detailed two-part account written by Tom Service in *Southwinds*, the owners were experienced bluewater sailors, and their boat, a Tayana 42 cutter, was stout and well equipped for passagemaking. The owner's brother and sister-in-law were also aboard. During the night of November 5, the skipper decided that he could not continue to fly any sail and would lie ahull. The crew tied themselves into their bunks and hung on. They made it through most of the night and felt that the worst was behind them, but just before first light a sinister wave reared up and struck *Kampeska* on the beam, sending her into a 360-degree roll. When she finally righted herself the hull was intact, but the mast and rigging had been torn away along with everything that had been stowed on deck, including the life raft. The mast, still connected to the boat by remnants of the rigging, was battering the hull as the boat careened about in huge seas. The crew was battered, too, and thankful to be alive. They immediately set off their EPIRB. Five hours later a Coast Guard C-130 rescue plane made contact, but it would be another 24 hours before they would be airlifted to safety.

There's plenty to be learned from our encounter with Mitch. We employed three storm strategies, adjusting our actions to meet the changing wind and sea conditions. From running to forereaching to finally lying hove-to, we coped with the storm despite being limited in our sail plan. I would like to have had an inner forestay and a storm jib, and also some form of protection in the cockpit, although I am not sure if it would have survived the many waves crashing over the deck. The seaworthy hull shape and stout construction of the Hylas 46, and the wherewithal to stay engaged with the storm, were the keys to our survival.

I think the takeaway lesson of our encounter with Mitch is the plight of *Kampeska*. Lying ahull is a bad idea, period. If you feel that you can't carry sail, then try to run under bare poles, and at the least try to present the stern or stern quarter to the breaking seas. Launch a drogue. Allowing the boat to drift and consequently take a huge breaking wave on the beam is suicidal. I don't want to judge the *Kampeska* crew's actions because I don't know what was going on aboard. There might be more to the story; there's almost always more to the story. Fortunately the crew was rescued, and although there were serious injuries, no lives were lost.

North Sea Force 10

Date: February 27, 1991
Location: 50 miles east of Ramsgate, England
Boat: Isobell, Ocean 71 ketch
Crew: 2

The North Sea is depressingly gray in fair weather. In a winter gale, it's a bleak shade of gray, the mere sight of which, as the storm pitched and heaved with barely concealed rage, can suck the spirit out of you. Back aboard *Isobell*, an Ocean 71 ketch I was delivering in midwinter to Sweden (see the first story in this chapter), Joe and I were bound across the North Sea from Plymouth, England, toward Kiel, Germany.

Molly had left the boat in the Azores and was replaced by my friend Steve Maseda for the passage up to England. Steve left the boat there and Joe and I pressed on, smelling the finish line. Once through the Kiel Canal we would be in the Baltic Sea, and from there Sweden seemed just around the corner. But it never pays to look ahead, and the North Sea had no intention of letting us slither over to Kiel without testing our resolve. Rereading my journal, I now realize that those were some of the toughest 300 miles I have ever sailed.

I remember clearing the Strait of Dover and looking at the churned-up North Sea ahead with a sense of bewilderment. I am Dante, I thought, entering the Inferno, with no hope in sight. The wind was from the north, and as we lost the lee and made our way offshore we felt the power of what would later grow into a Force 10 storm that would cause extensive flooding in Belgium and Holland. Why did we press on, you might ask? That's a fair question. The answer may be hard to swallow, but we were on a tight deadline. The owners wanted their boat in Sweden and Joe had to get back to work. Deadlines and sailing can be a toxic mix.

A deep low-pressure system that had begun as a nor'easter off North America had tracked across the Atlantic. After coming ashore in Ireland, it defied the official forecast and swept southeast instead, hammering us with hard north winds. Within an hour we were down to a double-reefed main, a staysail, and a reefed mizzen. Two hours later we dropped the mizzen and tied the third reef in the main. The north wind was steady at 40 knots and we beat right into it, trying to claw our way off the coast of Belgium.

I assumed the route from the English Channel to Germany was mostly an east-west affair, but a quick look at the chart reveals how wrong this assumption was. In another one of those tricks of geography, the coast of Europe bends north and, once clear of Dover, you have to sail on a heading of 30 degrees true or north-northeast for more than a hundred miles to clear the Frisian Islands off Holland and Germany. The entire European coast on this stretch is a treacherous lee shore with low-lying islands and plenty of off-lying shoals. We had to maintain sea room, but that was not easy to accomplish even in a powerful boat like *Isobell*.

Conditions rapidly deteriorated. Winds increased to a steady 45 knots, Force 9, and the seas became increasingly steep. The visibility was reduced to less than a half mile, a distance we knew with some degree of accuracy because we were tracking many ships on radar. This is one of the busiest commercial shipping lanes in the world, and the lack of visibility was a major concern. We considered turning around and reaching back toward the English Channel, but that option was not appealing due to the lack of visibility. I would have liked to heave-to, but I didn't feel we had enough sea room and I didn't want to lose the ability to move quickly if we found ourselves in the path of a ship. I chastised myself for my cavalier decision to leave port, and now Joe and I were in a precarious situation.

We had both the staysail and the storm jib repaired while we were Horta in the Azores, and we decided it was already past time to drop the staysail and replace it with the storm jib. The wind then ratcheted up another notch, and was steady at 50 knots with some gusts to hurricane strength. Luckily, as the center of the low dropped down on top of us, the winds backed to the northwest, giving some room to come up and gain some much needed sea room. I knew the sea state would have to improve eventually because, with the winds moving in a counterclockwise direction, they would soon be blowing from over the nearby English coast.

We next dropped the mainsail because the ride was rugged as we were making too much speed. With just the storm jib set, we forereached 60 degrees off the wind, which was actually our desired heading, and slowed our speed to around 4 knots. The ride was remarkably tolerable, although many waves continued to break on deck. Joe and I were both impressed and incredibly relieved how well *Isobell* forereached in truly severe conditions. We felt that as long as we could maintain that heading, we could take even more wind.

One of the reasons we were confident was because we were actually pretty comfortable inside the makeshift cockpit cover that Joe had fashioned back in Newport. Using lightweight cedar, he bent a wooden frame around the cockpit, ingenuously securing the planks without marring the fiberglass. Then he stapled shrink-wrap to the frame and lashed a canvas tarp over everything with just a small slit for visibility.

To our complete surprise the covering made it across the Atlantic, and looked like it was on its way to crossing the North Sea until a sudden gust that must have been 70 knots finally tore the canvas free. The shrink-wrap blew apart in seconds, and we were exposed to the elements and all their fury. "Hold on, John," Joe had shouted. "It's going to go." And it did. The entire frame blew right off the boat and into the air. It looked like Dorothy's house in *The Wizard of Oz*. We were both convinced that it must have landed in Holland, and hoped that it didn't kill any witches.

Although it was shocking to be in the now-open cockpit, *Isobell* was behaving herself. I had made mistakes previously when forereaching by either going too slow or too fast. By finding the right speed through the waves, I realized then—and still firmly believe today—that forereaching is the best storm management strategy (see Chapter Seven).

The low persisted for 30 hours. We were able to maintain our course most of the time, and actually found ourselves sailing a bit north of our rhumb line. When the storm started to moderate, we replaced the storm jib with the staysail and then hoisted the main with three reefs. Conditions were still rough when we reached Kiel two days later, but aside from having lost our cockpit cover, we were none the worse for wear.

The primary lesson learned from the North Sea Gale was that a cavalier disregard for the weather can land you in serious trouble, even in an incredibly seaworthy boat. Fortunately, forereaching allowed us to manage the storm successfully, and because the low was tracking south, the winds backed in a favorable direction. I am sure *Isobell* would have been able to heave-to effectively, but the thought of being immobile in a busy shipping lane seemed dangerous.

Capsize in Force 10

Date: November 1, 1983
Location: 250 miles southeast of Bermuda
Boat: Gigi, *Contessa 32*
Crew: 2

This storm, encountered early in *Gigi*'s Cape Horn expedition, is a good example of how a series of poor decisions nearly resulted in me being washed away. Although I have written extensively about this life-changing event, I have never been sure if I described the situation accurately. To reenact the storm here, I went back and read my Cape Horn journal and also looked at the 8-mm film footage I have of the storm and its aftermath. I had made an SSB call to a Detroit radio station the day after the storm, and from those comments I think that, if anything, I have tended to downplay how serious the situation really was, maybe in an attempt to not appear so stupid. Anyway, here's the story.

Molly and I cleared Bermuda on October 30, bound for Rio de Janeiro, more than 5,000 miles away, where she planned to leave me and the boat. Like many of these storm stories, there's a geography lesson in this one as well. South America does not lie directly below North America; it's actually almost entirely to the east of it. Our route to Fernando di Noronha, an island just off the eastern bulge of Brazil, was 135 degrees true, or exactly southeast. We had to traverse 35 degrees of latitude and 35 degrees of longitude before we could head due south along the coast of Brazil, and that didn't leave much margin for error. For that reason we hoped to gain as much easting as possible early in the passage.

The forecast was not favorable, but we pressed on just the same, using the flawed logic that if we couldn't cope with a gale off Bermuda, how would we ever round Cape Horn? I never dreamed that a "gale" off Bermuda would turn into a Force 10 storm and become one of the most challenging encounters of the entire expedition. The wind was from the southeast, naturally, so we were obliged to tack east and sail as close to the wind as possible. It was sloppy going and I felt terrible. I was seasick for one of the only times in my life as we sailed into steadily building seas.

We plunged to weather all day and night, tacking as the wind backed farther to the east. Although I didn't know it at the time, the gale was actually a developing tropical storm. In those pre-GPS days I was able to grab a sun sight at noon and total up a first day's run of 148 miles, really good going in a 32-foot boat sailing uphill.

Later that afternoon we found out why we were feeling sick. The spare five-gallon diesel jerry can that we carried for charging the batteries had sprung a pinhole leak and was dripping its wretched contents into the cockpit. In a fit of environmental terrorism that I am not proud of, I tossed the plastic can into the sea, and we scrubbed the cockpit clean. If only we had known about the thorough rinse the cockpit was about to receive, we would not have wasted the time and energy.

The night of November 1 was a night that I'd like to forget but never will. In addition to dealing with steadily building winds and seas, we were having serious gear issues. The headsail furling system was poorly designed and kept chafing the furling line. One minute we'd be beating with a deeply furled headsail and the next we'd have a 135 percent genoa fully deployed. Twice I effected splices in the line before dropping the sail completely and setting a small staysail on a mobile inner forestay. This experience, early in my sailing career, is one of the reasons I am always wary of furling line chafe.

It was obvious that things were going to get worse before they got better. The barometer was plunging and the clouds were black and swirling in cyclonic fashion. According to my journal, which I was dutiful in updating throughout the voyage, the winds were steady at Force 10, and I noted that there were more gusts above 50 knots than there were lulls below 40 knots. It was honking, and other than a gale in the Bay of Biscay the year before, was surely the most wind I'd encountered. We were approximately 250 miles southeast of Bermuda and continuing to claw to weather with a triple-reefed main and staysail. *Gigi* was amazingly firm-footed for such a small boat, and although the ride was brutal I didn't feel threatened, especially since I didn't have to worry about the furling gear.

As darkness descended it became obvious that if we hoped to get any rest, we had to ease the motion aboard. Our hard-won progress to windward had come at the expense of sleep. I made a curious decision and decided to drop the staysail and let *Gigi* ease along under only a triple-reefed mainsail. My thought was that we could continue to make progress while also softening the ride a bit by slowing down.

At first it seemed like a good idea. We inched along course making about 2 knots and riding nicely in the water. We had shortened our watches to two hours, and I had the 2000 to 2200 shift. When I shined a light on my watch, I was relieved to see that it was nearly 2200. All I had to do was pump the bilge, our end-of-watch ritual, and I could head below.

I heard the wave before I saw it. It's a sound I'll never forget, and I didn't hear it again for 28 years, until that night in the Gulf Stream that I wrote about at the beginning of this book. The wave crested with a roar that was alive, an animal about to strike, deep throated and hungry, a 20-foot wall of water poised perfectly in a tight curl, a catapult ready to unload. I remember turning my head just as the wave hit. *Gigi* went over violently to leeward, and I went with her, clutching the mainsheet out of desperation. I can recall with clarity the few seconds that I was completely submerged, and my reaction was strange. I was surprised, even amazed, that I was suddenly underwater, and slightly pissed off about it.

I am not sure what exactly happened underwater, but I do know that *Gigi* didn't roll through 360 degrees. She righted herself, and I came with her because I was harnessed to the boat and also tangled up in the mainsheet. When she broke the surface, she was facing 180 degrees in the opposite direction. Somehow she had pivoted underwater, as if in a desperate urge to find her way upright. The wave hit so hard that the leeward aft stanchions were bent nearly flush to the deck, caused in part by the weather cloths we had rigged. The boat was dead in the water, and I was able to pull myself back aboard, an advantage of a boat with 28 inches of freeboard with flattened stanchions and droopy lifelines.

My first reaction was to get to Molly, but I couldn't because the spray dodger had been crushed and blocked the companionway. I finally forced the hatch open and was immensely relieved to see that she was okay. She was thoroughly shaken but miraculously unhurt. There was so much water in the boat that she thought we'd been holed and was collecting the emergency ditch bag. I assured her we were not going down, although I didn't know if that was true or not.

A logical question to ask is why there was so much water below and, further, did we have the washboards in place. Of course it seems sensible to always have the washboards in place during heavy weather, but strangely that doesn't always feel right out there in a gale. First, the person below is completely cut off from what is happening on deck, and that's disconcerting. Second, the person on deck is completely cut off from the crew and the sanctuary below. I know this sounds silly, but storms are terrifying, and maintaining human contact is important. I have definitely had times when I have all the boards in place, especially with a big crew. And that's one feature of *Quetzal* that I like—she has stout but small teak doors that can be closed and secured in an instant but opened quickly too. I also have a heavy-weather washboard, made of StarBoard. But that long-ago night on *Gigi*, we had just two of three boards in place; the top one was removed for communication purposes, and that's why so much water flooded into the boat.

The mainsail was shredded, the steering vane was ripped off the stern, and everything on deck had vanished with the wave, but *Gigi* was basically intact. Her mast was still standing and the tiller was still responding. We were lying ahull.

When another wave crashed aboard, I realized that we couldn't just drift, and I took the tiller and steered downwind. We ran under bare poles all night, and several times waves broke across the transom, pooping us. We were most vulnerable after wallowing in the troughs, which left us slow to gather way before the next wave wracked us. I knew we actually needed more speed, but I was afraid to set sail in the dark, and I didn't know how badly the rig had been damaged. Molly spent hours emptying the interior by bucket because both bilge pump handles had been washed away. It was a long night.

We ran under bare poles for another 24 hours. Fortunately the conditions were moderating and we were able to assess the damage. The rig seemed relatively undamaged, and we bent on the spare mainsail. The furling extrusions, the aluminum sleeves that fit over the forestay and allow the sail to roller furl around the stay, were crumpled, but we had thought about this possibility before leaving and had fitted our spare jib with grommets and nylon straps to be able to set the sail in a conventional way over the extrusions. We even had a spare autopilot, and soon we were underway again. We ended up detouring to the Virgin Islands, a logical place to put *Gigi* back together again. We needed a break.

Writing about this storm always makes me a bit angry because I am certain that I was responsible for what happened. That's the lesson of this story. I slowed the boat too much. The wave that flattened us was actually the second one in a pair, albeit the larger and more dangerous one. *Gigi* had been hit by the preceding wave and knocked her off course. She was wallowing beam-to the waves when the next wave hit. She didn't have enough speed to respond and as a result ended up taking the wave at the worst spot, on the beam. If we had taken the wave off the bow, we would have been knocked down, but that would have been a much better fate.

I always sail with the lesson of this storm in mind. I had let my guard down and made a very poor decision. I knew we needed more speed before we were capsized, but I was just hoping to make it through the night. I also see in my journal that I had thought about heaving-to, but I didn't want to go up on the foredeck and deal with the storm jib. I was lazy and scared and indecisive, and we paid the price.

Unexpected Hurricane Bob

Date: August 16, 1991
Location: 200 miles southeast of Nassau, Bahamas
Boat: Southern Light, Hylas 44
Crew: 5

Whether or not you hate the cliché about it being a small world, it is particularly apt when it comes to sailing. Just the other day I received an e-mail from a reader asking my opinion about a used 1990 Hylas 44. I told him how much I admired the boat but warned him that most Hylas 44s of this era were ex-charter boats. I assured him that he should not write the boat off because of its possible ownership history, but I felt that he should be aware of it. I studied the listing he attached, and it piqued my interest. Although the boat was currently called *Atlantis*, it looked familiar. I asked if he knew whether the boat had a different name in the past, and he told me that it had several previous owners and had been named variously *Blue Mirage*, *Nike*, and *Southern Light*.

Of course, *Southern Light*. I knew the boat very well indeed.

In 1991 Dick Jachney, then the owner of Caribbean Yacht Charters, came up with the novel idea of offering an offshore navigational training passage as a cost-efficient way to transport two of his boats from his Virgin Islands charter base to Newport, Rhode Island, and then later to Annapolis, Maryland, for the fall boat shows. I became the director of the program and the skipper of *Southern Light*. With a crew of four relatively inexperienced sailors and the 16-year-old son of a dear friend for my mate, we set off from St. Thomas, U.S. Virgin Islands, bound for Nassau, Bahamas, the first leg of the CYC Navigation Passage. It was August 12, the heart of hurricane season.

Naturally we checked the tropical weather outlook before shoving off and felt that we had a clear window for what we expected to be a five- or six-day 850-mile passage that promised to be a nice reach before the southeast trades. The irony of hurricane season is that when there is not a tropical system brewing, the trade winds are milder and the weather is usually settled. If you ask powerboaters when the "season" is in Florida and the Bahamas, they'll almost assuredly tell you May through July, with some stretching things into late April and early August as bookends. Powerboaters like calm weather.

Just as we hoped, the trades settled in early and escorted us northwest toward the Bahamas on a gentle reach. Rolling along at 5 to 6 knots, I longed for a spinnaker, or at least a whisker pole. Still, life was pleasant aboard, and we even hove-to for a quick swim as we passed over the Puerto Rico Trench, which at nearly 30,000 feet is the deepest spot in the Atlantic. It's a bit creepy to dive into a translucent sea knowing that the bottom is nearly six miles beneath you. We stopped briefly in San Salvador, Puerto Rico, possibly the site of Columbus's original landfall, before carrying on toward Nassau in the late afternoon. We knew about a low-pressure system to the northeast, but it was not forecast to develop rapidly. Besides, we were heading away from it. Nassau was just 180 miles away, 30 hours at 6 knots.

When the purplish red light of dawn introduced August 17, 1991, it was clear that we were in for some dirty weather. One of the crew, Tim, a dentist from San Francisco, asked, "Is there any truth to that old saying 'red sky by morning, sailors take warning'?" Oh yes, there's plenty of truth to it. References go back to Biblical times. Shakespeare wrote about it in his poem "Venus and Adonis":

> Like a red morn that ever yet betokened
> Wreck to the seaman, tempest to the field,
> Sorrow to the shepherds, woe unto the birds,
> Gusts and foul flaws to herdmen and to herds.

A red sky horizon is never welcome in the morning, but in this case it didn't indicate a classic weather system moving from west to east. Typically a red sky in the morning reflects the dust particles of a system that is passing from west to east in the Northern Hemisphere—the direction that weather travels—and the red color is caused by moisture in the atmosphere. That long-ago morning's gloomy sky was a combination of weather systems, including a deepening low that was developing right on top of us.

Our weather-receiving equipment consisted of a handheld shortwave radio that didn't work very well, and a VHF radio to solicit information from passing ships. Although *Southern Light* was well designed and constructed, she wasn't set up for offshore sailing. She was set up like a charter boat, without any stormsails. As we motored over a calm sea, steering toward the northern tip of Eleuthera, which we had to round before heading southeast toward Nassau, we didn't know that the National Hurricane Center was issuing tropical storm warnings for the Bahamas between Eleuthera and Andros Islands. A band of low pressure east of the Bahamas had gradually developed into a tropical depression as we tarried in San Salvador. By the morning of August 17, it had been upgraded to a tropical storm and given the prosaic name of Bob. Ironically, we were positioned very near to where, seven years later, I'd ride out Hurricane Mitch.

Our situation changed rapidly. The winds picked up and abruptly backed from the east to the northwest. We were suddenly beating into a rising wind and choppy seas. Fortunately, because the center of the storm was not far off, there wasn't sufficient sea room, or fetch, for the seas to build, and the waves never became unmanageable. But the onset of the fierce wind gusts was impressive to witness. Within an hour the calms had given way to 40 knots of steady gale force winds with occasional hurricane blasts. And then it started to rain.

The rain was intense, an assault from which foul-weather gear offered minimal protection. I've never felt such a vicious, skin-piercing rain. We did everything we could to prepare the boat. We folded the bimini and frame and lashed them in place. Every item on deck was stored in a locker or below, and we lashed the chain locker and lazarettes. We dropped the main and lashed it to the boom with a dock line. We rigged up makeshift lee cloths in the main saloon, and stowed all personal gear. *Southern Light* was ready for Bob. Or so we thought.

Beating into the wind, we shortened the headsail as the wind increased, and eventually it was just a tad larger than a bath towel. One of many problems with furled sails as stormsails is that as the sail area is shortened, the lead angle changes, and even with the genoa track all the way forward it is difficult to maintain enough shape to sail upwind effectively. And, as mentioned before, the more you roll in a sail, the more you raise the center of effort and the more you reduce stability. Roller-furled headsails make terrible stormsails.

The ride was rough, and we crashed to windward on a course just east of due north. Roger, who was inadvisably perched on the companionway steps, lost his balance and took a hard fall. He was in severe pain, and it was clear that he had broken a couple of ribs. This is a terrible injury ashore, but it's even worse at sea. Fortunately, Tim, our hastily appointed medical officer, took control and eased him into the aft cabin bunk. He supported him with a combination of pillows and duffel bags and tended to him on his off-watches throughout the storm.

Tim and 16-year-old Max were my steady helmsmen. Max had grown up on a boat and had made his first passage to Bermuda when he was an infant. Today he's a successful software engineer and writer, and recently made a passage from Florida to New York City aboard his father, Edd Kalehoff's Swan 46. Edd and I have been friends for 30 years, the circle of sailing keeps spinning.

Out on deck, we had no protection at the helm. We took turns steering in 30-minute intervals. Waves swept the deck repeatedly, as the Hylas 44 is relatively low slung. A center-cockpit boat is dramatically wetter upwind in a gale than an equivalent aft-cockpit design. It's simple: you're closer to the point where waves break on the bow and deflect aft. I told Max to remember to adjust the furling line every time we changed helmsman. The headsail was under tremendous load, and if the furling line chafed through, suddenly unveiling the genoa, it could be disastrous.

Although we later learned that the storm was upgraded to hurricane status just as it passed over us, we had already suspected we were experiencing steady hurricane force winds. At times, when a wave would break on the bow, the boat would actually shift sideways—not heel excessively, just move—as though the wave energy was more of an escalator than a cascade.

The hours wore on and we were wet and cold to the core. We kept two people tethered in the cockpit and alternated steering, with Tim and Max on one, and big Harold—who had spent most of his life in a Washington bureaucracy instead of where he longed to be, at sea—and me on another. Fortunately we didn't have a lee shore to worry about, and we were well positioned to endure the fury. By forereaching north, and then later northeast, we were clawing our way away from Eleuthera. If we continued north, we'd clear the Abaco Islands and track out into the Atlantic. Ideally we'd have been heading northwest, but just knowing that we were making progress, more or less in the direction we needed to go, buoyed our spirits.

Our plans changed when Tim poked his head out of the companionway and announced that Roger was in great pain and it would really help to ease the motion aboard.

Once again this was before the days that GPS had become ubiquitous aboard boats, and we had not had a celestial fix since leaving San Salvador. At this point the wind had backed to the north, so coming about and running, which would definitely ease the motion, would take us south or southeast back toward the island. We had been dutifully updating our dead reckoning position, and I calculated that we had room to run southeast for at least 12 hours. But we had no choice and reluctantly turned south. With the wind aft, the tiny headsail jibed repeatedly. Steering required concentration and a seat-of-the pants sense of anticipation.

Soon the winds eased and became eerily calm. It was surreal. We had entered the eye of the hurricane, a reprieve that lasted about 45 minutes before the back side of Hurricane Bob blasted us with east-southeast winds. At least we were able to bring the boat back on course and run northwest.

The back side of the storm was short-lived. Bob was in a hurry and picking up forward speed. After leaving us behind, it moved up the East Coast, striking the south coast of Rhode Island and Massachusetts as a Category 2 hurricane on the Saffir/Simpson scale. Bob then regrouped, skirted Maine, and whacked the maritime provinces of Canada before ambling most of the way across the North Atlantic.

Some lessons just keep hitting me over the head, and our experience in Hurricane Bob reinforces the importance of having dedicated stormsails. Relying on a furled headsail is like playing Russian roulette. If the sail, furling line, or furling gear fails, your options are reduced dramatically. I knew we needed better stormsail and rig options, but I didn't have the authority to insist on the changes, and as a working skipper I was mostly concerned about getting a paycheck.

The second takeaway from our encounter with Bob is that winds are not nearly as dangerous or damaging as seas. Although the waves that washed the bow were powerful, they didn't have time to build into deadly, destructive walls. By the time Bob reached the New England coast, the accompanying storm surge was deadly, and it left a swath of devastation that covered hundreds of miles. And as with the other storms described, no one single tactic ensures safety in severe weather. You must adjust your strategy as conditions change.

Cape Hatteras Storm

Date: October 24–25, 1990
Location: Off the North Carolina Coast between Cape Hatteras and Cape Lookout
Boat: Swan 411
Crew: 3

With all due respect to Cape Flattery in Washington State, Cape Mendocino in California, and Point Conception in California, the continental American headland that stirs sailors to certify their life rafts and update their insurance policies is Cape Hatteras, North Carolina.

Physically, there is nothing dramatic about it. In fact, you wouldn't even know it was a headland without looking at a chart of the North Carolina Outer Banks. It's a sandy spit at the bend of elbow-shaped Hatteras Island, and on a summer day when it is covered with tourists it is difficult to understand why Cape Hatteras is infamous. I confess that I was something of a Hatteras skeptic, having rounded it without incident countless times as a delivery skipper and in a slew of different boats. However, the storm that I describe here made a believer out of me.

The waters off Cape Hatteras are treacherous because of a combination of meteorological and geographic factors. Start with Diamond Shoals, the shipwreck-littered collection of shifting offshore sandbars and shallow ridges that stretch east and southeast off the Cape. Then add the confluence of the warm Gulf Stream and the cold Labrador Current that make the waters near the Cape naturally turbulent and difficult to navigate, especially on southbound passages when boats are forced to cut Diamond Shoals dangerously close to avoid being set by the Gulf Stream. Finally, consider the jet stream, which passes overhead and escorts depressions out to sea near Cape Hatteras.

Together with my friend Bobby and my first mate, Dave, I picked up a 1978 Sparkman & Stephens-designed Swan 411 near Sandy Hook, New Jersey, south of New York City. We were bound for Fort Lauderdale with plans to drop Bobby in Morehead City, North Carolina, after rounding Cape Hatteras.

A cold front greeted us as we cleared New York Harbor, and we flew south on a deep reach. We tried to keep up with the front but ended up motoring in light airs. Still, 48 hours out of Sandy Hook we were tied up at the city docks in Morehead City after another easy rounding of Cape Hatteras. So much for it being the so-called Cape Horn of America.

Nancy replaced Bobby, and with the forecast calling for strong but favorable west-northwest winds, we shoved off. We figured that the challenging part of the passage was behind us, and we anticipated sailing south inshore of the Gulf Stream until we reached South Florida, where the current kisses the beach.

As we punched out of the Beaufort Inlet, the National Weather Service revised its forecast and called for near gale force winds and seas to 10 feet. Dave and I were not overly concerned, although we expected some tough windward sailing. I had met Dave in Sri Lanka several years before, and although he was in his early twenties, he was an experienced sailor and had already completed a circumnavigation. Nancy, on the other hand, was a new sailor and unprepared for the choppy seas we encountered. She was seasick immediately and retired to her bunk.

S&S-designed Swans are known for their solid construction and ability to sail to weather, and this one lived up to expectations. Blasting into steadily building seas, we were able to carry a reefed main and a furled headsail in 30 knots of wind. Unfortunately, the wind backed to the south, forcing us to tack to the southwest too close to the coast for my liking. We kicked up sheets of spray as we fought for every inch by pinching as close to the wind as possible. Soon it was obvious that we would never clear Cape Fear and off-lying Frying Pan Shoals near the South Carolina border. We tacked off-shore and then headed east, back toward the Gulf Stream. We managed to work our way past Cape Lookout Shoals (you do have to love the names of the Carolina capes) before darkness fell.

We found ourselves in the heart of the Gulf Stream as the weather turned truly nasty. It seems a low-pressure system had stalled along the coast, and the latest forecast was for gale force southeasterlies. Gale force turned out to be an understatement, and the storm that developed that night was one for the archives. The Diamond Shoals Light Station would report gusts to 80 knots, and the bridge linking Hatteras Island to the rest of the Outer Banks was wiped out, isolating the island for weeks. We didn't record 80 knots, but the wind did peg our wind speed indicator at 54 knots repeatedly

As the storm intensified, we kept shortening sail. We had to keep moving because the Gulf Stream was sweeping us north as we angled east. Cape Hatteras was drawing us back, as if to say not so fast JK, it's time for a little respect. Reduced to the third reef in the main and a storm jib hanked on to an inner forestay, we clawed our way across the current, crashing to windward in an aggressive form of forereaching. Dave and I stood two-hour watches, hand steering and getting completely soaked in the process.

The low-slung Swan offered no protection at the helm. The large bridge deck made it difficult to mount a spray dodger, and I am not sure it would have survived the Atlantic's onslaught anyway. It was almost like swimming at the helm as wave after wave washed over the boat. Yet I never felt unduly nervous. The boat was managing the wild conditions beautifully. The helm was light, and we had enough speed to steer into the worst breaking seas and fall off and gain speed when trapped in the troughs. Dave was an excellent helmsman, and we had confidence in each other. Despair never raised its ugly head, and we cheerfully swapped watches all night long. Sadly, Nancy was not able to overcome her seasickness and missed taking part in the amazing spectacle unfolding on deck.

Although we'd been carried all the way back to Cape Hatteras before we cleared the Gulf Stream, we were able to tack south as the winds continued to back. The seas were massive and confused. We decided not to fall off and instead continued to forereach through much of the next day, tracking well offshore. When the winds finally abated the next evening, we exchanged the storm jib for a bit of headsail and pointed the boat southwest toward Flor-ida. The following morning we were becalmed, wallowing in the leftover storm swells.

There are two lessons of the Cape Hatteras storm. First, the boat really does matter. You just can't escape this conclusion the more experience you have and the more miles you log. The Swan 411 was able to track into the teeth of the storm, never pounded, responded to the helm, and never shuddered under the force of waves crashing on deck. She didn't leak very much either, which, considering that at times it felt like we were on a submarine and not a sailboat, is impressive. Coping with the same conditions in a less capable boat would have been much more challenging. The second lesson is that the crew matters too. Having a talented helmsman is critical, but, just as importantly, having someone who maintains optimism when the weather deteriorates is a tremendous asset on any boat. Dave and I reached a weird but wonderful psychological state during the storm. We felt intensely alive, fully engaged, and utterly humbled by the power of the sea. If you can reach that point, trusting in your boat, your mate, and yourself, then a storm can actually be a good memory.

Bay of Biscay Force 10

Date: November 1982
Location: 100 miles southwest of l'île d'Ouessant (Ushant)
Boat: Gigi, Contessa 32
Crew: 2

This storm is memorable for me primarily because it was the first Force 10 gale I'd ever experienced, and it marked, at least in my mind, my transition from a stumbling midwestern kid into a bluewater sailor. True, this passage was many years ago, but not only have I documented it in many magazine articles and in *Cape Horn to Starboard*, I recently reread my surprisingly detailed and surprisingly legible account from my journal.

The brutal weather that we encountered southwest of the French island of Ouessant, which the English prefer to call Ushant, for some reason, was actually the culmination of a week of gale force conditions. Ty and I left Lymington Yacht Haven on the south coast of England on November 15, bound for the Canary Islands and then on east across the Atlantic. He was thrilled and I was nervous. He was 42, and wise and saw our voyage as a grand adventure. I was 23, not very wise, and I saw it as my first test as a skipper. Maybe I was wiser than I thought because I knew I was in over my head.

Gigi, Ty's stalwart Contessa 32, was brand new (see page 89 for illustration). Other than a two-hour test sail the day before, this was to be her maiden voyage, and she was in for a stormy christening. Although she was well equipped for the 5,000-mile trip, and her pedigree was beyond reproach, the same cannot be said about her crew. Our combined offshore experience could have been jotted down (with room to spare) on the back of the business card that I had printed up to impress Ty.

We battled a procession of southwest gales after leaving the protected waters of the Solent, near Chichester Harbor. We clawed west, tacking across the English Channel and crawling up the south coast of England. We lost one full day of hard-earned westing by heaving-to overnight in a Force 8 gale, and I learned just how strong the tidal currents are in the Channel. Running into the harbor of Dartmouth, in the pitch of dark and under bare poles, we were pooped. As a wave washed over the stern, *Gigi* rolled hard from side to side, but she kept her footing. I didn't know then that *Gigi* was as surefooted as a sherpa on Everest, and my confidence was shaken. If we couldn't heave-to, or run-off under bare poles, how would we ever deal with these nasty gales? Eventually I figured it out, but not without a shot of chutzpah from Ty.

We were holed up in Falmouth, having fought our way to the southwest corner of merry old England. The only thing left to do was to push off south, clear Ouessant, cross the Bay of Biscay, and make our way to the sunny Canaries. But the weather was brutal, and the forecast even worse. I was depressed, and wondering if we should give up and ship *Gigi* across the Atlantic on a freighter, when Ty suggested that the weather was improving and we should get going. I had just listened to the shipping forecast on the big, bulky, very expensive all-band Motorola shortwave receiver that I insisted he buy before the passage. "Did you hear the forecast?" I asked, both amused and shocked that he thought we should leave the security of the Falmouth Marina docks for the madness of the gales lurking just offshore. Ty was weary of the dreary forecasts that I listened to hour after hour, day after day, and asked to see the radio. We were sitting in the cockpit, tucked beneath the dodger and trying to stay warm and dry.

"You see the break in the clouds?" he asked, and indeed the sun was poking through the cumulonimbus for the first time in days. "That's a good sign. I'm sick of this box telling us what to do." And with that he stood up and tossed the radio into the harbor.

I shook my head in disbelief, and then I had to laugh. He was right; it was time to get moving. We climbed into our soggy foul-weather gear, readied the boat, and backed out of the slip. Soon we were clear of the harbor and heading past Lizard Point, beating south-southwest into the teeth of a stiff westerly. Ty was right. The sky was clearing, and for the first time in a week we were laying our rhumb line, although not by much.

Pushing the tiller down, I rode each lift to bank more sea room. I'd seen too many gruesome pictures of waves exploding against the rocks of Ouessant and didn't want to get anywhere near the place. Pre-GPS navigation required more caution, intuition, and seat-of-the pants sailing. I was also learning how to sail the Contessa: we needed to carry sail and maintain speed.

Shortening up at the first sign of heavy weather was counterproductive. *Gigi* was capable of making progress, especially upwind, when other boats would be hove-to. I had only read about what a fine sea boat the Contessa was; finally I was beginning to use her best attributes.

The westerly held through the night, and in the morning the sun made another rare appearance. I was able to take a sextant sight and cross it with a solid RDF bearing. (Can you imagine such primitive navigational techniques?) Plotting them on a universal plotting sheet, I determined that we were at last officially out of the English Channel.

But there was no time to celebrate with another southwest gale brewing. The clouds swallowed any open blue spaces overhead and the winds began to escalate. By lunchtime the wind speed indicator was steady above 40 knots. In the late afternoon the gusts were frequently above 50 knots.

The depth contours of the Bay of Biscay contribute to its fearsome reputation as a stormy and dangerous body of water. The continental shelf cuts across the bay, extending well offshore in the north but not in the south near the Spanish coast. Deep ocean waves spawned by the southwest gale became steep and deadly when they encountered the shallows just ahead of where *Gigi* was slugging along.

These were the worst conditions I had ever seen, but I was determined to keep moving. We set the bulletproof storm jib on the staysail stay and put the third reef in the main, but that was too much canvas. We dropped the main and drove forward under the storm jib alone. It was a wild ride, crashing into breaking seas, kicking up spray, being completely submerged time and again. It was easy to see how the Contessa had earned the nickname "submarine with sails."

I had, almost by accident, discovered the technique of forereaching. Fortunately Ty had the foresight to insist on serious lee cloths for the settee berths, and although the ride was brutal we managed to stay put and actually rest in the bunk when off-watch. Luckily it was a short-lived gale, 12 hours, the last breath of the sea monster that had dogged us since we left Lymington more than a week before. As the gale eased, the seas moderated as we made our way off the shelf and into deep water. Soon we were heading south under full sail, and I was a much smarter sailor.

The prime lesson I learned in this, my first serious gale, was that you have to use your boat's best attributes, both from a design and a construction standpoint, and not rely on a strategy that worked in other boats that you may have read or heard about. Second, I realized that an active approach to storm management is superior to a passive approach. Time and again as *Gigi* and I coped with gales during the Cape Horn passage, I used the technique of forereaching. And because I was able to bull my way through dicey situations, I've always looked at a boat with an eye toward whether it will be able to forereach when you really need it to.

Other Notable Heavy-Weather Experiences

- Gulfstar 50 ketch—the Pacific near Guam—ran before the full gale force winds of Typhoon Roy. Also hove-to in massive seas to wait for daylight before making landfall.
- Hylas 47/49—the Atlantic—ran before the remnants of Hurricane Grace and the deep low that resulted in the "perfect storm," made famous by Sebastian Junger. Also, several Force 8 gales in the North Atlantic, forereaching, heaving-to, and running.
- Beneteau Oceanus 46—the Atlantic—severe gale, Force 9, knocked down. Forereached through the worst of it.
- Roberts 45 ketch—the Caribbean—the so-called Storm of the Century, a wicked cold front offshore Belize. Forereached through Force 10 winds under double-reefed mizzen and storm jib.
- Fountaine Pajot Venezia 42 catamaran—the Atlantic—Force 9 November gale that sank two other yachts being delivered to the islands. We forereached until the seas became too difficult to manage, then ran-off under bare poles. Considered setting a sea anchor, but towing long lines slowed us enough that we never felt threatened.
- Moody 422—the Atlantic—midocean Force 9 gale. We hove-to for 12 hours and later forereached for 12 hours before conditions moderated.
- Jeanneau Gin Fizz—the Caribbean—encountered Tropical Storm Arlene, heaving-to at first and then later running before it. Twice we pooped, and nearly broached before the fast-moving system overran us.
- *Quetzal*—the Atlantic—several Force 8 and Force 9 storms, some of which you have read or will read about in this book, and others, including a tough passage south from Ireland across the Bay of Biscay, a full-throated gale in the Aegean, and a challenging passage from Bermuda to Fort Lauderdale.

The Best Storm Sailing Literature

Sailing literature has a proclivity for emphasizing—and in some cases overemphasizing—extreme conditions. From the wreck of St. Paul on the shores of Gozo to Joseph Conrad's savage imagery in the novel *Typhoon* to the recent sinking of the *Bounty* in Hurricane Sandy, storm stories have long captivated sailors and land people alike.

Let's face it, storms are a lot more exciting to read about than beautiful trade wind passages or lazy days on calm seas. Storm stories make us feel uncomfortable, vulnerable; the notion that it might very well have been us battling treacherous seas and shrieking winds instead of *(continued next page)* the unfortunate souls in the book connects us to the narrative, and we can't turn away until the protagonists either overcome adversity, or don't. In recent years, true storm stories have mushroomed into a genre all their own, led of course by Sebastian Junger's best seller *The Perfect Storm*. The only thing perfect about Junger's book is the title, and most sailors quickly recognize it as a gripping tale powerfully told from the perspective of a total lubber. Still, the combined commercial success of *The Perfect Storm* and accounts of several recent sailing disasters has spawned an outpouring of storm books, a veritable golden age of heavy-weather wisdom.

If you are new to the literature of storm sailing and want to find solid advice as well as some good reading, you have to tack through this body of work carefully. There are some great books, and some not so great books. Further, some of the classic sailing books by the masters, Slocum and Moitessier, still stand the test of time and offer solid advice cloaked in wonderful stories and beautiful prose. When it comes to advice about handling your boat in a blow, it is hard to beat Hal Roth and Lin and Larry Pardey. Of course *Heavy Weather Sailing*, described in this chapter, is still the best of the best, but here's a list of other storm books that I like and the reasons why I think they're worth reading.

***How to Sail Around the World*, by Hal Roth.** Roth's advice is timeless, and although some of it seems out of step with more modern boats, his four chapters on storm management present clear and concise strategies for heaving-to, lying ahull, setting drogues and sea anchors, and running-off. The term *management* is perfect because Roth keeps his emotions in check, something hard to do when talking about storms.

***Sailing Alone Around the World*, by Joshua Slocum.** Slocum's masterpiece is the book that all sailing books are judged by. His understated description of being driven back toward Cape Horn after clearing the Strait of Magellan is more powerful and instructive because of the author's humility and deep respect for the ocean and his stout sloop, *Spray*. All alone he contends with a great Cape Horn tempest, first by reefing, then running, towing lines, and finally negotiating the deadly breakers of the Milky Way on his way back to the Strait of Magellan. The lesson of remaining calm and fully engaged comes through loud and clear even though the adjectives are neatly furled.

***Fastnet, Force 10*, by John Rousmaniere.** Arguably the "first" modern storm book, Rousmaniere's well-respected account of the tragic 1979 Fastnet Race, which claimed fifteen lives, is told from two perspectives. He's an experienced sailor who actually sailed in the race, and also a professional journalist who later reconstructed the events and conditions leading up to the tragedy. Rousmaniere follows the fate of several boats, notably *Grimalkin*, *Trophy*, and *Ariadne*. His chapter "Lessons Learned and Unlearned" tries to summarize what in the end can only be described as a natural disaster and is refreshingly free of after-the-fact judgment.

The Long Way, by Bernard Moitessier. Readers know that Moitessier is my favorite sailing author, and this book is anything but a heavy-weather how-to book. It's more about attaining a state of mind that accepts storms and calms as equals, as part of the pact of going to sea, and without which the experience would be diminished. Moitessier was in some ways the first modern cruiser, and his discovery of running-off before the giant waves of the Southern Ocean without slowing the boat changed the way we all sail. He writes about heaving-to, knockdowns, and how seabirds tell him that a storm is on its way. We all need to read Moitessier.

Icebird, by David Lewis. This may be the most insane quest in the long annals of sailing quests. Lewis, an experienced sailor, passagemaker, medical doctor, and author, sets out in 1972 to sail alone around Antarctica. His boat, a doughty 32-foot steel sloop, is battered by severe storms. He survives capsizing, dismasting, and constant freezing temperatures. This is a testament to man's will to survive and gives readers a view into just how brutal conditions are in the extremes of latitude.

The Ship and the Storm, by Jim Carrier. Although not a book about small sailboats, Carrier's story is incredibly well told. This is the tale of the windjammer *Fantome,* a tall ship that gets overwhelmed by Hurricane Mitch. Yes, the same hurricane that we encountered in a Hylas 46 earlier in this chapter. Mitch seems intent on tracking down the *Fantome,* and despite doing everything possible to avoid the track of the deadly hurricane, *Fantome* meets its fate off the coast of Honduras. A great, if incredibly sad, story.

The Proving Ground, by Bruce G. Knecht. This is the best account of the tragic 1998 Sydney–Hobart race. This race ranks behind the '79 Fastnet when it comes to sailboat race disasters, and Knecht does a terrific job of following three boats into the heart of the storm. He had extensive interviews with Larry Ellison, whose maxi *Sayonara* was the eventual winner. Ellison is surprisingly frank about how terrified he was during the storm. Another good book about the race is *The Fatal Storm,* by Rob Mundle.

Storm Tactics Handbook, by Lin and Larry Pardey. Although I am not in agreement with the idea that heaving-to is always the best way to deal with severe conditions, especially in modern boats, I really like this book. I have great respect for the Pardeys, and their track record speaks for itself.   *(continued next page)*

Storm Tactics Handbook, now in its 3rd edition, is filled with great advice. The chapter on avoiding chafe is brilliant, and their thoughts on how stormsails should be designed and constructed speaks to their vast experience.

Bluewater Handbook, **by Steve Dashew.** This book is one of the few that looks at storm tactics from the perspective of a modern boat. Dashew is brilliant. He has logged as many offshore miles as anybody, and he's not bound by tradition. This is one of the few resources that give advice on forereaching, which can be the only option at times, and also talks about the limits of passive storm strategies. Although we differ on the types of boats we like, our thoughts are similar when it comes to handling severe weather.

Once is Enough, **by Miles Smeeton.** This account of Miles and Beryl Smeeton's two attempts to round Cape Horn is legendary. Together with John Guzzwell, they set off in 1956 aboard *Tzu Hang,* their 46-foot ketch, to cross the Southern Ocean. This is one of the early accounts of the huge seas that haunt those latitudes, and I remember reading this book as a boy and feeling the chills creep down my spine. And this was before they encountered the first of two destructive waves. As they approached the Horn, *Tzu Hang* was pitchpoled while running before a storm under bare poles. Beryl was flung out of the boat but managed to swim back to the wreckage and was hauled aboard. The story of jury-rigging the boat and repairing it in Chile is instructive and fascinating. The story of their second attempt on the Horn is downright heartbreaking. My version of this book is tattered from rereadings.

nine

Mediterranean Cruising—Dangers of an Inland
Sea | Mistrals | Cockpit/Deck Enclosures | Leaving
a Boat for Long Periods | Tornado Damage to a Boat
on the Hard | Fitting and Erecting a New Mast

Odyssey Redux

"Sailing conditions in the Mediterranean have been reviled and ridiculed by modern sailors more than any other part of the world and the most repeated saying is, 'in the Mediterranean one either gets too much wind or none at all, and what one gets is on the nose.' "

—Jimmy Cornell, World Cruising Routes

IF THE WINDS ARE RIGHT, from the northwest, and the pollution from nearby Cadiz is not too bad, you can smell the brandy from ten miles out to sea. Is that just my imagination, or maybe my anticipation? Puerto Santa Maria is not only home to the bodegas of the famous Osborne sherries and brandies, it is also the shellfish center of Spain. And yes, one more thing, Puerto Santa Maria is supposedly where Columbus's flagship was fitted out before his big trip in 1492.

The harbor is lined with open-air cafes that serve every kind of crustacean. I discovered this out-of-the-way corner of southwest Spain that's a day's sail from Gibraltar many years ago and always seem to find my way back to Puerto on my way to and from the Mediterranean. Seven days outbound from Horta, *Quetzal* slipped between the massive breakwaters into Puerto Sherry, an aptly named marina just outside Puerto Santa Maria.

As we eased alongside the control dock, four kids, obviously in a desperate race not to be the rotten egg, charged toward the boat and caught our lines. Their home away from home had finally arrived, and they were ready to throw their bags aboard and move in. Trailing behind, my wife, Tadji, smiled, and I sensed the relief in her eyes as we embraced on the wobbly dock. It had been a difficult passage. *Quetzal* was battered by storms and gear failures on her recent Atlantic crossing, the passage you read about in Chapter Six, and our grand summer plans of cruising the Mediterranean had been in jeopardy.

I rarely schedule training passages over the summer, taking time out for cruising instead. Tadji is a middle-school teacher, and although she's incredibly devoted to her students nine months of the year, the day school lets out she's ready to board the first plane to wherever *Quetzal* is docked. While the girls and I had made summer cruising a ritual, having explored New England, Nova Scotia, the Caribbean, and the Mediterranean, this summer was going to be different. Tadji and I had married in 2006 and suddenly we became a family of six, with her sons Nick and Alex joining my girls Nari and Annika.

The boys had sailed aboard *Quetzal* a few times on those rare occasions when she passed through Fort Lauderdale, but this was to be their first extended time on the boat. Although Tadji assured me that things would be fine, I confess that I was a bit nervous about the idea of "the Brady Bunch goes to sea." I anticipated turf wars, short tempers, and hurt feelings that can make a 47-foot boat seem very small. The girls had their own cabins when we lived aboard, and the boat had been their sanctuary after the divorce. Now the boys, Neptune help them, were moving into their sacred world.

Fortunately, my fears were overblown, and not surprisingly the kids saw things more clearly than their old man. Even at ages thirteen, eleven, ten, and eight, they sensed intuitively that the opportunity to spend the summer knocking about the Mediterranean outweighed any petty squabbles they might have, and as if on a mission to prove me completely wrong, they got along famously. It turned out to be our best family summer, and I miss those halcyon days when the kids actually liked being with their folks and were still unshackled from the scheduled activities that take over their lives.

The new crew finally pried me out of Puerto Santa Maria after a week of R and R. My time was mostly devoted to eating *gambas con ajo* (shrimp with garlic) and my favorite, *boquerones* (lightly grilled sardines), both of which had to be washed down with dry, pale, refreshingly cold Fino. If your idea of sherry is sickly, sweet, and warm, something like Harvey's Bristol Cream, do yourself a favor and sail across the Atlantic to Puerto Santa Maria. I suppose you could simply buy a nice bottle of Fino at Total Wine, but it just wouldn't be the same as sitting on the terrace at Romerijo with a plate of freshly caught shellfish in front of you.

Quetzal was also given some well-earned love. We had the injection pump rebuilt, proper freeze plugs installed, the dodger repaired, the staysail re-cut, and the stay replaced. Tadji cleaned the boat in a way that she'd never cleaned before, and *Quetzal* glistened as we threw off the bow mooring line, slipped the stern lines, and got underway.

Childbirth must be like passagemaking. There's something about both that creates paramnesia. The miseries of the last trip fade as quickly as the screams of a colicky child as all eyes are focused on the future, the next passage, the next kid. In my case, the knockdowns and breakdowns in the Atlantic, although just a few weeks removed, were already a distant memory. It was time to press on.

We made our way south, toward the Strait of Gibraltar, taking care to give shoals off Cape Trafalgar plenty of sea room. Our passage through what the ancient Greeks called the Pillars of Hercules was thrilling. A light westerly increased as we neared the Strait, not uncommon as winds tend to funnel between this narrow 8-mile-wide passage. Soon it was blowing near gale force, a local wind called the *vendavales* (see "Local Winds of the Mediterranean" on page 212), and we charged into the Mediterranean with too much sail up and too little margin for error. With a favorable current also giving us a boost, the GPS registered our speed over ground consistently above 10 knots and with a top burst of 14.3. I was hand steering and anxiously wondering how I should slow the boat down. The kids, on the other hand, cheered every time we raised the speed bar on the GPS. They weren't nervous, and I was reluctant to suck the thrill out of the afternoon. I decided to maintain the good cheer aboard and literally go with the flow. Laughing and joking with my brood, I was also steering extremely diligently with the wind directly astern and the main and genoa rigged wing and wing. We blasted past the blunt headland of Punta Almina, swung the boom over, and found a welcome lee in the shadow of the African continent.

Our landfall was Smir, Morocco. From the modern marina complex we made a trip back in time to the medina of nearby Tetouan. Walking through the maze of narrow alleyways, we would have been hopelessly lost without our guide, Mustafa. From street vendors hawking sheep heads and their brains, to women in *hijab*, to the haunting melodies of the Azan calling the faithful to prayer, Tetouan was an eye-opener for the kids. Then we drove inland to Chefchaouen, a village nestled in the foothills of the Atlas Mountains, before heading back to sea.

From Smir we made an overnight passage across the Mediterranean to Almerimar, Spain, where sprawling masses of hideous holiday homes encircle a friendly marina near Almeria. The winds were light and the sailing was easy, a perfect night for the kids to stand watch. Annika and Alex accompanied Tadji on the first shift, from 2100 to midnight. I had taught Alex how to plot, and he neatly and dutifully updated our position on the chart every 30 minutes. Annika, with sharp eyes, kept track of the many ships heading to and from Gibraltar. Nari and Nick stood a watch of their own and were chatting away happily when I relieved them at 0300. Nick had disengaged the autopilot and was steering on a sweet reach.

"There are a couple ships over there," Nari casually informed me, "heading toward Gib. And I'd keep an eye on those clouds over there. They might turn into something."

I bid them goodnight and laughed. My oldest daughter was definitely a sailor, and the others were following her lead. The brainwashing was working.

From Almerimar we made our way to the Balearic Islands, where we dropped the hook off chic Formentera. In what I swore was a complete navigational accident, we had anchored off a full nude beach, which was certainly a contrast to the medina in Morocco. In Ibiza we skipped the all-night discos and headed instead to the walled medieval citadel, Dalta Vila, a UNESCO World Heritage Site offering commanding vistas of the harbor below.

We eventually sailed north to Barcelona, where, with mixed feelings, we put the kids on a plane. They were heading home, to the other spouses, the reality of divorce. While Tadji and I were sad to see them go, the notion of having the boat to ourselves for almost a month helped us deal with the pangs of separation. And I will always deny those reports that we were seen high-fiving before the plane had even left the ground.

Tadji and I carried on along the rugged and starkly beautiful Costa Brava, the coast of Salvador Dali. Spain's northeastern region near France is one of the Mediterranean's most dramatic shorelines and the setting for Dali's famous works *Bathers of La Costa Brava* and *Leda Atomica*, among many others.

From Palamos we set off across the infamous Golfe du Lyon, and right on cue a mistral developed, making for a rough ride through the night. Local winds with wonderful names and dubious histories ply the Mediterranean. The mistral is a much-feared north wind that stalks the Golfe and whose effects can be felt as far away as the Balearic Islands, about a hundred miles to the south. The mistral is formed when a cold front in the Bay of Biscay is drawn south by low pressure in the Mediterranean. The winds funnel down the Rhone river valley and gallop out to sea at gale force. Mistrals generally occur in the winter months, and although the winds may be howling in excess of 50 knots, the skies are usually crystal clear. In the summer a "mistral light" occasionally forms, especially in July, but rarely lasts for more than 24 hours.

Although there wasn't much fetch, surprisingly nasty waves formed quickly and descended on us from the north. Tadji wasn't feeling well and ducked below to get some rest, a very sensible move. Even in July the breeze was quite cool, and sitting behind the wheel I lamented the destruction of the "patio" during the Atlantic crossing knockdowns. *Quetzal*'s patio was a full enclosure made of several panels that connected to the bimini frame and the spray dodger. Although I had paid a fair bit of money for it, it still had the look of a homemade contraption. A low-freeboard boat like *Quetzal* is not well suited for this type of cockpit cover, and waves seem to enjoy treating it like a bowling pin.

Still, I often make the case for the onboard patio. What is it that I like about them? That's easy: I like staying warm and dry. I know, you're screaming right now, what about the aesthetic poet back in Chapter Three who claimed that one of the ten most important design features states that a boat must be beautiful? I apologize, and I agree: nothing can mar the lines of an otherwise graceful boat more than an upright, see-through bomb shelter planted above the cockpit like a bad growth. But the tradeoff is—yes, I am saying this—worth it.

I spent years mocking cockpit enclosures and even wrote an article declaring that if you didn't like Neptune's signature elements, wind and spray, then you should stay off the water. With the all-knowing arrogance of youth, I suggested that if you no longer wanted to feel the breeze on your face, then maybe it was time for you to take up another pastime. Then I started sailing *Maya*, a Hylas 49 with the fullest of full enclosures. It was an ingenious creation, with panels that rolled down from the bimini top at a moment's notice. The first time we sailed through a gale and stayed dry and relatively comfortable, I began to change my tune. After sailing more than 15,000 miles, through some serious weather and rarely, if ever, donning foul-weather gear, I became a believer.

Now mind you, I am talking about removable enclosures, not fiberglass or aluminum permanent additions—some of which are beautifully sculpted and flow naturally with the lines of the boat and some, sadly, that are not quite as handsome. While I would consider adding a sleek and robust hard dodger to *Quetzal*, especially when we sail to the Arctic in a few years' time, that's a serious structural addition that requires a talented boatyard and a designer with a deft eye to properly execute. A simple set of marine fabric-rimmed clear panels that zip into the existing dodger and bimini top are easy to fashion and install. They're also easy to remove. Sometimes the ocean does it for you.

The mistral blew itself out in the night, and shortly after first light we made landfall off Porquerolles, the western most island in France's Iles d'Hyeres and part of a marine national park. We ambled east, calling at St. Tropez, Port Grimaud, and Cannes, in coastal Provence, before setting off across the Ligurian Sea. The wind was fresh and we were close-reaching at hull speed, 8.5 knots.

Looking behind, Tadji spotted the unmistakable rig of *Maltese Falcon*. Built by famed Italian yard Perini Navi for American venture capitalist Tom Perkins, the private yacht is nearly 300 feet long, with three massive free-standing carbon fiber masts and fifteen electronically controlled squaresails. She cut an impressive wake, and she must have been doing 20 knots or more under full sail. She blew by us as though we were dragging a sea anchor. It was a bit surreal that there was only one person visible on deck, and he waved feebly as one of the most impressive sailboats ever designed and built strode silently past us. Now owned by hedge fund operator Elena Ambrosiadou, who bought her for the bargain price of $100 million, you can charter *Maltese Falcon* for just $500,000 or so for a week.

As *Maltese Falcon* put a "horizon job" on poor old *Quetzal*, the weather began to change abruptly. In classic Mediterranean fashion, the wind shifted 90 degrees and piped up to 25 knots from the south. The seas were suddenly confused, and *Quetzal* pitched about searching for her footing. Tadji, who had been lying out in her bikini and asking why she wasn't aboard *Maltese Falcon*, wondered what was going on. Just as she sat up and pulled on her sweatshirt, a steep wave curled off the stern and crashed aboard the boat, catching us completely by surprise. It was another one of those damn rogue-ish waves, and it rocked the boat from gunwale to gunwale and flooded the cockpit. Tadji, completely soaked, was stunned. Although we weren't in any danger—the only damage was to the sat phone and the pilot book—the incident was unnerving for her. I read her thoughts. "If you can encounter a wave like that on a nice Mediterranean afternoon, what's possible in the middle of the ocean?" I tried to reassure her, and debunk the entire notion of rogue waves, but, suddenly cold and wet, she wasn't buying my so-called logic.

Naturally the wind soon died, and we ended up motoring into the large commercial port of Genoa, Italy, hometown of Christopher Columbus and that other famous Italian mariner, Andrea Doria, who is best known for having ships named after him. We spent several days in Genoa, preparing for a training passage that would take us south to Corsica and back to Barcelona. We left the boat near Barcelona, in a new marina just up the coast, and flew home.

In what had become the pattern of my life, I was home for three weeks and then headed back to the boat for a month. My next passage took me to the Balearic Islands of Majorca and Menorca before crossing to Sardinia and on to Rome, well Ostia anyway, the ancient port city.

After that, I left the boat in a new marina near the airport and flew home again. I was back a month later for *Quetzal*'s last passage of the season, a voyage to Greece by way of the Straits of Messina, Sicily, and the Ionian Sea. We raced across the Ionian, trying to outpace a forecasted gale that never materialized. We came to rest in Lefkada, an olive tree- and vine-covered island with a well-protected port. I hauled *Quetzal* for the winter after crisscrossing the Med like a drugged lab rat during the summer.

This was not the first time I had left *Quetzal* in a distant country for a long period. She had previously spent months unattended in Trinidad, Antigua, St. Martin, Spain, and Panama. And since her winter in Lefkada, *Quetzal* has been abandoned by her owner in Italy, Turkey, Canada, Ireland, and Malta. Of course this is the only way that I can make my two worlds work. I need to be home, close to my family, but I also need to be away, at sea, because that's what I do, that's what I have always done, that's how I make my living and maintain my sanity. Finding secure marinas to leave the boat lets me live my double life.

Leaving your boat for long periods is also a new model for cruising known as "commuter cruising." Even the most devoted long-distance sailors will confess that they need a break from the boat from time to time. Time off the boat can keep cruising fresh and extend your traveling options. For many cruising couples, one person usually has a harder time leaving their world behind than the other. Instead of forcing a partner to be miserable, a compromise arranged around part-time cruising can satisfy both. Also, leaving the boat can free up cruisers to travel inland when they reach intriguing destinations.

My mother and her partner, Tim, frequently left their boat during their circumnavigation to travel ashore. They bought inexpensive used cars in New Zealand and Turkey and made long overland trips. They also left the boat for months in Australia while they explored Southeast Asia by plane and ferry. Mom returned home every six months, leaving Tim to watch the boat. She needed to check on her business, visit her family, and recharge her batteries with a dose of land life.

The major decision when you leave your boat is whether to haul it out or leave it in the water. I have done both over the years. The deciding factors for me are how long I am going to be away, the marina facilities, and the season. Anytime I expect to be away less than a couple of months, I tend to leave it in the water. It is a lot less hassle to prepare the boat for sea when you return. If I am going to be away for more than a couple of months, I usually haul the boat out, just for peace of mind. During shorter absences when I leave the boat in the water, I make sure it is well secured with spare lines, chafing gear, and extra fenders. I prefer marinas to moorings and feel that the boat is more secure in a slip. I am wary of leaving the boat on a mooring unless I know that the mooring and tackle are in good shape and the boat will be watched. I have left *Quetzal* in Lunenburg, Nova Scotia, for many months at a time riding on my dear friend Alan Creaser's robust mooring. I know it's robust because *Quetzal* rode out a direct hit from Hurricane Earl in 2010 on Alan's mooring. Alan has no choice but to keep an eye on the boat. She's like a painting framed by the picture window in his living room.

I do a lot of research to find the right marina for leaving the boat before I arrive at my destination. I am often moving fast at the end of a passage and don't have time to poke the boat into one marina after another, shopping around. Fortunately, most marinas have websites these days, and it's easy to make contact from afar.

Sometimes I make arrangements to have someone watch the boat while I am away, but usually I don't. I am not by nature suspicious, but at the same time it doesn't seem wise to announce the fact that I will be away for a long time. I am usually coy about letting others know exactly when I will be back. If I meet fellow sailors whom I can obviously trust, I might enlist their help, but usually I don't like to burden them. I have had decent success in scheduling low-tech repairs while away, and at least this shows some life on the boat when a technician turns up and others see that the boat is not abandoned.

After a terrible experience in Trinidad, where a lazy yard worker took a belt sander to my teaks, I will never again commission serious repairs unless I am there to oversee the work.

I launched *Quetzal* in March from Lefkada and with a great crew sailed toward Athens. Steve, Dan, and Jerry joined my friends Bob and Rick for a cool and blustery passage across the Gulf of Corinth. We squeezed into the ancient Venetian harbor at Nafpaktos, an alluring place designed for dories, and secured *Quetzal* to a couple of fishing boats.

We were ashore having lunch when blue skies suddenly gave way to ugly greenish gray storm clouds. You could smell the wind. It was going to blow, and the weather deteriorated almost instantly. We paid our bill, left the rest of our lunch on the table, and dashed for the harbor. We made it just before *Quetzal* crashed into the ancient rampart standing sentinel over the tiny port. We leaped aboard and powered into the Gulf. Within minutes it was blowing a gale, then a full gale, and finally a Force 10 storm.

Luckily the winds were from the west, and we shot east. Conditions continued to deteriorate, but the seas hadn't had time to build, and the boat was well balanced under the staysail alone. I recalled a Greek sailor I had met in Lefkada who assured me that gales on the Gulf lasted at least three days. We made our way to the tiny island of Nisis Trizonia, which had a very secure harbor, and found an open spot along the harbor wall. We were smart to pick the lee side of the concrete wall so that the gale force winds blew us off the wall and not onto it.

My Greek friend was right; it blew hard for 72 hours. While the crews of other boats struggled to keep their fenders in place, we were able to get to know some of the local fishermen, and some of the local wines, in a small *taverna* in town.

We eventually made our way through the one-way Corinth Canal to Athens, where once again I left *Quetzal*, this time for a month. When I returned, another crew joined the boat and we set off for Turkey. Harry, Velinda, John, Nan, and Kevin had signed aboard to help me retrace at least some of the route of the most famous sailor of all, Odysseus. His protracted route from Troy, located along the Dardanelles on the Turkish coast, back to his home island of Ithaca in the Ionian Sea, is much disputed. A bevy of historians and sailors, from Ernle Bradford to Tim Severin to Hal Roth, have made voyages based on close but always subjective interpretations of Homer's epic *The Odyssey*. Our voyage was not that serious. We were looking for the spirit of Odysseus as much as his actual sailing track.

Our first night we anchored in the shadow of the ancient temple of Poseidon, overlooking the small cove at Cape Sounion, at the southeast tip of the Attica Peninsula. The next morning we hoped to set sail for a passage directly to Troy, or at least to the nearest marina at Ayvalik, 200 miles across the Aegean.

Maybe we should have offered a sacrifice to Poseidon when we visited the temple, but virgins were in short supply. Poseidon was clearly upset, and instead of the 15 knot westerly forecast, we encountered cold north winds gusting to Force 7, or 30 knots. It felt a lot like the summer *meltimi* (see Etesian in "Local Winds of the Mediterranean" on page 213), the feisty local wind that makes sailing the Aegean challenging and rewarding. The meltimi is caused by high pressure over the Balkans and low pressure over Turkey and brings strong winds to the Aegean Sea, which lies between them. Typically a meltimi is at its meekest in the spring. For this reason I had hoped we would be able to sail north-northeast toward Troy without too much trouble.

The winds built all day, and by late afternoon we were down to a double-reefed main and a staysail, pounding to weather against rising seas. We decided to detour to Gaviro, a quaint and supposedly well-protected harbor on the island of Andros. It was a smart decision as the heavy winds persisted for a couple of days. We had front seats to the Greek Orthodox Good Friday parade, as the faithful, ignoring the cold rain, marched through town with a cross and tabernacle on their shoulders. We were definitely finding the spirit of Odysseus as the winds thwarted our every turn.

We decided to head for Kusadasi, Turkey, instead of Troy, and sail in the lee of the Greek islands to make progress. At Ikaria, named for Icarus, the high flyer from Greek mythology, we moored in the harbor just as locals were hanging a stuffed Judas in effigy on the breakwall as part of their Easter celebration. As soon as it turned dark, they doused him with gasoline and set him on fire. Fireworks stuffed inside Judas shot in every direction, with a couple just missing *Quetzal*. It was an Easter to remember.

At Samos, the home island of mathematician Pythagoras, we explored the handsome port city named Pythagoreio. A week out of Athens we made it to Turkey. We spent a couple days enjoying Kusadasi, and made a side trip to the impressive Greek and then later Roman ruins of Ephesus, which in its heyday was one of the seven wonders of the ancient world.

Tracking Odysseus was not a casual cruise. It was work, and soon we were back at it, motoring across tranquil seas, thoroughly frustrated. Where was Aeolus, the god of wind, when you needed him? We empathized with Odysseus; the gods in this part of the world are fickle. We skirted Cape Malea, known as the Cape Horn of the Mediterranean, in waters so calm you could have shaved in their mirrored reflection. We anchored off Methoni, on the bottom of the Peloponnese Peninsula, and explored the well-preserved Venetian castle. We had no proof, but all concluded that Odysseus would likely have stopped there, if just for the delicious kalamata olives.

Back in the Ionian Sea, we sailed north to Ithaca, our hero's home island, where his faithful wife, Penelope, was warding off the suitors who, after his twenty-year absence, were trying to convince her that he wasn't coming back and thus she should marry one of them. We anchored in the expansive harbor of Vathi, rented a car, and drove to the Cave of the Nymphs, were Odysseus finally washed ashore and plotted his revenge on the suitors.

Our next passage took us from Corfu north to the spectacular Kotor fjord of Montenegro and along the craggy coastline of Croatia. Amy, a frequent shipmate, as well as Dave, Diane, Tom, and Steve joined me as we concluded a most enjoyable passage by sailing into Venice.

It was June, that wonderful time of year again, and Tadji and the kids soon turned up and we spent a delightful week in Venice. We had found a small, local marina in Sant'Elena, on the southeast tip of the island, and staying aboard the boat was the only affordable way to spend time in this enchanting city by, and of, the sea.

We had only a month to cruise because Tadji and I had big plans that summer. We had organized an "around-the-world" (sort of) charter sailing trip and had to be in Los Angeles by early July. We sailed back to the Istria peninsula of Croatia. In Pula, the kids and I watched Croatia lose to Turkey in Euro Cup soccer on a giant screen in an ancient Roman coliseum. We left before the game ended. A good move, because the Croats did not take the loss well and violence erupted.

Sailing north, we visited the lovely city of Piran in Slovenia, and then finally made our way to Grado, an Italian beach resort perched on the northern shore of the Adriatic.

Although I had several Mediterranean training passages scheduled for the fall, I decided to haul *Quetzal* at the small, family-run boatyard of Porto San Vito. I just didn't want to take any chances and wanted to know that *Quetzal* would be secure while I was out of touch. The five-week around-the-world-trip would take us to Tahiti and nearby islands, the Great Barrier Reef of Australia, Phuket, Thailand, and finally back to the Sporades Islands in the Aegean. We would spend a week chartering a boat in each locale and then fly to the next destination with seven others set to join us for this unique voyage.

I was impressed with Gianfranco, the yard owner, and his son Andrea, who spoke a bit of English. I felt secure leaving the boat in their capable hands. *Quetzal* was propped up in a steel cradle, which I thought was better than being supported by randomly placed jack stands. Unfortunately, that did not turn out to be the case. Tadji thought it was a bit absurd when I gave the boat a couple of pats on her hull and told her to behave herself before the taxi pulled away.

The word *tornado* has no direct translation from English to Italian, but *disaster* translates perfectly. And you don't need a Rosetta Stone course to know how to interpret *"disastro."* We had been home from the around-the-world trip all of one day when Andrea called from Italy.

"John, my friend, your boat, actually your tree . . . Oh, John, I am so sorry, but there's been a terrible *disastro."* He was speaking rapidly, pausing for exaggerated breaths and to corral his thoughts in English. "John, you must come to Grado quickly."

"Andrea, relax, slow down. What do you mean, what about the trees?"

"No, John, not the trees. The tree on your boat. It has been destroyed by a terrible wind, by what you call a tornado. It is a crazy wind. Never before have we had such a wind. It came like a thief, at midnight. I hate that wind, John, I hate it."

By the end of the conversation, I knew that *Quetzal* had been damaged in a freak tornado and at the very least the mast was destroyed. Andrea said he would e-mail pictures to me, but I wasn't in the mood for pictures. After a bout of screaming and throwing things around the house, I calmed my nerves and booked the first flight to Venice.

The transatlantic flight dragged on, and I couldn't shake the worst-case scenarios from my mind. I had visions of the boat sprawled across the tarmac. It didn't seem possible to lose the rig without seriously damaging the hull and other parts of the boat as well. I know it's irrational to love a hunk of fiberglass, teak, and stainless steel, but as I've said several times in this book, you either get it or you don't. I love my boat, and on that long flight, wedged in the middle seat, my heart ached.

It was impossible to read on the plane, and I passed the time torturing myself by replaying my many passages aboard *Quetzal.* By the late summer of 2008, I had owned her five years and already logged 50,000 miles. But the miles were not important; days at sea spent with customers who had become close friends, and with my family, kept racing through my mind. We'd been all over the Atlantic, from Nova Scotia to Panama, and sailed from Florida to Turkey. We'd endured some serious storms, and it galled me to think that my beautiful boat had been ambushed while stranded ashore. I felt guilty as hell.

I couldn't actually get myself to turn into the boatyard parking lot, and instead drove the rent-a-car around Grado one more time, stopping for a cappuccino to compose myself. Finally I pulled into the lot and there, right before me, was *Quetzal.* She was propped up in a different cradle, but aside from a hideous stump of a mast, she looked proud and defiant. I took a deep breath and felt a tidal wave of relief wash over me. At that moment I knew two things: I had a mountain of work ahead of me, and *Quetzal* would soon be back where she belonged, at sea.

Gianfranco greeted me with a hug, and although he spoke no English we understood each other perfectly. I couldn't blame him; blame is for fools and attorneys. He was devastated and felt terribly responsible. Soon Andrea arrived and explained what had happened. A freak tornado had ravaged

Grado and the boatyard, killing two tourists. Five boats went down in the yard before the tornado spun out to sea. Miraculously *Quetzal* had fallen to her right and toppled into the superstructure of a large motoryacht parked next to her. The mast became entangled in the boat's bridge and served to keep the hull from hitting the ground. The rig was completely destroyed, but the hull, aside from two small gouges and some impressive scratches, was otherwise undamaged. I gained a new appreciation for top-heavy motoryachts.

Gianfranco insisted on repairing the hull at his own expense and assisted me in every way possible to find and install a new rig. My Italian was only slightly better than his English, but we are similar men, with similar passions, and we communicated on an intuitive level. When it came to specifics, Andrea was our translator. The three of us became fast friends, and I had many meals in their home over the next couple of months. Instead of distancing themselves from my troubles, they did all they could to help me. One of these days I am going to sail back into Grado and take them out to dinner. I think I will leave the boat in the marina this time, however.

The logistics of my task were daunting. It was mid-August. I had to find a new mast, get it to Grado, rig the boat, and sail to Gibraltar by the end of November. I had canceled two Mediterranean passages and couldn't afford to scrub the transatlantic passage scheduled for December. The trip was booked and I desperately needed the money. My liability-only insurance offered no financial assistance. I was on my own. Or was I?

Gianfranco had to cut the mast and rig with a Sawzall to extract *Quetzal* from the clutches of the motoryacht, and as a result the rig was a complete write-off. I had originally hoped to save the section of the spar above the splice, but I quickly realized this wasn't an option. Alspar, a defunct Australian company, had built *Quetzal*'s mast more than twenty years earlier, and trying to track down the right aluminum section was a waste of precious time. I needed a new mast, all the standing rigging, and a headsail-furling system. This realization was a low moment.

Tom Sharkey, the general manager of Seldén Mast, USA, a division of the world's largest mast builder, based in Sweden, came to my rescue. I have known Tom since I had worked for him at his small Florida rigging company 20 years earlier. He'd install the rigs on all the new Hylas yachts, and I would deliver them to the Caribbean charter base. We were always on deadline: he'd be slipping in the last cotter pin as I was slipping off the last dock line. He understood my plight. I needed a rig, I needed it fast, and I didn't have a big insurance settlement to pay for it. "We'll figure this out, John," he assured me. "Relax."

My first job was to measure the old mast as accurately as possible. Although designer Mike Kaufman provided the original mast specs, he cautioned me not to rely on them exclusively. "They should just confirm your measurements," he told me.

I am not good at measuring, tending to ignore the carpenter's mantra of "measure twice, cut once." But this time I measured my heart out, double- and triple-checking each one. I measured everything I could think of—the length and width of the spreaders, the exact position of the chainplates on deck, even the length of the mast splice. Like most big-boat masts, my old mast was built in two pieces and then joined with an inner sleeve. The new Seldén mast would be built the same way. Finally I took my trusty grinder and cut a clean section of the old mast and made a tracing of the extrusion. I flew home and mailed all of this information to Tom and his capable sales manager, Bernie Beasley.

Custom masts are not built overnight. A typical production schedule is two months, and that's after the design and engineering process is complete. I didn't have that kind of time, and fortunately Tom and Bernie pushed my job to the front of the custom production list. Although based in Sweden, Seldén has far-flung operations. My mast was designed in Sweden, built in La Roche-sur-Yon in western France, and then trucked to Grado. There were countless details to sort out, and nobody who knows me would call me a detail guy. Fortunately my dear friend Bob Pingel came to my assistance. Bob is a software engineer by day, a rigger by weekend, and a renaissance man all the time. His mind can process manufacturing details like a computer, he can whip up a gourmet meal in a cramped galley, he can fashion a finely fin- ished piece of furniture, all the while talking about music and literature. Bob, Tom, and Bernie made sure all the details were right.

With a mast delivery date of October 20, I made another trip to Grado to prepare for the new rig. My primary objective was to remove, inspect, and if necessary replace the chainplates. I knew that they must have been subjected to unnatural loads when *Quetzal* lurched to starboard, especially the port- side chainplates, and the thought of a new mast being supported by question- able chainplates made no sense.

When I first arrived I hired an Italian rigger to inspect the chainplates. Marveling at the 4-by-½-inch stainless channel, he assured me they were fine. I didn't trust him. (See illustration on page 55.)

Removing the chainplates was a huge job. First I had to destroy the beau- tiful teak panels that covered them and then loosen thirty bolts per side. They still didn't budge, so I had to remove the covering plates and dig out all the old caulk on deck and push the chainplates down into the boat. The rigger was right; they were in excellent condition, so I cleaned and polished them and put them back in place.

I needed help to put the new mast in the boat. Three friends—Bob Pin- gel naturally, Rick Thompson, and Dan Stillwell—responded to my desper- ate pleas. Without their help *Quetzal* would still be propped up in Grado. Rick is a great shipmate and a great friend. He has sailed on *Quetzal* many times, and you may recall he was part of the transatlantic crew in Chapter

Six. He knew I needed help, and that was reason enough to fly to Italy. And when my funds ran low, he loaned me money with no questions asked. Dan, a friend of Bob's and a friend of mine, owns a 62-foot motoryacht in Milwaukee and knowingly suggested that we might need an extra hand. He was aboard *Quetzal* during the mischief in the Gulf of Corinth, and he is a closet sailor at heart. Bob was the heart, soul, and brains of the operation.

The mast crate arrived before we did. Yes, I said crate. While the spar arrived in two sections, we were surprised to see an enormous wooden crate sitting next to it. To ease shipping, nearly all the mast fittings, from the spreader bases to the pole track, were stashed in the crate. They had to be unpacked, assembled, and installed. The whole assembly was like a giant erector set. While I fretted, Bob methodically started going through the bits and pieces, formulating a logical approach to the project. That night at dinner we discussed the scope of the project and the time frame. We had five days to pry the old mast out of the boat; install a new mast step; assemble the new mast; measure, cut, and then build the new rig with Sta-Lok fittings on the lower ends of the wires; assemble the new Furlex headstay furler; reeve all the running rigging; find a crane to step the mast; and set up and tune the new rig. I did say five days—five days before Bob and Dan had to head home, and five days before two paying crewmembers showed up to help Rick and me sail to Gibraltar.

Those five days were some of the most exhausting days of our lives. First the stump of the old mast wouldn't budge. I cut it off from inside the boat so that we could install the new mast step, and we decided we would wait for the crane to lift it out. Bob and Dan set up the new sections on sawhorses and set about building the new mast. Gianfranco opened the tool shop and let us have the run of the yard. We would typically get started at 0600 and work until midnight. The cappuccino machine in the storeroom was indispensable.

We launched the boat on day four, and with the help of the chain pull on the Travelift we managed to remove the mast stump. The next day I hired a small construction crane. The entire yard turned up to help us hoist the mast. The definition of confusion is thirty screaming, gesturing, well-meaning Italian experts. Despite their help, the mast was successfully stepped.

Bob had done a great job measuring the new stays and shrouds. Everything fit perfectly. We had to calculate the expected stretch before cutting the wires, and the equation we drew with chalk took up 10 feet of the tarmac. Bob worked out the numbers, and then I worked them—and we didn't cut the wires until we came up with the same answer.

The last job was to build the furling system. Bob extended his flight by a day, maybe a fateful day in his life, but that's another story. We installed the furling gear just hours before he had to head to the airport. New crewmembers Dennis and Susan, who had done me a great favor by agreeing to sail on the delivery trip to Gibraltar in lieu of asking for a refund for a canceled trip, jumped right in and went to work.

Staring at my boat in the haulout slip, with her new spar standing tall, I had to choke back a tear, really. But there was no time for sentimental sobs. I hugged Bob for all I was worth, and he squealed out of the yard to catch his flight. We loaded provisions aboard, fired up the engine, and pushed off into the Adriatic Sea. Severe thunderstorms developed that night, with thunder and lightning crackling all around the boat. I was too tired to be scared and felt completely fatalistic. If *Quetzal*'s new mast was going to be struck by lightning, I was going to give up the sea and buy a vineyard. At least I had a plan.

The winds blew us down the Adriatic and across the Ionian Sea to Sicily. We stopped briefly in Palermo before beating to southern Sardinia. Dennis and Susan left the boat there, and I thanked them profusely for their help. Rick and I pressed on for Gibraltar. A distant mistral sent strong north winds our way, and we flew toward the coast of Spain. Despite our best efforts, we were running behind schedule.

Me holding court in the cockpit, my office. I would like to think I am giving some kind of important tip or nautical insight, but it's much more likely that I am telling one of my stories to a captive audience. Note that we are zooming along on a nice reach. Quetzal is sailing flat with a reef in the main and the autopilot in control. (Left to right: Kristy, JK, John, Steve)

Tadji was in contact with the transatlantic crewmembers, and they all agreed to meet us in Almerimar, farther up the coast. One week out of Grado, Rick and I pulled into the huge marina complex and were greeted by six eager sailors. *Quetzal* was back in business.

The ensuing transatlantic was textbook. I had a terrific crew, all of whom had sailed with me previously. Harry and Venlinda, gluttons for *Quetzal* adventures, were aboard, along with Todd, James, and Alan from Australia. Mark, who had found his stride after the adventure I recounted in Chapter One, was also part of the crew. I don't think anyone has ever enjoyed a crossing more than he did. We made landfall in Antigua, seventeen days out from the Canary Islands.

I was able to collect my thoughts on the crossing and realized how lucky I was to have friends and customers ready to step up and help keep *Quetzal* and me at sea. Over the next two years, *Quetzal* and crew would make some impressive voyages. We would sail to every corner of the Caribbean and as far north as Labrador on a passage that took us around the rock of Newfoundland. It was the return from that passage that left me with a death grip on Diane's thighs, with the moment and the future hanging in the balance, as I recalled in Chapter Two.

Local Winds of the Mediterranean

Nikos Kazantzakis opens his wonderful novel *Zorba the Greek* in the port of Piraeus. "A strong sirocco was blowing the spray from the waves as far as the little café, whose glass doors were shut." He doesn't feel the need to explain that a *sirocco* is a south wind that originates over North African deserts and picks up moisture as it moves over the sea. Everyone in the Mediterranean knows the sirocco. The word itself implies its direction and weather characteristics. Siroccos arrive in advance of low-pressure systems and bring rainy, unsettled weather, and occasionally gale force winds. I once had a Greek charter boat captain tell me, "I can smell a sirocco coming as clearly as I can see a beautiful woman walking toward me." I never saw a beautiful woman walk his way, but he was good at predicting weather.

The Mediterranean is prone to local winds. Mountains to the north, deserts to the south, and scores of convoluted bays and snaking peninsulas brew up pressure gradients that wrack the Med with an olio of intriguing winds. Early Mediterranean sailors didn't need a magnetic compass. Wind direction and the associated weather conditions served as a ready-made direction finder. Identified and characterized by the ancient mariners, the names of these winds are still very much in use today. A forecaster in Gibraltar, complete with a British accent, will mention the *vendavales*, a hard westerly wind blowing in from the Atlantic. French sailors never refer to a cold north wind in the Golfe du Lyon as a "north wind." It is the *mistral*. In Malta they talk about the *gregale*—the wind that supposedly shipwrecked St. Paul in AD 66—just as New Englanders know of nasty nor'easters. These winds are personal, which makes perfect sense to me. Just as we name our boats and our seas, it seems natural to name the wind—it completes the sailor's trinity.

Here is a list of the many local winds of the Mediterranean, with some information about each.

Bora: Named after Boreas, the Greek god of the north wind, *boras* haunt the Adriatic Sea. Katabatic winds—sometimes called fall winds—boras are north-northeast downdrafts that rip down the steep mountain faces of the Dinaric Alps that border the eastern Adriatic. They occur primarily in the winter and are usually at their most dangerous near shore.

Cers: Another katabatic wind, *cers* is the local name for the northwest wind that makes the border sea between France and Spain a consistently windy stretch of the Mediterranean. The cers is the result of winds from the distant Bay of Biscay funneling between the Pyrenees to the south and the Montagnes Noir to the north. It is similar to its more famous brother, the *mistral*.

Etesian: From the Greek word *estesios*, or annual, these strong and steady north or northwest winds arrive in the Aegean every May like clockwork. They are more commonly called *meltimi* in Greece and Turkey. These winds reach their peak in high summer, July and August, and occasionally reach gale force. The many islands of the Aegean can either provide a welcome lee or act as a launch ramp for these fierce katabatic downdrafts.

Gregale: This storm wind takes its name from the Italian word *grecale*, for the Ionian island of Zakynthos. It is a northeast wind of the western Ionian Sea, most prevalent near Malta. It's caused by low pressure south of Malta and a strong airflow from north to south. The history of Valetta, Malta's dramatic capital, is littered with storms and deadly waves from the *gregale*.

Levante: An ancient name implying the East, or the countries and regions of the eastern Mediterranean, *levante* is also the name of a local easterly wind that flows along the southwest coast of Spain and through the Strait of Gibraltar. Its counterpart, the *ponente*, which implies west, is a westerly in the Strait. Levantes form in advance of approaching cold fronts. Ponentes are the fair westerlies after the front passes.

Libeccio: This is a strong west or southwest wind that blows along the north and south shores of Corsica, another consistently windy area. Off Cap Corse, in the north, and in the Strait of Bonifacio, in the south, it often reaches gale force.

Marin: This is a south or southeast onshore wind in the Languedoc coastal region of France. A counterpart to the northwest *(continued next page)* cers, the *marin* is a winter wind and responsible for flash floods. The name is a local variation, meaning onshore.

Mistral: The most infamous local wind, the mistral is a cold north or northwest wind blowing down the Rhone river valley. Mistrals can be destructive, especially in the winter when a low-pressure system over northern Italy collides with a ridge to the west. Mistral winds reach out to the Balaeric Islands, more than a hundred miles to the south.

Sirocco: Known by various names along the north coast of Africa, including *chille*, *ghibli*, and *khamsin*, *siroccos* form in advance of eastward-moving depressions in the southern Mediterranean. They are hot, dry winds along the African coast but transform into moist, sticky winds when they reach the islands of Malta, Greece, Italy, and Spain. Italians use the word *ostro* to describe both the sirocco and any wind from the south. Siroccos occur throughout the year and occasionally reach gale force.

Tramontana: Associated with the mistral, *tramontanas* form after a depression has passed the Gulf of Genoa. The tramontana blows along the northwest coast of northern Italy and reaches out to Corsica. In the winter, it can bring frigid conditions to sailors in the Ligurian Sea.

Vendavales: Strong southwest winds that blow in through the Strait of Gibraltar and make it difficult to leave the Mediterranean. Vendavales follow the levante and precede the ponente. Gale force winds are accompanied by thunderstorms.

Here is an excellent website, both as a general weather site, including GRIB files, and as a resource for interesting meteorological facts and lore: www.weatheronline.co.uk

Crew Retrieval | Steep Waves in the Gulf Stream | Dismasted and Drifting in the Gulf Stream | Solo Sailor Lost at Sea

Survival of the Luckiest

"Like every living thing its prime characteristic is a blind, unreasoned instinct to survive."

—Robert Heinlein, *Stranger in a Strange Land*

"Survival is the celebration of choosing life over death. We know we're going to die. We all die. But survival is saying: perhaps not today. In that sense, survivors don't defeat death, they come to terms with it."

"The word 'experienced' often refers to someone who's gotten away with doing the wrong thing more frequently than you have."

—Laurence Gonzalez, *Deep Survival*

As I RECOUNTED in Chapter Two, we were aboard *Quetzal*, en route from Nova Scotia, when we were hammered by a huge wave, and I thought that if Diane was washed away I was going with her and it would all be over.

"You are not leaving this boat, Diane," I screamed and tried again to lift her back aboard. "You are not going anywhere."

My voice was fading along with my strength. Her inflatable harness was keeping her head just above water, and she had a death grip on the same lifeline that her legs were hooked around. We were fighting each other. Each breaking wave hissing by the boat completely submerged her and terrified me.

Help me, *Quetzal*, I thought to myself. Do something. As if the boat had to rescue me once again. It had been only a minute, maybe two, but it seemed like Diane had been suspended in this limbo, not quite on board and not quite overboard, forever. I was afraid to let go of her legs and reposition myself for better leverage. She was not letting go of the lifeline. Period.

My hoarse cries finally reached the crew below, and Kevin emerged from the shambles of the interior as he struggled into his foul-weather gear. The look on his face described better than words the wild conditions and battered cockpit. At the same time, Ric at last extricated himself from the wreckage of

215

the bimini. With help from a wave that momentarily floated Diane most of the way out of the water, the three of us managed to lift her back onto the boat.

Quetzal was wallowing in the troughs and skidding down the massive faces. I knew that if another wave broke over her, she might be rolled. The cockpit was a disaster. The spray dodger was shredded and the clear panels were gone. The stainless steel bimini frame, the supports for which I had beefed up just before the passage in Lunenburg, was twisted like a pretzel, with most of it dangling over the side and slamming into the hull. The frame also supported the solar panels, and luckily they were still attached, although just barely; they were hanging by a couple of cable ties. The stern pulpit was cracked and bent. Anything that had been in the cockpit—cushions, winch, and bilge pump handles, even a teak cockpit grate—had washed into the sea. I remember thinking how much it was going to cost to replace all this gear before realizing that if we didn't do something fast, the cost of repairs was going to be the least of my worries.

Ric helped Diane below while Kevin, Giorgio, and I hastily wrestled the solar panels back aboard. I took the helm, and they lashed everything in place with the lazy sheets. Then they cut away the remnants of the bimini fabric. They worked efficiently and without a trace of fear or panic. I was impressed.

I finally noticed that *Quetzal* had been taking care of herself, more or less. When we were knocked down, we had a tiny bit of headsail up supported by the whisker pole—my normal arrangement for running downwind. Now I realized that having the blanket-sized headsail poled out was in fact forcing us downwind, a lucky break that may have kept us from being rolled by taking another wave beam-on. But we needed more than luck; we were in for a brutal ride, and the seas were just warming up.

As we ran before the wind into the heart of the Gulf Stream, the seas became deadly. This is not hyperbole, for I have never seen such consistently steep waves so far offshore, and it seemed they were all breaking. This was the most challenging steering of my life, with simply no margin for a momentary loss of concentration. When I look back at the conditions that morning from the perspective of this desk in Fort Lauderdale, I can state honestly that I don't know if we would have survived running without sails, and I doubt we would have survived lying hove-to, not with consistently breaking 30-foot-plus waves. We may have been able to forereach back north, but that would have been a brutal slugfest, especially in our battered state. The only course was ahead. Our fate was in our hands.

I steered as much by sound as by sight. I could hear the waves astern, and I quickly realized that I had to position *Quetzal* to take each wave just off the transom. I made a point of trying to cut each wave with the corner of the transom and hull, shouting, "Corner, corner, John. Take it on the corner" to remind and encourage myself. "Yes, *Quetzal*, you can do this." Even when breaking waves overran the boat and flooded the cockpit, despite taking them on the corner, we maintained steering control. I actually eased out a few more feet of sail. We needed more speed, especially in the troughs, to better position *Quetzal* for the next onslaught.

Running before foaming, breaking walls of destruction, I realized just how stupid I had been. By aiming for the narrowest band of the Gulf Stream, I had steered directly into harm's way, into an area of current running hard and fast and thereby creating the ultimate collision of wind and sea. It was ugly, a no-man's sea, and I was responsible for whatever fate awaited us.

I steered for several hours and was finally relieved by Giorgio. A renowned heart surgeon, Giorgio had grown up on the island of Sardinia and had sailed all his life. He was an excellent helmsman, and between the two of us we conned *Quetzal* south, eventually clearing the minefield of breaking waves after eight hours of intense concentration. We were both exhausted and incredibly relieved as the waves began to subside ever so slightly. We didn't know that just a few miles away from us, the battered wreck of a once-proud ketch, the *Emma Goldman*, lay ahull, dismasted and drifting, truly at the mercy of the sea.

Captain Dennis White, *Emma Goldman*'s experienced owner, and his best friend, Will Thorns, and Thorns's daughter Amanda had left Lake Tashmoo near Vineyard Haven on Martha's Vineyard on November 6, 2010, three days after we left Lunenburg. They sailed to Tarpaulin Cove, a snug anchorage off Naushon Island across Vineyard Sound. There they finished preparations for their upcoming passage. With a favorable forecast calling for northwest winds, they decided to get underway. Just after midnight they weighed anchor and headed south toward the open sea.

White and crew were headed to the Virgin Islands, a 1,350-mile passage as the fulmar flies. White, however, was also considering a landfall in Bermuda, a nice halfway-point option if the weather turned bad or they needed to refuel. White's wife, Julie Robinson, later told the *Vineyard Gazette* that her husband had told her that if she didn't hear from them in five days, which was how long they expected to take to reach Bermuda, then she would not hear from them for two weeks, the time, plus a few days, that they expected they needed to reach the Virgin Islands.

White is a vastly experienced sailor and boatbuilder. He and his family sailed around the world in a modified L. Francis Herreshoff H-28 that he built himself. He had made the passage south from New England to the Caribbean many times and didn't underestimate the potential for heavy weather. Still, he was expecting a good run all the way to Bermuda and told the *Gazette* that he had a six-day forecast calling for favorable northwest winds. I know that forecast he was looking at, and neither one of us thought the winds would clock quickly to the northeast, dramatically ratcheting up the stakes.

White built the *Emma Goldman*, named after a defiant anarchist and activist of the early twentieth century, in his backyard in West Tisbury on

Martha's Vineyard. It took him six years to complete the 41-foot ketch patterned closely after an L. Francis Herreshoff design called the Leeboard Ketch. The handsome hull had a long, shallow full keel, low freeboard, and a narrow beam. White had dispatched with the quaint idea of leeboards and slightly deepened the keel instead. The hull was a cold-molded cedar plank-and-epoxy construction, very strong and nicely finished. White and his wife had logged more than 25,000 miles in the *Emma Goldman*, including five trips from the Vineyard to Barbados and back. It was almost as if the boat knew the way back to the islands.

Will Thorns was a boatbuilder and an experienced sailor, but he was not an offshore sailor. Also a carpenter, Thorns had a love of wooden boats and was eager to help his friend of 25 years deliver the boat south to the Caribbean. Thorns's daughter, Amanda, 25, had sailed frequently with her father around the islands of Buzzards Bay and Vineyard Sound in his H-28. Like his friend Dennis White, Thorns had also built his own version of this L. Francis Herreshoff classic. Amanda was excited to be making her first bluewater passage.

They ran into the same confluence of a strong cold front moving across Canada, a mid-Atlantic ridge of bad weather, and the remnants of low pressure caused by Hurricane Tomas that would flummox us a few days later. Although *Emma Goldman* had left three days before we did, they made slower, more deliberate progress. According to Amanda Thorns, White and her father decided to try to avoid or at least delay their entry into the Gulf Stream, where they knew the seas would be dangerous. They decided to slowly motor south-southwest in an attempt to skirt the current until the weather moderated. The same idea would flash through my mind a few days later, but I worried that the conditions would be even worse near Cape Hatteras. Instead I made the fateful decision to head for the narrow band of supercharged current, also a bad call.

After three days of slow progress, running slowly before the storm under bare poles and with the engine on to steady the boat in the wave troughs, the *Emma Goldman* encountered the Gulf Stream. White was quoted as saying they were approximately 350 miles south of Martha's Vineyard when they were "sucked into the current." We were catching up with them fast, and by my best estimate we were just one day behind them when they were overwhelmed, and we would ultimately pass less than 50 miles to the west of the stricken *Emma Goldman*.

White later told the *Gazette* that once he realized they were in the current, they decided to "take it," to just get across. Every skipper knows that once you get south of the Gulf Stream on a fall passage, the world improves. I would later make the exact same decision aboard *Quetzal*. According to several reports, the *Emma Goldman* encountered 30- to 40-foot seas. On the night of November 10, 2010, the boat was violently rolled by a break-ing wave. White and Amanda Thorns were below. Will Thorns was on deck alone, on watch. He was harnessed to the boat but it didn't matter. When the *Emma Goldman* finally righted herself, sans both masts, Will Thorns was trailing astern, entangled in the web of shattered rigging, his harness lanyard long gone.

Amanda Thorns told Matt Lauer on the *Today* show that her father extended his arms for help. His head was barely above water and was bleed-ing badly. Amanda, who had scrambled on deck in her pajamas, and White tried to pull Will free, but he was hopelessly snarled by wire and lines. Amanda said she was waiting for superhuman strength to come to her, "but it didn't come." A wave finally washed Thorns away as his daughter screamed on deck. "Daddy, daddy, don't leave me."

The next several days were torturous for the two survivors. They cowered below, trying to ignore the battering of the hull. The rigging, the spars, and the ground tackle and anchor continuously smashed the hull as the *Emma Goldman* pitched about in the still raging conditions. It's a testament to the strength of the boat that it survived this assault. Shattered and grief stricken, they bailed from time to time as the water was above their knees in the cabin, but they had little incentive to do more.

Eventually White found the will to survive. He went forward and some-how wrestled the anchor and chain back aboard the boat, relieving the worst of the pounding. With the weather finally moderating, they summoned the energy to cut away the rig, and just in time, as Amanda later told the *Royal Gazette* in Bermuda. A nasty squall hit just after they finished the huge job.

Emma Goldman was not equipped with an EPIRB, an emergency satel-lite beacon, which would have alerted the Coast Guard to their plight. This was a near-tragic oversight of the skipper. She was also not fitted with a sat phone or a SPOT transmitter. The VHF antenna was gone with the masts, wiping out the ability to communicate, and although White later found the handheld VHF radio floating in the bilge, it didn't have much range or charge. They were alone at sea, and a once proud ketch was a barely floating hulk.

Twice they were taunted by near rescue. The first ship appeared a few days after they had cut away the rig, and although they fired off half their stock of parachute flares, the ship didn't stop. This was before White found the floating VHF. Thorns said they watched the ship "cross from one end of the horizon to the other over the course of an hour before disappearing into the still, clear night." Before that encounter, she said, "death or rescue seemed imminent, one or the other. Both felt distant after that. It became a long game of waiting."

A week later a second ship appeared. White reached the ship with the little power left in the handheld radio. The ship answered their Mayday just before the radio died. The weather was rough again, and in the big seas they lost sight of the ship when in the troughs. They decided not to waste another of their dwindling flares on an unlikely rescue.

Eventually the long waiting game became unbearable. Ten days after the capsize, they were running low on food and water, so White decided to take their fate into his own hands. He fashioned a jury rig using the 10-foot mast from the sailing dinghy that had somehow stayed with the boat when it was rolled. They lashed it to the stump of the mainmast and hoisted a small jib, flying it sideways, and the *Emma Goldman* was moving again. They logged 50 miles in 24 hours, slowly sailing toward Bermuda.

The next morning, November 21, 2010, they spotted another ship. They were still nearly 200 miles from Bermuda. Uncertain whether their provisions would hold out, they decided to risk deploying another flare. This time it worked, and the 80,000-ton Greek oil tanker *Triathlon* spotted them. The ship maneuvered alongside the *Emma Goldman*, a remarkable bit of seamanship, and lowered lines down to the stricken vessel. White and Thorns were hauled to safety, and the *Emma Goldman* was abandoned.

I learned about the *Emma Goldman*'s tragic plight several weeks after *Quetzal* reached Fort Lauderdale. As if our passage had not been ordeal enough, the sad story shook me to my core. I had been having a hard time freeing the image of Diane hanging from the lifelines from my mind's eye. But it was not the only tragedy that haunted me. Exactly one year before *Quetzal* and *Emma Goldman* battled the same deadly Gulf Stream gale, we made the same passage, south from Lunenburg to Bermuda, in early November 2009. Once again, we were the lucky survivors.

Sometimes I ask myself why I love Nova Scotia and northern sailing so much, because it is never easy retreating to the tropics in advance of winter. Once again *Quetzal* and her crew were holed up in Lunenburg, waiting for a break in the weather. Finally, on November 7, the so-called "weather window" cracked open and we fled south. It was a crisp, cold, classic northern day with a light but dense wind escorting us toward Bermuda along the rhumb line, which is sometimes dubbed I 65 south because it follows the 65th meridian to Bermuda and on to the Caribbean islands. We were ultimately bound for St. Martin.

I had a talented and geographically diverse crew. Rolf and Mike were from Minnesota and sailed their 37-foot Delphia sloop on Lake Superior. Pete lived in Alabama, Kristi was a lawyer in southern Georgia, and John, a reformed lawyer now selling wine, hailed from Jacksonville, Florida. The southerners on board were bundled up like Arctic explorers while the Minnesota boys thought it was downright balmy. Soon we would all be decked out in full foul-weather gear, racing before a northeast gale. But first, of course, we had to cross the Gulf Stream.

A sinister loop in the Gulf Stream arched north and then east, and despite having the latest satellite imagery at hand, and an experienced friend serving as a weather router back home, I managed to steer right into it. That takes a real navigator. We spent a frustrating 24 hours sailing smartly through the water at 7 knots but making less than 4 knots toward Bermuda. We were wasting precious hours of perfect weather, something I knew intuitively would come back to haunt me in northern latitudes in November. But this time we were lucky. We crossed the Gulf Stream exactly 24 hours before a nor'easter developed and turned the Stream into a raging mayhem.

Sadly, the same can't be said for Canadian solo sailor Herbert Marcoux. Like Dennis White, he was an accomplished sailor and had circumnavigated in his stout, if funky, 46-foot steel boat. Unfortunately, the deep low that Environment Canada predicted would track north dipped south instead, creating gale force northeast winds.

South of the main body of the Gulf Stream, we experienced winds near 40 knots steady with higher gusts. The seas were large, certainly 20 feet on

Another cockpit shot, another heavy-weather passage, this one from Lunenburg, Nova Scotia, to St. Martin by way of Bermuda. We have escaped a major storm in the Gulf Stream, and the conditions are moderating, but everybody is still in full foul-weather gear. Note the duct tape holding the sailing instrument pod together. One of the many changes over the years has been a new pedestal and single, larger instrument pod. (Left to right: Mike, Rolf, Kristy, John, Pete)

average, with occasional larger combers piling up astern. As the gale intensified, we reefed the main once, then twice, then finally tucked in the rarely used third. The winds were just aft of the beam, so we rolled in the headsail and raised the bulletproof storm jib. The sailing was exhilarating. With a willing and capable crew, *Quetzal* didn't miss a beat. We dashed before the storm, sailing at an angle that was clearly taking us away from the low-pressure system, and sailing fast. In fact, the 180 miles we logged was the best 24-hour run of the passage.

Two days behind us, Marcoux was in a different ocean. A later CBC report stated that the Canadian Coast Guard reported winds at 60 knots and seas greater than 10 meters, or 33 feet. Marcoux was also bound for Bermuda, but he never arrived. *(continued page 224)*

Ten Items/Essential Systems for Bluewater Passagemaking

1. **Autopilot.** This may seem an odd choice for number one on the list, but without excellent self-steering, most of the magic of passagemaking disappears. The development of reliable self-steering and the popularity of cruising go hand in hand. Today's autopilots are remarkable, and it will quickly become the most important piece of equipment aboard. If I could choose one electronic gizmo, I would not pick GPS, SSB, radar, or a sat phone. I would pick an autopilot. If I could pick two items, I'd pick a backup autopilot. A wind vane self-steering device is a wonderful addition to any boat, but it does have limitations and drawbacks, although the well-equipped cruising boat has an autopilot *and* a wind vane self-steering device.

2. **Rugged Headsail Furling Gear.** Roller-furling gear is the biggest revolution in cruising, right behind the development of fiberglass hulls. Good roller furling is what makes shorthanded cruising possible, and it's a huge safety feature. It is, in fact, the most important safety feature on the boat. However, inadequate or worn-out gear is aggravating and unsafe. Spend money on the best furling gear you can afford. Top brands include Furlex, Harken, Hood, Schaefer, and Pro-Furl.

3. **Bulletproof Electrical System.** There is no denying it, our boats today are dependent on electronics of every kind. A bulletproof system is critical. By bulletproof I mean three things: (1) it has to deliver the amps where and when they are needed; (2) it has to easily regenerate what it puts out, and (3) it has to be as simple and reliable as possible. Resist the urge to complicate the electrical system; instead, engineer it with superior components in a straightforward manner. Complementing the basic charging system with

solar and wind also offers a vital backup system should the engine or alternator or generator become inoperable.

4. **Storm Headsail/Staysail.** A system that removes the furling headsail from your heavy-weather storm management program is essential. This can be achieved by a staysail, either fixed or mobile, or with a storm jib designed to wrap around a furled headsail. The former is much preferred. Staysails, especially storm staysails, are wonderful tools, and much more useful than the trysails (storm mains) that we all used to carry. An additional and obvious point is that every passage should begin with fresh sails in general, as nothing breathes new life into an old boat like new sails.

5. **Mainsail Reefing and Preventing System.** Once you complete an offshore passage, you will realize just how important it is to be able to reef the main off the wind. You almost never read about this, but it is vital. There are times when coming upwind to reef is not practical, safe, or even possible. A slippery luff track with robust slides, shackle, and halyards is essential. Retractable lazyjacks and possibly a downhaul system help. An overall well-designed slab reefing system is still the best. The main boom is the most dangerous piece on the boat and also one of the easiest to break. A proper main preventer made of stretchy line and led forward to allow for soft pseudo jibes is the way to go.

6. **Cockpit Protection.** A spray dodger and bimini are vital, and nowadays storm panels protecting the cockpit have become common. This system has to be well designed, however, to actually withstand severe weather. I have lost three cockpit enclosures to date! Keeping the crew warm and dry changes the very nature of a passage.

7. **Whisker Pole.** It is vital to be able to sail efficiently downwind, and you will not be using a spinnaker very often—plain and simple. A heavy-duty running pole, or whisker pole, is one of the most important pieces of equipment on every trade wind passage. I have crossed many oceans with the mainsail resting on the boom, and a poled genoa providing all the necessary horsepower. Storing the whisker pole on a track on the mast to allow for easy deployment without hefting it off the deck means you will use it more often. Some think that the whisker pole should be stored on deck to be available as a jury-rigged spar should the mast go down, but I disagree. Using the whisker pole makes sailing much safer and more efficient, and if you can rig it without much fuss, you are much more likely to use it.

8. **Sea Berths.** It is amazing and sad how few boats are rigged with adequate sea berths these days. This sounds like an old bugger's lament, and I not crying out for the return of old narrow designs, just for a place to sleep while underway in every condition. Sleep is one of the three essentials to happiness on a passage, but you have to put some thought into this before shoving off. With the imaginative use of lee cloths, some doubles can be made into secure singles for offshore sailing.   *(continued next page)*

9. **Personal Gear.** As the Scandinavians say, "There is no bad weather, only bad clothing." With today's gear, there is no excuse for being miserable at sea. It can be costly, but money spent on top-quality foul-weather gear and under layers is money well spent. Sooner or later offshore cruisers will learn from dinghy sailors and start wearing gear that not only keeps them warm and dry but allows for a full range of motion. One interesting note is that slowly but surely survival suits are making their way aboard cruising boats. Survival suits are affordable and rachet up your life expectancy if you end up in the water, and when boarding a life raft.

10. **Deck Safety Gear.** You can spend a fortune on safety gear, and while it enhances your peace of mind, it does not always make you safe. Think hard about this, and put your money into a top-quality life raft, stout, well-designed jacklines, top-quality inflatable harnesses and PFDs, and a simple, easily deployed retrieval system. New wireless MOB systems will gradually become standard on cruising boats. Most importantly, as discussed throughout this book, have a plan for man-overboard emergencies.

We reached the island oasis in a slow seven days after battling headwinds the last couple of days. I called my friend Alan Creaser in Lunenburg to let him know that we had arrived safely. He asked if we'd seen or heard from Marcoux, and I told him that we had not but we'd keep an eye out for him in Bermuda. A few days later the Canadian Coast Guard launched a search-and-rescue operation. By the time we reached St. Martin nine days later, the Coast Guard had called off the search and pronounced the 68-year-old sailor "lost at sea."

With a large and talented crew, a well-found boat, and a storm strategy that worked, it would have been easy to feel as though we survived and Marcoux didn't because we were somehow better prepared, maybe even better sailors. But none of us felt that way when we got the news in St. Martin. We knew the truth. We were lucky. We had a two-day head start and missed the worst of the storm. Marcoux was in the wrong place at the wrong time. One window opened and another slammed shut.

Any thoughts of bravado were squelched in our 2010 trip. *Quetzal* was seconds, maybe milliseconds, away from suffering the same fate as the *Emma Goldman*. Why she didn't roll over I will never know. It had nothing to do with my skill as a skipper. If anything it had to do with Mike Kaufman's terrific seaworthy design. But I suspect it had more to do with chance. Will Thorns and Herbert Marcoux were the unlucky ones, and their sad fate reminds all of us who ply the sea in small sailboats that it is a serious ocean.

eleven

Gathering a Crew | Preparing for Passages—The
Work List, Including Rigging Dynex Dux Backstays |
The Many Meanings of Ocean Passages

Atlantic Crossings—
Part Two, Back Where
We Belong

*"Tomorrow will have an island. Before night I always find it. Then on to
the next island. These hidden places in the day separate and come forward if you beckon. But you have to know they are there before they
exist.*

*"Some time there will be a tomorrow without any island, so far I
haven't let that happen, but after I'm gone others may become faith-
less and careless. Before them will tumble the wide unbroken sea, and
without any hope they will stare at the horizon.*

*"So to you, Friend, I confide my secret: to be a discoverer you
hold close whatever you find, and after a while you decide what it is.
Then, secure in where you have been, you turn to the open sea and
let go."*

—William Stafford, *Tomorrow Will Have an Island*

QUETZAL WENT RIGHT BACK to what she does best, taking people to sea. Less
than two weeks after arriving in Fort Lauderdale following our near demise in
the narrow Gulf Stream, we shoved off on a training passage to the Bahamas.

I confess that I was having a difficult time shaking off the gloominess
that pervaded my thoughts after the rugged passage south from Nova Scotia.
Not that I doubted myself, and certainly not my stalwart boat, but more that
I had somehow violated the natural contract that I feel exists between me,
my friends and customers, and the sea. I respect the ocean and have always
accepted my own vulnerability as a core belief, as part of the pact in going

225

to sea. I understand that every passage comes with risk, some more than others. The essential meaning of how I have spent my life is hidden somewhere in this element of danger, that the deck edge is a cliff, an abyss, and daring to look over the edge gives you a beautiful perspective and rare insight into how fragile life is. But after the Atlantic crash, I was having difficulty accepting the notion that I was exposing people to risks they might not understand, or at least not in the same way that I did.

I believe in individual responsibility and the concept of a crew or team, of operating both for the benefit of the group and for each person. This is why an ocean voyage is so fulfilling. It satisfies on two basic levels: we're all Joshua Slocum on one hand, and part of Columbus's crew on the other. The crew on the passage south from Nova Scotia responded brilliantly to our near disaster, and for them it was a defining moment, a moment of clarity. Ric and Diane were not swayed from their dream of sailing away, of slipping from the hollow material demands of their upper-middle-class existence in Toronto and seeing the world in their own boat, on their own terms, and accepting the risks and rewards for such an enterprise. My spirits were buoyed when they bought a Caliber 47 sloop in New Orleans, sailed it across the Gulf of Mexico to Florida, and began refitting it for serious cruising. They knew exactly what they were getting themselves into, and they tackled the project with gusto.

Kevin, probably the least-experienced sailor in our crew but well versed in other rugged outdoor pursuits, also pushed on with his dream to buy a boat. And he didn't do it the easy way. He zeroed in on a Passport 40 and scoured the country, and then the world, looking for the best value in this handsome Perry-designed classic. He eventually bought a boat in Panama, and after his delivery skipper left him high and dry on the small island of Providencia in the western Caribbean, he delivered the boat back to Fort Lauderdale with just one other crewmember. Now he and his wife, Rose, are completely retrofitting the boat for future Caribbean adventures. Over dinner he assured me that he couldn't have done it without the experience he'd gleaned on the trip down from Nova Scotia a few months before. "Broken autopilot, a suspect rig, and miserable headwinds seemed like nothing after what we'd been through on *Quetzal*." I took it as a compliment and realized that you can't promise people sea stories, then hope they don't find them. Stories are based in truth, in salt and spray, in the moment. They're reality relived—they're not hype or a sales pitch. The story is only the vehicle for the delivery of truth. Underestimate a sea story at your own peril. It seems that my friends and customers understand more about going to sea than I suspected.

I also realized that I needed another transatlantic passage. It may sound strange, but crossing the Atlantic is soul soothing to me. It's my passage, like going to the office. It's what I do, and it makes my world right again. And with *Quetzal* on the other side of the Atlantic, I wouldn't be tempted to sail up to and back from Nova Scotia again and might stay out of trouble for a few years.

My 2011 crossing to Ireland sold out the day I posted it on my website. But before setting off on her fifth crossing in seven years, *Quetzal* needed some love and a bit of a makeover. Naturally, I turned to my friends.

Steve Sullivan, who owns a near-perfect Baba 40 that he sails on Lake Michigan, and a dear friend, decided to spend a couple of winter months warming up in Fort Lauderdale, and he went to work on *Quetzal*. He mounted a new steering pedestal with an instrument pod that for the first time properly housed my electronics. He also replaced the steering chain and cables and beefed up the brackets supporting the cable sheaves. I had been worried about the steering system, and it was comforting to know it was in good order before setting across the Atlantic. Steve also replaced the Plexiglas sidelights and added four opening portlights. He oversaw the building and installation of a new stern pulpit, and rebuilt the windlass for good measure. Down below, he put in a new headliner in the main saloon, spruced up the galley counters with fresh Formica, and gave the old girl a nice cosmetic face-lift. I didn't pay him anywhere near as much as I should have, but he swore that the experience was worth it. He knows he's always welcome on *Quetzal*.

Not surprisingly, Bob Pingel, my guardian angel, was the next friend to spend some time working on *Quetzal*. An electrical engineer by trade, Bob

Quetzal under sail as a cutter in front of infamous Fastnet Rock. This was on our summer cruise off Ireland after crossing the Atlantic in 2011. She was sailing as a true cutter, with a high-cut 100 percent jib/Yankee because we blew out the genoa on the crossing and were awaiting a new genoa to be built and shipped.

Quetzal's side deck. It looks busier than it actually is. Note the substantial mast rails, or granny bars, just to leeward of the mast, which also make a good support for the spare plastic fuel jug and a place to lash spare lines. The Seldén boom vang makes handling the boom easy, especially off the wind. It's large and easily supports the boom, making the topping lift redundant. I like the strong, structural-aluminum toe rail that's incorporated into the hull and deck joint. The rail can support sheet leads, is handy for mounting snatch blocks, and is also a better place to secure fenders than the lifelines.

went to work on *Quetzal*'s 12-volt system. We replaced the 6-year-old AGM batteries with new ones and rewired the boat from the batteries to the electrical panel. *Quetzal* had been crying out for this upgrade for years. Bob added a new charge controller and battery switches, and not only beefed up the system but simplified it as well. He also replaced a couple of the interior lights with LEDs, added fans in the cabins, and helped me tackle several plumbing issues.

Once he finished the electrical system and the interior items on my master project list, Bob went back to his specialty, rigging. He made up new running backstays out of Dynex Dux, the new super line with a tightly braided synthetic construction and in many applications stronger than stainless steel. Some new boats are using Dynex Dux for standing rigging, and I will give serious consideration to doing likewise when it's time to re-rig *Quetzal*. Some may scoff at the use of running backstays on a cruiser like *Quetzal*, but I am religious about deploying the runners, even when it seems like overkill. Something about losing a mast in a tornado makes running backstays seem like they're worth the minimal effort involved in setting them up. Bob also fashioned new lazyjacks to tame the mainsail.

I had a new bimini and spray dodger and cockpit cushions made for the third time in nine years, and fashioned a more secure system for mounting the solar panels. I had a surprise when I serviced the life raft. One of the tubes was ripped. It is a double-floor, twin-tube raft, so it would have only partially inflated. I had it repaired and repacked and all the safety equipment upgraded, including new fire extinguishers and flares. I opted for the top of the line SOLAS (Safety of Life at Sea) flares, inspired by the poor results of Dennis White and Amanda Thorn's aboard the ill-fated *Emma Goldman*.

In preparation for the crossing, we sailed from Fort Lauderdale to the Chesapeake Bay. John, Cindy, Jim, Don, and Kelly joined me for this passage north. Sailing with the Gulf Steam, we flew, and reached Cape Hatteras, more than 600 miles away, in three days. *Quetzal* completed her final preparations at Spring Cove Marina in Solomons Island, Maryland, just south of Annapolis. Owned and operated by my sister Liz and her husband, Trevor, whom you met in Chapter Three, Spring Cove is one of *Quetzal*'s homes away from home, and has had many upgrades completed by the skilled crew there. Just the year before, they had installed a new 60 horsepower Beta diesel, replacing my tired Westerbeke. I left *Quetzal* on the hard and returned home for my daughter's high school graduation. I knew the boat was in good hands because the yard general manager, Don, was part of the transatlantic crew and I figured he would make sure *Quetzal* would be in top shape for crossing.

The crew that turned up at Spring Cove was one of the best I have ever assembled. All had sailed with me before, and most were experienced, confident sailors. Charlie, from nearby Annapolis, is a navy captain who flew helicopters in Afghanistan and had sailed aboard *Quetzal* several times before. Although still on active duty, he was able to secure the needed time off, and I

Quetzal has logged many miles under this simple rig. The beefy traveler and mainsheet blocks are on holiday as the mainsail is taking a rest. You can see the main, lashed rather sloppily around the boom, as Quetzal reaches before the wind under the poled-out genoa. When the trades are in full glory, this is our preferred sail plan. We knock off 160 to 180 miles a day, and the stresses on the rig and crew are minimal.

was delighted to have him join us. Charlie is a steady hand in an emergency and an enthusiastic navigator. Kyle, an air force colonel and also an active-duty officer, had just accepted an assignment in London and figured that sailing across the Atlantic was a more interesting way to get to Europe. Kyle had sailed with me to Nova Scotia the year before. A PhD chemist, Kyle had taught at the Air Force Academy. He and his wife, Jen, an air force colonel and a poet, have dreams of taking their young daughter cruising one day.

David, at age 72 when we crossed, is the oldest person to sail across the Atlantic with me. But he puts the truth to the line "72 is only a number." I think the crew would agree that he was the most youthful among us in spirit. David had a keen sense of the value of this adventure in his life, and he knew he was unlikely to make the trip again (although he did join me this year on an expedition to the Galapagos and then later in the Med). He thoroughly enjoyed the passage. Sergey, my Ukrainian friend, is an impressive young man. Although just 38 at the time of the crossing, he had already lived in four countries, leaving a trail of success in his wake. He is a natural on a boat, and although he may have been the least experienced in sea miles, his judgment was almost always sound, though the same cannot be said about his jokes.

Don, as mentioned earlier, the boatyard manager at Spring Cove Marina, is one of the most capable people I have sailed with, and he brings a quiet confidence to every situation. In difficult conditions he was our steadiest helmsman, and he also tirelessly repaired the array of broken bits that accompany every crossing.

Don's cabin mate in the forepeak, Rick, is a dear friend. Rick and I have made many passages together, and readers may remember he was part of the crew on *Quetzal*'s rough crossing back in Chapter Six and one of the group of friends who came to my rescue in Italy after the tornado dismasted *Quetzal*. The son of a Chesapeake Bay waterman, Rick is at home on any boat, unflappable in a crisis, and reliable. More than that, Rick has been like a father to me, offering support and assistance every time I've made a mess of things. I am always relieved knowing Rick is part of the crew.

Liz, Trevor, and Don's wife, Linda, and David's son Adam saw us off from the marina fuel dock on June 12. Four hours later we were caught in one of those legendary Chesapeake Bay summer thunderstorms, which produced 50 knot gusts, hail, and machine-gun bursts of rain. An hour later it was behind us. We topped our fuel again at Little Creek Marina, at the bottom of the bay, and then headed for the Azores, narrowly avoiding a collision in the bay approach channel before finally gaining some sea room. As if on cue, the prevailing southwest winds filled in, and *Quetzal* found her stride and charged toward Horta.

In preparing for this chapter, I had each crewmember send me some of their favorite memories of the passage. Their views are interesting. David called the passage "one of the most memorable experiences of my life." He especially enjoyed the vastness of the sea, and how the ocean "cradled" *Quetzal* and treated us to a daily display of soaring seabirds and dolphins putting on an aquatic ballet. He also recalled flying backward out of the head, pants down to his knees, when *Quetzal* hit a nasty wave as he was relieving himself. He flew into the galley like a cannon shot, but luckily he bounced off me and was not hurt. His most overriding memory was the camaraderie of the crew. "We will always be shipmates having shared the crossing."

Kyle's memories are more specific. His low point, he said, was when we accidentally jibed and ripped the traveler car and end stop off the track. It was serious for a few minutes, and he was at the helm and felt responsible. We quickly corralled the wayward boom and, led by Don's clever thinking, fashioned a repair and didn't miss a beat. Steering dead downwind in rolling seas without a preventer in place puts the blame squarely on me. Kyle also has a graphic memory of standing watch with Don during a gale in the early morning hours of June 22, when we were still a few days away from Horta. He admits to being a bit apprehensive as the winds piped up to 35 knots, but he also notes that once we shortened sail and bore away to 120 degrees, things settled down. That was when he realized why he was there, to learn from experience and not from reading yet another book about voyaging. He gained new respect for what it means to be in a gale offshore. "Now I can tell stories about PFDs inflating when waves break into the cockpit, sails being torn, gale force winds, etc.," he wrote. Kyle also noted that eating lunch with Don at Café Sport in Horta before we shoved off for Ireland was unforgettable. "The view of the harbor, Pico in the background, people milling about. We could see that the few boats at anchor had swung around, indicating the wind shift that would make it easy for us to take off for Ireland in a few hours." At that point in the passage, he was thinking like a sailor.

Sergey told me that the Atlantic crossing has made it difficult for him to enjoy casual sailing. "You ruined sailing for me, John. Now I don't like knowing that I always have to return to the dock. I want the option to just keep going, all the way across an ocean." Sergey kept us amused with stories of life in the Ukraine and Israel and noted that four weeks was the longest he'd ever gone in his life without speaking Russian. He also said that being a Russian on a boat with six Americans and a six-man life raft made him nervous. And he was impressed with how one tuna could feed the entire crew and just how small 47 feet can feel in the middle of the ocean.   *(continued page 234)*

A Sailor's Guide to the Gods

Although I rejected organized religion at an early age and am a secular humanist through and through, I confess I don't hesitate to drop Neptune's name and plead for help when things turn dicey at sea. I am not above urging Aeolus, the god of wind, to either ease up when it's blowing a gale, or have a heart and throw us a breeze in calms.

I am not a spiritual person, and these rants are mostly in jest, but I have deep respect for myths. They're our shared cultural heritage, and I have always been a sucker for a good story. I like the idea that ancient mariners saw the sea as divine and ruled by a slew of mischievous gods. The fickle and often cruel ocean was hard for sailors to understand, and conjuring gods, heroes, and stories to explain natural phenomena makes sense to me. The Straits of Messina, between Sicily and the Italian mainland, had serious whirlpools that still exist today. It's more fun to think of them as Charybdis, the sad daughter of Poseidon whose face is all mouth. She swallows all the water in the strait and then spits it out again to create the whirlpools. Poor Charybdis is guarded by the sea monster Scylla, who snares sailors and their ships if they pass too close to her cave. I tend to rely on local gods from the classical myths while I'm in the Med, Norse gods when sailing in the North Atlantic, and Polynesian gods in the South Pacific.

Every ancient culture venerated sea gods of some type. Here's a list of some of the big names, just in case you need to call for help on a dark and stormy night.

Classical Mythology

Poseidon, called Neptune by the Romans, is the Greek god of the sea and a brother to Zeus and Hades. He ruled over an array of lesser gods, nymphs, and heroes. Like the sea he ruled over, Poseidon was a tempestuous deity, prone to outbreaks of bad temper and not shy about stirring up storms, floods, and even earthquakes when things didn't go his way.

Triton, the merman son of Poseidon and also his herald.

Proteus, one of my favorite gods, didn't wield much influence but was known for his wisdom and the ability to change shape, which seems useful for a sea god. The word *protean* comes from this old man of the sea.

Sirens, beautiful sea nymphs who charmed sailors with their songs and in the process lured them onto the rocks. Odysseus made his crew put wax in their ears to avoid their sweet music, and had himself bound to the mast so that he could hear the music but not allow himself to be drawn to it.

Amphitrite is an important sea goddess for sailors. She traveled the seas in a boat made of mussels and was known to calm stormy seas. Good to keep her on speed dial.

Aeolus, son of Poseidon, the god of winds who lived in the Aeolian Islands north of Sicily.

Norse Mythology

Aegir, the Viking god of the ocean, ruled over the moods of the sea, an important job if there ever was one. The waves of the sea were considered his offspring, and he is sometimes described as an ale brewer as well, which of course makes him a favorite of sailors.

Ran, Aegir's consort, was known as the storm goddess. She drowned mariners in whirlpools, gathered them in her net, and dragged them to the bottom of the sea. Apparently she demanded sailors throw money into the sea as a sacrifice, which some boatowners might find very appropriate.

Pacific Mythology

Tangaroa, the god of the sea from a Maori myth, was worshipped throughout the Pacific islands. A Tahitian myth claims that he fashioned the world from a giant mussel shell. He is the progenitor of humans, and rules over them. He is also in constant conflict with Tane, the god of birds and trees, who also claims to have fathered humans. Maoris saw this as the natural conflict between those who remain on land and those who go to sea, something that I know a lot about.

Daucina, the god of seafaring from a Fijian myth, clearly helped give sailors a bad name as he is also the god of seduction and known for adulterous behavior.

Other Sea Gods

Yamm, a sea god who became popular in ancient Egypt, was known as the creator of primal chaos, about the perfect definition of the ocean. His name is literally from the Canaanite word for sea.   *(continued next page)*

Lir, the god of the sea in Celtic mythology, is known mostly for giving his name to places, including Leicester, England. Some think that Shakespeare may have had the Welsh version in mind, Llyr, when he wrote King Lear.

Mazu is a benevolent sea goddess from Chinese mythology who looked after sailors and fishermen.

Agwe is the Haitian god of the sea. Haitians have a lively mythology, and Agwe is still venerated by fishermen and sailors today. Offerings are loaded on rafts and sent out to sea. Agwe particularly looks over sailors, especially during hurricane season.

Varuna is the god of the ocean in Vedic tradition, and seen as a brother to Poseidon and Neptune. He rides on a sea monster and is often depicted with a trident. My friend Tania Aebi named her Contessa 26 after him, and he safely guided her around the world. Tania was the youngest person to ever do so at the time.

Idliragijenget is the Inuit god of the ocean, and officially the most difficult god to pronounce or spell. And yet despite this drawback, Idliragijenget is now a very trendy name for Inuit male children. My daughter Narianna has nothing to complain about.

Don really enjoyed getting back to sea on a sailboat. He and Linda and their young son left Southern California in the late 1980s in an Ericson 41 sloop that Don had completely rebuilt. They spent a couple of years sailing south to Panama and then across the Caribbean before finally fetching up in the Chesapeake Bay. The Chesapeake can be a frustrating place to sail, and with limited free time, Don turned to powerboats to stay on the water. But his heart was always in sailing. He confided to me that he had thought seriously about buying *Quetzal* when she was still called *Madrigal* and owned by St. Mary's College.

Charlie needed the crossing, he wrote, because he needed the uncluttered horizons that only the ocean can serve. His new assignment, chasing terrorist threats, could be incredibly stressful, and he decompressed at sea. He also navigated with a vengeance, and my approach charts to both Horta and Cork, Ireland, are crisscrossed with coordinates, courses, and danger bearings.

The voyage was especially rewarding for my friend Rick. As a member of the crew of the 2007 crossing, he had nothing to prove but still felt like he had not quite finished the job by leaving the boat in the Azores. This time nothing would stop him from reaching Ireland. Rick's note, typically, commends the crew for their competence and courteousness. Despite being a licensed captain with many sea miles under his belt, he saw the passage as a great learning experience. He was impressed again with how we dealt with the traveler incident, and also noted that a ripped mainsail, which we repaired a couple of times, and a blown-out genoa did little to slow us down. "They were just distractions, not calamities." He remembers one particular watch, "the wettest ever," with David. "I have felt drier scuba diving than I did on watch that night. The rain was just pouring, coming in around and through the bimini and dodger. Even in top-notch foul-weather gear, we were cold and soaked." Rick also remembered the tuna, and claims to have never seen a fish cleaned and eaten faster. As for most of the crew, the Azores were a highlight for Rick, especially being rafted alongside the Norwegian sail training schooner *Opal*. And he recalled the exuberance he felt making landfall in Ireland. "The night we came into Cork, I remember sitting on deck with the FLIR [night scope] in hand picking up unlit markers and floats and thinking, we did it, we sailed all the way to Ireland."

What do I remember? Captain's Hour, repairs, stories, cooking, reefing, my beautiful boat blasting along on a sweet reach for days at a time, paying attention in heavy weather, landfalls, and laughing until my sides ached. These are the ingredients that have gone into every crossing I've ever made, and the summer of 2011 was my twentieth. It doesn't seem to matter if I am sailing with a full crew, or just my mate, crossing the Atlantic under sail remains one of the most fulfilling ways possible to spend a month or so of your precious allotment of time.

Quetzal is still in Europe as I write these final words, hauled out in Malta and buttoned up for the winter. We will head to Turkey in the spring, then back toward Gibraltar in the fall. In January we'll cross the Atlantic again. Those of us who sail aboard her are the lucky ones, the quixotic ones, the knights-errant of the sea. We'll stand our watches, keep an eye out for squalls, muscle the wheel to keep her squarely before trade wind–driven seas, and feel the thrill when we surf down a wave, leaving a trail of bioluminescence. There will be dirty nights, no doubt, and we'll be cold, wet, and miserable. But there's one thing I know for sure. None of us would trade places with anyone ashore.

Acknowledgments

This book was long in the writing, and that's putting it mildly. My editor, Molly Mulhern, with a mixture of gentle prods, timely suggestions, and occasional commands, kept the book together. I can't thank her enough, and she knows she has a berth on *Quetzal* whenever she is ready to cross an ocean. I also need to thank my daughter Narianna Kretschmer. She devoted a summer to reading and editing. She knows a lot about boats and her old man, and she's a good writer; her input was incredibly helpful. One day she will write her own book. I'd also like to thank my friend Fred Grimm of the *Miami Herald*. He reads my drafts, shakes his head, and quietly cleans up my prose. And finally, I must thank my wife and best friend, Tadji. She tolerates my sea time and always supports me. Our circumnavigation is not far off baby.

Index